AF350411

**Bronze Winner, Readers' Choice Award
(5-Star Rated)**

"Most Christians don't know this story—
and it would be good if we did."
— John Goldingay

Praise for *In the Shadow of the Most High*

"There are three kinds of stories in this book, and they are all worth reading… Most fascinating is the account of Doug Einfeld's discovery of his Jewish ancestors in Germany four centuries ago. But equally valuable is his readable retelling of the history of Israel and the Jewish people—from its beginnings through the centuries that followed the Roman Empire.

Most Christians don't know much about that story—and it would be really good if we did. I am especially glad Doug has retold this story."

— John Goldingay, **PhD**
Senior Professor of Old Testament
David Allan Hubbard Professor of Old Testament Emeritus
Fuller Theological Seminary

****

"A deeply personal and pious telling of the Jewish roots of early Christianity and the ongoing interconnectedness of these two traditions, told as an autobiographical journey—one that is shared by hundreds of thousands of contemporary Christians, whether they know it or not."

— Rabbi Brad Hirschfield
President, National Jewish Center for Learning and Leadership

In the Shadow of the Most High

In the Shadow of the Most High

Uncovering My Jewish Ancestors' Perilous Journey Through History

———————————

Rediscovering Our Roots: Judeo-Christian History Revisited
Volume One

———————————

Doug Einfeld

Independently Published

In the Shadow of the Most High

Copyright © 2026 by Doug Einfeld

Printed in the United States of America

First Edition

ISBN: 979-8-218-91217-8

BISAC Cataloging Subjects: HISTORY / Jewish | RELIGION / Christianity / History | BIOGRAPHY & AUTOBIOGRAPHY / Memoirs | RELIGION / Biblical Studies / History and Culture | RELIGION / Judaism / History

Cover design by Ares Jun
Editing by Positive Proofing
Map designs by Bree Rose Creative

In loving memory of my parents

Frank and Angie Einfeld

who showed me the way of truth and grace

Israel at the Time of Jesus
1st Century AD

ii

Diaspora Synagogues (1st–2nd Centuries CE)
The Roman Empire
Provincial capital
Evidence of a synagogue:
Archaeological
Papyrus
Inscriptions/carvings
Historical texts/literature
Augusta Vindelicorum
Virunium
Caralis
Aleria
Carthago
Ostia
Rome
Syracuse
Salona
Mursa
Sitmium
Viminacium
Sarmizegetusa
ADRIATIC SEA
Berenike
Cyrene
Nicopolis
Corinthus
Aegina
Athens
Delos
Gortyn
Beroea
Stobi
Thessalonica
Philippi
Philippopolis
AEGEAN SEA
MEDITERRANEAN SEA
Paraetinium
Schedia
Naukratis
Alexandria
Athribis
Alexandrou Nesos
Arsinoe
Nitria
Leontopolis
Ptolemais
Pelusium
Caesarea
Paphus
Salamis
Ephesus
Miletus
Priene
Smyrna
Sardis
Philadelphia
Halicarnassus
Parium
Antiochia
Konya
Attaleia
Nicomedia
Ancyra
Caesarea
Tarsus
Antiochia
Bostra
Damascus
Dura Europos
Tomis
Olbia
Panticapaeum
Phanagoria
Gorgippia
BLACK SEA

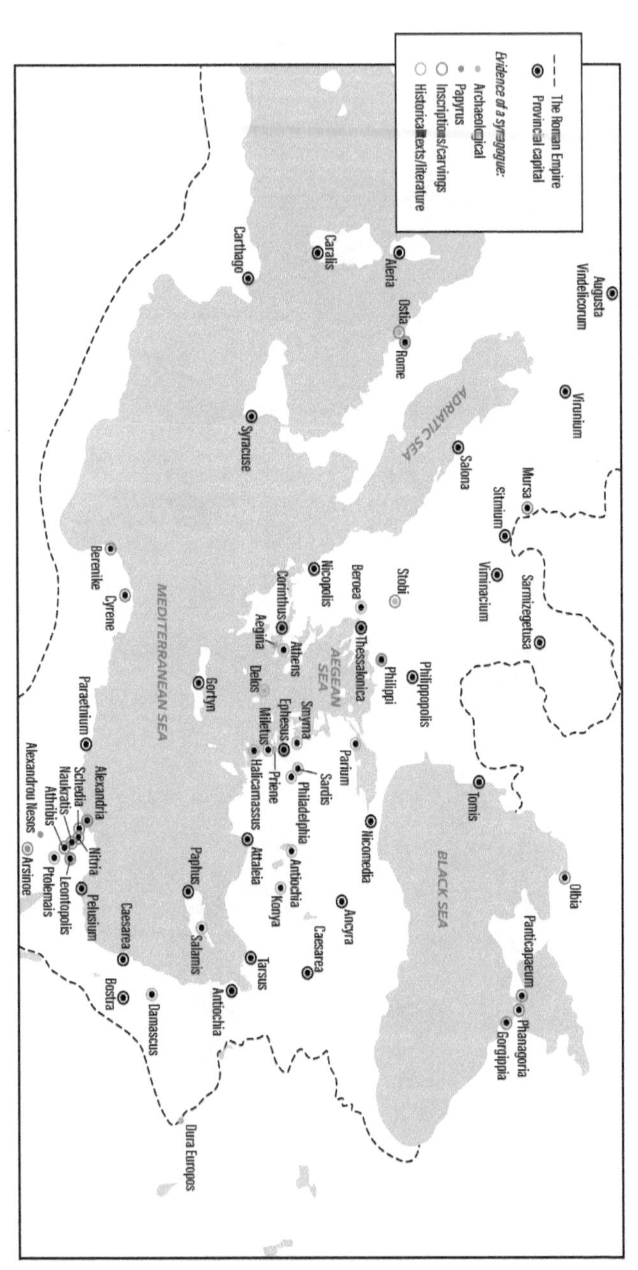

Jewish Settlements in the German Rhineland
ca. 900–1300

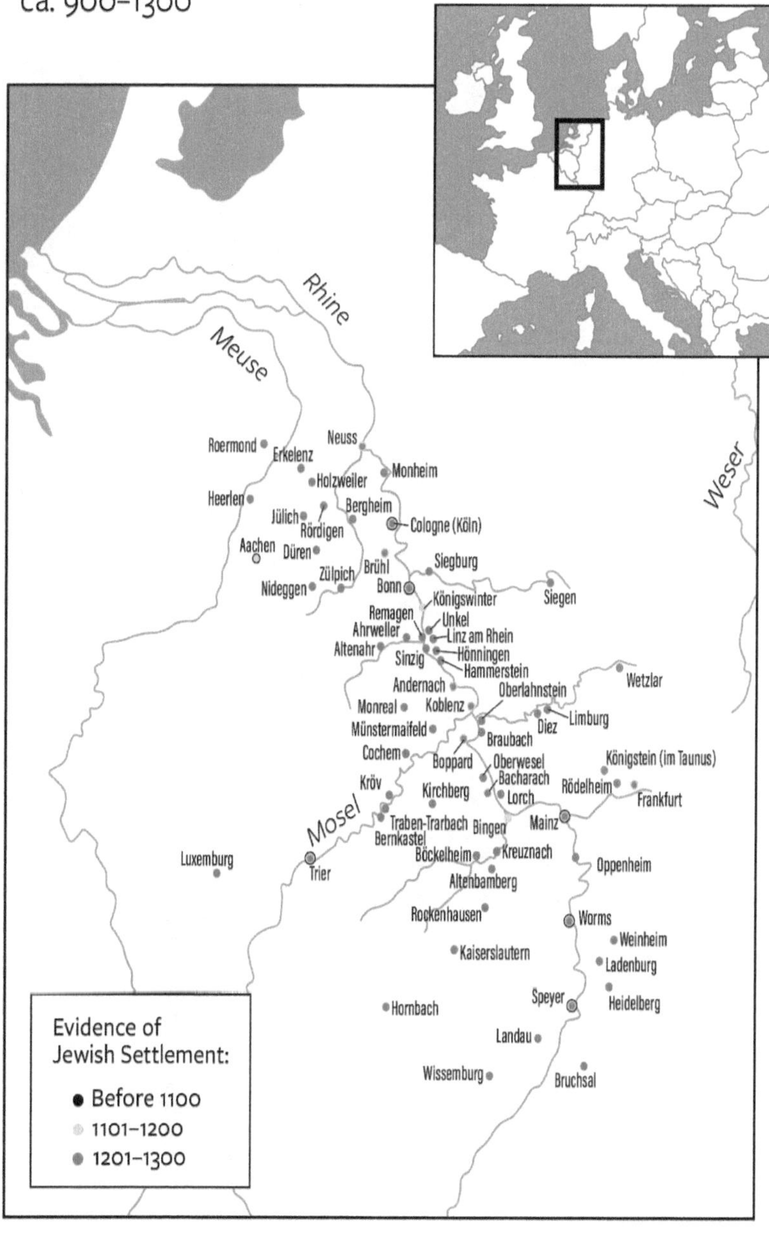

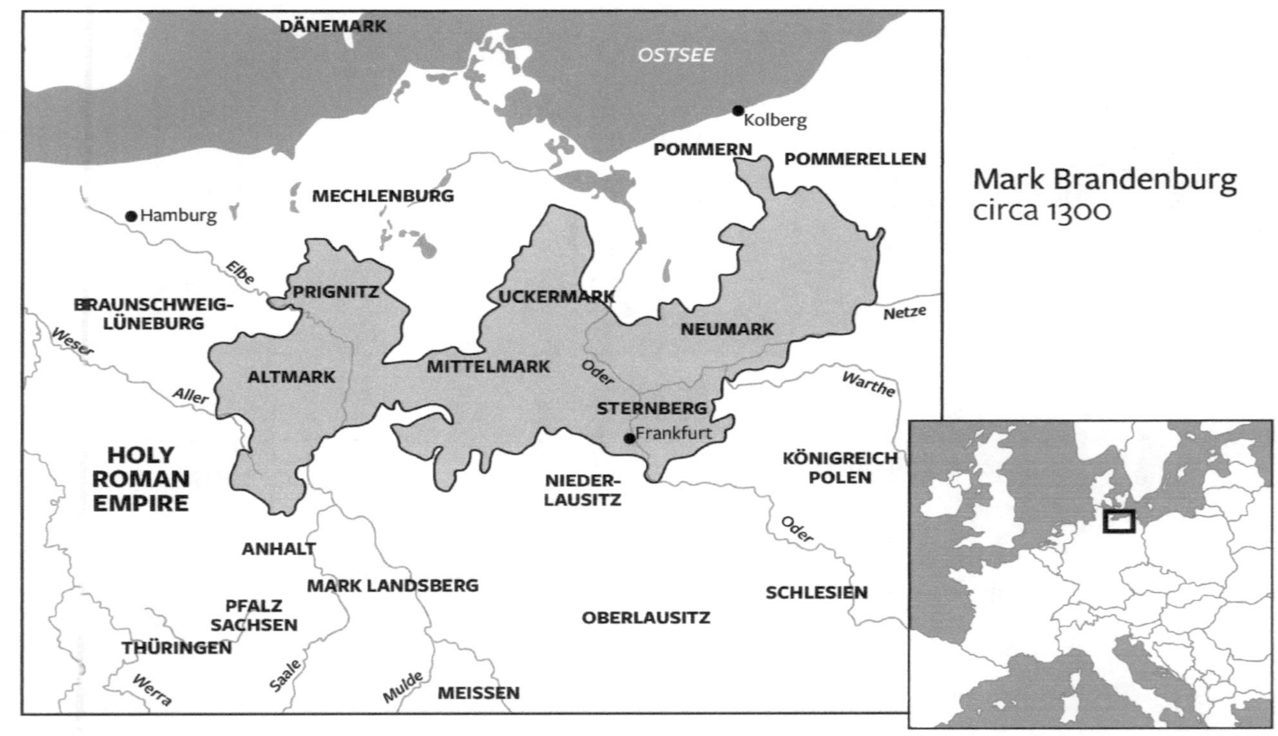

DÄNEMARK
OSTSEE
Kolberg
POMMERN
POMMERELLEN
MECHLENBURG
Hamburg
Elbe
BRAUNSCHWEIG-LÜNEBURG
PRIGNITZ
UCKERMARK
Netze
NEUMARK
Weser
Aller
ALTMARK
MITTELMARK
Oder
Warthe
STERNBERG
Frankfurt
HOLY ROMAN EMPIRE
NIEDER-LAUSITZ
KÖNIGREICH POLEN
ANHALT
MARK LANDSBERG
Oder
SCHLESIEN
PFALZ SACHSEN
OBERLAUSITZ
THÜRINGEN
Saale
Mulde
MEISSEN
Werra
Mark Brandenburg
circa 1300

Ostfriesland Region
1500s
NORTH SEA
Esens
Dornum
Ochtersum
†
Stedesdorf
Norden
Schweindorf
Dunum
Wittmund
OSTFRIESLAND
Aurich
Wiesmoor
Emden
Leer
Weener
GERMANY
THE
NETHERLANDS

Contents

Introduction

Around forty years ago, while in my late twenties, my dad's oldest sibling, our Einfeld family's matriarch at the time, Aunt Clara, showed me a picture I had never seen before. It was the lone surviving photo of my long-deceased great-grandpa Einfeld, taken sometime around 1900 in the Netherlands. She seemed eager to reveal a closely held family secret. My great-grandpa, she said, had been a "German Jewish seaman." Jewish?! I was flabbergasted. How could that be true? My dad was a Christian Reformed Church minister. His Dutch immigrant parents had been devout, lifelong Christian Reformed people. But my aunt sure sounded convincing.

When online genealogical databases later emerged, I began checking out her story. I discovered that my great-grandpa had been born in the North Sea coastal town of Norden, Germany and was baptized Lutheran as an infant. In fact, he was the sixth consecutive generation of Einfeld sons who had all been baptized German Lutheran. However, the names of the three earliest generations of those sons (living during the 1600s–1700s) revealed something more. They all shared the same hereditary name: Juede—the German word for Jew. It was the handy ID tag often used back then to underscore the alien minority social status of those of Jewish ethnic descent. Aunt Clara had been right about my great-grandfather's Jewish ethnic origins!

The implications jolted my sense of identity. My lifelong Christian identity had been rooted in the conviction that patriarchal Abraham had been my *spiritual* father. But now I realized I also had a *genetic* connection to him. I had inherited his DNA. Suddenly, the entire biblical account took on a more personalized feel. All those familiar Bible stories I had grown up hearing and reading—my own flesh-and-blood ancestors had experienced them firsthand. Egyptian bondage. Mount Sinai. The desert wanderings. Crossing the Jordan. Babylonian conquest. Herod's psychopathic tyranny. The ministry, death, and resurrection of Jesus. And speaking of Jesus, perhaps my own ancestors had seen and heard him in person. If so, how had they responded? What stories might they have been able to tell?

Additional questions begged for answers. How did it happen that a descendant of those first-century Palestinian Jewish contemporaries of Jesus turned up in the far-flung North Sea coastal region of seventeenth-century Germany—as my earliest documentable paternal ancestor? I set out to find the answer. I wanted to uncover and retrace the full and complete story, the entire saga of my Jewish ancestors' trek through history. My research took me on a fascinating journey across continents and centuries, and deep into the heart of the matters of identity, faith, and survival. I unearthed a rich, long legacy, which was forged in exile and resilience, and lived beneath the ever-present shadow of their Most High God.

This book is my effort to convey their story. It begins in antiquity with the patriarch Abraham and offers behind-the-scenes glimpses into everyday Jewish life throughout the biblical era, including the time of Jesus. It retraces their near-annihilation by the Roman Empire and follows their migratory journey from ancient Palestine to Italy—and eventually to Germany. Along the way, it recounts their suffering under brutal anti-Jewish violence during the Middle Ages. It culminates in their arrival in

1

From Desert Nomads to Village Dwellers

Ancient Beginnings

The journey of my Jewish ancestral family began, inconspicuously, in what many might consider the middle of nowhere: a relentlessly hot, dry, and dusty Middle Eastern desert region. This desolate, seemingly lifeless and God-forsaken wasteland was perhaps one of the least desirable places on earth for them to inhabit. Yet there they were—amid these forlorn surroundings. Being cradled in their infancy. Being molded into a distinctive tribal identity. And beginning to frame the story of how they came to be.

Vivid, dramatic stories sprang to life here. Accounts of personal experiences and supernatural phenomena. The kind you can't help telling your children and grandchildren, and they to theirs. On and on, the telling and retelling persisted, generation after generation, century after century. Eventually, they were written down. Still later, they became preserved for the ages, incorporated into what would become the definitive chronicle of their tribal journey through ancient times: the sacred Hebrew scriptures.

The introductory book of Genesis lays them out for us, taking us back to around 2000 BC. There, we encounter the towering life and legacy of Abraham, the Hebrew people's patriarchal founder. We discover he was born in one of the most sophisticated cities in ancient Babylonia (today's southern Iraq). His father, Terah, as a resident of the cosmopolitan city of Ur, would likely have been a man of some means. He was certainly more than a mere low-level, small-time sheepherder.

At some point, Terah decided to relocate his family to a land called Canaan. It was a place he'd apparently heard about. But what drew him there? We have no clue. It lay eight hundred miles to the west, on the other side of the vast Arabian Desert. Accompanied by Abraham and his wife, Sarah, Terah departed Ur. Off they went in a northwesterly direction along a major trade route, likely traveling as a large caravan entourage. After journeying about six hundred miles—for who knows how long— they arrived at the city of Haran in the southern part of what is now Turkey. Scratching their plans for reaching Canaan, they settled here instead.

Haran was a flourishing Mesopotamian caravan city, an important economic center. It was also the cult center for the Mesopotamian moon god, Nanna. He was considered chief among the multiple spiritual beings that comprised the people's deeply ingrained polytheistic worldview. He was the same chief god venerated back in Abraham's birth town of Ur. Abraham, in all likelihood, arrived in Haran as a typical Mesopotamian polytheist, with various household gods in tow—the sacred, venerated physical representations of the deities thought to be his family's protectors. There, in the middle of his new hometown, stood a towering ziggurat—a massive, stepped, mudbrick structure with a temple perched on top. It was dedicated to Nanna, the high god of his ancestors.

While living a settled urban life in Haran, Abraham experienced a dramatic religious encounter. It must have felt like a disquieting interruption to the predictable routine of his everyday life. Out of the clear blue, apparently, he heard what he took to be a divine voice addressing him. What did it sound like?

What was his immediate reaction? We're never told. But at some point, he realized this had not been the voice of Nanna or any of his household gods. It was, rather, a voice emanating from a deity he had never before heard of. (His descendants would later know him as "Yahweh," and "the Lord.")

According to the story passed along to Abraham's descendants and eventually incorporated into the Genesis account (12:1), Abraham heard a terse, bewildering directive: "*Lech lecha . . .*" This is more than the mere "go" or "go forth" found in most English translations. The literal reading is: "Get going!" "Get out!" It resounds with astonishing authority. "*Depart now* from your country, your people and your father's household and go to the land I will show you" (Gen. 12:1). What went through Abraham's mind when he heard this? This was all so counterintuitive, so illogical, so unreasonable. His country, his people, his father's household—these were the very bedrocks of his identity, his safety and security, his sense of peace and belonging. Wouldn't it be senseless to just walk away from all this? And frightening.

There must have been something about standing in the live presence of this voice that enabled Abraham to rise above his feelings of fear, doubt, and hesitation. Somehow, its intrusive, commanding sound had seized his immediate and total attention. Almost instantly, it seems, he was convinced. Surely this must be a divine, other-worldly being who must be taken with utmost seriousness.

Have you ever packed up your belongings to relocate, having no specific destination in mind? Who does that? Yet that's what Abraham had been instructed to do. Pack up all his things. Start heading down the desert trade route. But which one? And in what direction? Just go. Now. Get going. Yahweh will show the way. Abraham will have to wait until he gets there in order to discover what his destination is.

Isn't that so typically the case for people of faith? We trust that God has laid out a path ahead of us. We accept his invitation, step out on that road, and start moving forward. And then things take a sudden, unexpected turn, making us uncertain and fearful of what may lie next along the journey. Where exactly is this route taking me? It feels like I'm veering off course, heading to the wrong place. Often, it's only after passing through such a crisis point in life's journey, and reaching the other side of that crisis, that God reveals to us where he intended to take us all along.

It must have been the next part of Yahweh's statement that captured Abraham's imagination and moved him to comply. "I will make you into a great nation, and I will bless you; I will make your name great, and you will be a blessing. I will bless those who bless you, and whoever curses you I will curse; and all peoples on earth will be blessed through you" (Gen. 12:2–3).

Imagine being Abraham here. You are a childless man with an infertile wife. Biological descendants are obviously not in the cards for you. But what if they actually were? What if the things this deity is stating here could actually happen? Not just be able to have a child. But through that child, create the legacy of an entire nation of descendants. And then those descendants in turn become a blessing to the rest of the earth's entire population? That's a potential future that just might be worth the risk of stepping out in blind faith and going along with Yahweh on this mysterious, uncharted adventure. If . . . If this deity can deliver on what he is promising.

I wonder how Abraham processed all this. The biblical narrative leaves the impression that he made a rather quick decision. But was that really the case? This would be a major, life-altering choice. He would need buy-in from his wife and his father's household. There were significant pros and cons to be wrestled with.

All we're told, however, is that he "left, as the Lord had told him" (Gen. 12:4). He took the leap of faith. He made a deliberate choice to submit to the authority of this newfound Yahweh deity. Did he suddenly set aside his polytheistic belief system and toss out all his Mesopotamian household idols? Probably not. But it is clear who his new "patron deity" had become, and who his descendants' "ancestral deity" would be. The voice of Yahweh had made clear to Abraham who he should now consider the one supreme divine being—the one Most High above all others. This is who would be his family's divine protector and blessing-giver amid his impending desert journey.

Departing Haran undoubtedly presented a daunting challenge. For Abraham's household entourage, it meant a radical alteration, not only to their everyday lifestyle, but to their very identity. The comfort and security they had grown used to as wealthy, well-known residents of their urban settlement had ended. In exchange, they received the often-humiliating, second-class status that comes with being immigrants, strangers, outsiders in the unfamiliar space of someone else's land. From now on, they would be continuously on the road, living in goat-hair tents, moving from campsite to campsite, pasture to pasture, searching out water sources, engaging in nerve-wracking and sometimes hostile encounters with local villagers who spoke in different dialects.

Like his father before him, Abraham was no small-time herdsman who merely tended a few straggly sheep and goats. He was more likely a wealthy and influential merchant, overseeing a large sheep and goat herding operation. He probably had a security force of more than three hundred men to manage his herds and conduct business and trade deals with regional monarchs.

Even so, once he left Haran, he no longer had any land he could call his own. He and his descendants lived the next couple centuries as roaming herdsmen in the hill country and southern desert regions of Canaan. Raising sheep, goats, and grains became their livelihood. They wove sheep wool into cloth and turned animal skins into leather. They survived on grains and breads, goat's milk and curds, and fruits and nuts gathered along their travels or purchased from local villagers.

Constantly, they moved about in search of the vital resources of forage and water, scarce in such an arid climate. When found, they formed an encampment, pastured their flocks, and raised more grain. These resources were often controlled and only grudgingly shared with them by native Canaanite village dwellers. It therefore became incumbent upon them to draw as little hostile attention to themselves as possible. Any time these natives felt their own economy was being threatened by such newcomer nomads, they could force them to leave.

Yet this was the land Abraham believed Yahweh had led him to. It's the place where Yahweh solemnized a contractual relationship with him: Yahweh promising to remain his faithful God; Abraham committing to be his loyal follower and worshipper. This relationship became the foundation of the Jewish people's identity. It set the guiding parameters for their journey through history, as Yahweh repeatedly renewed and reconfirmed their covenantal relationship for generations to come.

Uprooted. Challenged to follow Yahweh on a wilderness journey. Not knowing where it would take him. Struggling to trust that Yahweh would keep showing him the way. That was Abraham's calling. It would become the primal experience of his descendants as well—both biological and spiritual—for millennia to come. It's the inescapable reality for all who say yes when Yahweh directs them to "get going" to that unforeseen place he intends to bring them.

Time in Egypt

Repeated cycles of drought, famine, hunger, and thirst haunted the Semitic-speaking inhabitants of ancient Canaan. Their search for food, water, and green pastures during desperate times often brought them to the fertile eastern delta region of Egypt. Such was the case for Abraham's immediate descendants. His grandson Jacob, along with his children and grandchildren, was granted permission to emigrate to this region during a time of severe famine.

It turned out to be a good time for them to be departing Canaan—for other reasons as well. Had they remained, they would have had to contend with the threat of being swallowed up by rising Canaanite city-states that were becoming increasingly powerful. And available Canaanite land on which to graze their herds was shrinking. The well-protected Nile delta region provided a more sheltered and stable environment for the early growth of their budding nation.

Originally intended to be just a short-term stay, their time in Egypt turned into a layover lasting multiple centuries. The scriptural narrative is virtually silent about this four-hundred-year period of Hebrew immigrant life in the land of Egypt. Probably because Yahweh himself had mysteriously gone radio silent. Since the days of Abraham's great-grandchildren, there's no record of any subsequent descendants hearing anything from him during these four centuries. Nothing but crickets. For the next four hundred years!

No wonder they drifted into a forgetfulness about Yahweh, the "God of their fathers." In fact, they became significantly influenced by Egyptian culture and religion. Some had adopted Egyptian names. Many had assimilated elements of Egyptian religious practice, even making Egyptian and other Semitic regional family gods the objects of their worship. Yet they did remain aware of their distinctive Hebrew identity. Make no mistake, they were still strangers in a foreign land.

By the seventeenth century BC, significant numbers of other foreign people from the Semitic-speaking world were now also living in the Nile Delta region of Egypt. Among them were thousands of captured Egyptian prisoners of war living under forced labor. Soon a new Egyptian king rose to power. Feeling threatened by the growing number of Hebrews among them, he felt compelled to conscript them into Egyptian forced labor as well.

Wilderness Reset

Most scholars believe it happened sometime during the thirteenth century BC. A man named Moses emerged to lead an escape from the Pharaoh's enslavement. On the run from Egypt as a murder suspect, he had been living incognito in the Sinai Desert—until his dramatic encounter with the same all-seeing desert deity that had spoken centuries earlier to Abraham. Notice the emerging pattern here. It's in the desert places where Yahweh typically shows up. Seeks people out. Reveals his presence. Grabs people's attention. And reveals his special calling on their lives. It had happened to Abraham, to Isaac, to Jacob—and now to Moses.

From inside an eerily blazing shrub, his voice suddenly shattered the desert silence: "Moses! Moses!" (Ex. 3:4). He had an astonishing message. A plan for orchestrating the Hebrew people's release from Egyptian bondage—incredibly, under Moses's leadership. Moses, skeptical and fearful, balked at the prospect: "O Lord, please send someone else to do it" (Ex. 4:13). But Yahweh persisted, unwilling to take no for an answer. Reluctantly, Moses eventually relented.

An unimaginable divine intervention ensued and became forever etched into the Hebrew people's collective memory. A riveting story of Yahweh demonstrating his superior power over the Egyptian deities and thereby compelling the persistently obstinate Pharaoh and his people into compliance. To the point where, in utter exasperation, they coerced Yahweh's people into a hurried departure. It was a defining historic moment, marking the birth of an independent nation.

And so, they successfully escaped into the Sinai Desert. But now what? Moses had a mess on his hands. He'd become saddled with skeptical, untrusting followers who had dug in their heels against him and his newfound Yahweh God. Why on earth had they been led to a dismal desert wasteland to face such a foreboding, forlorn future?

They were about to discover the answer: the desert is Yahweh's turf, a special place of habitation for him. Throughout the Hebrew scriptures, the wilderness is where Yahweh brought his people for preparation, training, and testing. A quiet, safe, isolated place of refuge where his people could retreat to—to encounter Yahweh, hear his voice, learn obedience, and discern his leading.

After four long centuries amid the cultural and religious influences of the Egyptian people and their deities, the descendants of Abraham had grown ignorant of this foreign-sounding Yahweh deity whom Moses claimed to have encountered in the desert. Who, exactly, was he? And what did he want with them? The desert was precisely the place for them to find out. A place to become detoxed from Egyptian spiritual and religious influences. A place to be instructed in the ways and purposes of Yahweh. A place where distrusting people could learn to trust, disobedient people could learn obedience, and spiritual wanderers could discover Yahweh's purpose for them.

At a mountain in the Sinai Desert, Yahweh, hovering high above in a dense cloud covering, startled them with a spectacular demonstration of his incredible power and transcendence. The mountain top stood concealed behind clouds of thunder and lightning. And what has all the markings of a volcanic eruption took place, with smoke billowing forth and the entire mountain jolting in convulsions. The audience was stunned, filled with fear and awe.

By the time they departed Mount Sinai, Yahweh was no longer merely Moses's God. He had become the God of the entire Israel community, their loose confederation of tribes coalesced into a unified people group with a distinct religious identity. The foundational framework for their emerging Israelite religion had been put in place: the "Law of Moses," the priesthood, the tabernacle. A personal bond between Yahweh and his chosen people had been formed. He'd already demonstrated his dramatic power to bring liberation from political oppression, and to cause mountains to shake and erupt in fire and smoke. Now he revealed something else about himself. He intended to remain up close with his wilderness followers, tenting alongside them in his own campsite quarters, personally leading their way to the land he had promised them.

Settling in Canaan

Canaan. What an interesting choice as Yahweh's "land of promise." Why this particular place? If Yahweh's intention was for his chosen people to live in protected isolation, unscathed by continual military and political turmoil swirling among the nations around them, then this was not a good choice. If his aim was the success, greatness, and glorification of the people of Israel as an end in itself, then this was the last place he should have brought them. But if Yahweh's purpose was for them to live smack dab in the crossroads of the world's cultures, positioned to play a major role in influencing world history, then this was a most appropriate choice. Where else could they have had as strategic a geographical and historical position from which to ultimately become the conduit through which "all peoples on earth" would be "blessed" by Yahweh?

The land of Canaan was about the size of the state of Vermont. Seventy-five miles wide from the Mediterranean Sea on its west to the Arabian Desert on its east. One hundred seventy-five miles long from the arid Sinai Desert in the south to the snowcapped mountains of Lebanon in the north. It was a narrow strip of territory forming a land bridge buffer zone between major empires to its east and west. Picture an hourglass resting on its side. Canaan is the narrow funnel area in the middle. The large and powerful succeeding Egyptian empires existed in the wide region on the left. Those of Asia—occupying modern-day Lebanon, Syria, Turkey, Jordan, Iraq, and Iran— existed in the wide area to the right. Canaan was the narrow corridor through which, century after century, the armies of warring empires from east and west repeatedly passed. It was a recurring hotspot of territorial conflict. It may have been Israel's promised land. But they would soon find out that it would not always be the most promising place to live and raise one's family.

For hundreds of years before Israel's Exodus group arrived at Canaan's border around 1200 BC, its inhabitants had lived under Egyptian domination. Their policy of deporting Canaanites into Egyptian slavery had caused a significant decline in Canaan's population. Eventually, Egypt's power waned and collapsed. As it did, Canaan's fortified walled cities began to weaken and disintegrate, leaving them more vulnerable to the intrusion of outsiders.

It was this apparent vulnerability that the Israelites were able to capitalize on under their new leader, Joshua. According to the biblical narrative, he led them in initial successful military assaults against key Canaanite city-state fortifications before they could organize to defend themselves. He bifurcated the land between its northern and southern regions. Without any apparent resistance, he seized control of the strongly fortified city of Shechem—the very place Yahweh had called Abraham into covenant relationship centuries earlier. There he led the people in a ceremony of covenant renewal at an altar built on nearby Mount Ebal. He then carried out further military operations in both Canaan's southern and northern regions. And he established a religious sanctuary at a place nineteen miles north of Jerusalem called Shiloh, where the people erected a tabernacle for Yahweh.

Although the Israelites successfully established a presence inside Canaan's borders, they were unable to fully capture and subdue the land. Superior Canaanite military capability and "chariots of iron" blocked their way. For whatever reason, they chose not to repurpose the remains of former Canaanite cities into their new places of residence. Instead, they made their way to the sparsely populated wooded areas in the central hill-country regions and created new settlement enclaves there. Archaeological evidence points to a major influx of new population elements arriving there during the late-thirteenth to the eleventh centuries. About 250 new small unwalled villages suddenly sprang up, extending from the northern Negev region in the south to the lower Galilee region in the north.

With Egyptian control now long eliminated, new regional Canaanite kingdoms emerged alongside the Israelite newcomers: Philistine city-states, Ammon, Edom, Moab, Phoenicia, and Syria. Territorial conflict was inevitable. The biblical book of Judges describes some of the clashes. Neighboring Moabite and Ammonite kingdoms tried subjugating the new Israelite settlers.

Midianite invaders came through their midst on a looting and burning rampage. Israelite tribal groups banded together to defend themselves. But their temporary militias, led by a succession of charismatic leaders (the "judges"), had inadequate weaponry to fully vanquish these threats.

While largely confined to their hill-country settlements in relative isolation over the next two centuries, they developed a strong, distinctive Israelite culture. The twelve tribes were loosely aligned politically in a city-state type of arrangement. Having no king, no monarchy, no sole political leader, or central government, they were led by tribal elders. Religiously, they were bound together in covenant with Yahweh. They shared a central place of Yahweh worship at Shiloh, overseen by the priestly tribe of Levi. Foundations were being laid for an eventual rise to prominence in the region, and for the attainment of a settled population of an estimated one hundred fifty thousand Israelites by 1000 BC.

Hill Country Life

Adjusting to Canaanite hill-country life required a radical shift in lifestyle. These settlers were used to living as semi-nomads, moving from place to place, husbanding sheep and goats. Suddenly, they were now sedentary—in a drastically different environment. It was largely uninhabited when they arrived. And for good reason. It was heavily wooded, water sources were scarce, and the land, in its current state, was unsuitable for farming. To adapt, they were compelled to shift their livelihood into other agricultural pursuits besides just the cereal grains they used to depend on. Alongside tending their flocks, they began cultivating a variety of fruit trees, olive groves, and vineyards. But they first had to clear forestation and construct stone terraces on the slopes where they could raise their crops on farmable strips of land. It was the only way to prevent the runoff of valuable rain that fell during only five months of the year, and to maximize its distribution.

Their typical village settlement consisted of fifteen to twenty dwellings on a two- to three-acre plot situated on a hilltop, with a population of seventy-five to one hundred people. Their houses were arranged in the same elliptically-shaped formation as their previous desert encampments. The back ends of their houses served as a natural city wall around the village perimeter. At the center of this circle of dwellings, occupying up to 80 percent of the total village area, was a large courtyard which kept their herds corralled at night.

Their uniquely styled four-room houses were unlike anything previously seen in the settlement history of Canaan. Constructed with bricks and sun-dried mud, their homes were designed with their new farming lifestyle in mind. The ground floor typically had space where food could be processed, small crafts could be produced, animals could be stabled, and storage room provided. The second floor was characteristically used for dining, sleeping, and other family activities. With few natural springs available, an interconnected cistern system was used to bring rainwater into the house.

Survival in these isolated settlements was continually threatened by limited water, periodic drought, erodible soils, and limited planting seasons. Each household lived in constant survival mode, focused intently on maintaining its own economic well-being. Family life was thus extremely task-oriented and labor-intensive. The bulk of daily life, virtually all available daylight hours throughout the year, was consumed by physical labor involving the entire household unit—men, women, and children.

Every day their flocks needed tending to: pastured, watered, milked, and securely penned at night. Agricultural chores kept them busy for ten straight months every year, planting, cultivating, pruning, harvesting, and storing.

Soil preparation involved clearing existing trees and undergrowth from new fields. Seed beds for wheat and barley crops were prepared using a wooden plow drawn by a team of oxen. The seed was then hand-tossed into the furrows and trampled into the soil by foot.

The vineyards needed constant care. Old or unproductive vines needed pruning to permit new growth. Weeds growing around the vines threatened to steal needed moisture from the fruit, and needed to be regularly hoed.

The ripened grapes were harvested using pruning hooks. Some were dried into clusters of raisins. The remainder was pressed or trampled into liquid form in a winepress, which was emptied or routed into a fermentation vat, and then later preserved in jars or skin bags. This was a time of great celebration in the community.

Ripened olives were gathered by whacking tree branches with sticks and collecting the fallen olives off the ground into baskets. A revolving flat stone crushed them into a stream of oil and juice that flowed into a cistern. The pulp left behind was then crushed a second time by a stone-weighted lever. The resulting liquid was then channeled into a larger catch basin. Over time, a settling process took place in the cistern. As the finer grade of oil came to the top, it was skimmed off for lamp fuel. The leftovers were further refined and used in cooking, as medicine, and as a base in cosmetics.

Harvesting and processing wheat was likewise a very involved process. Reapers took strands of the ripened grain into their arms and cut them away with sickle blades. The sheaves of grain were then taken to a centrally located village threshing floor. This was a circular, flattened, earthen floor in an open-air area. There, the grain stalks were piled and trodden underfoot by oxen to loosen the grain kernels from the stalks.

Following this, the grain kernels were separated from the chaff through a winnowing process. As the mixture of grain and chaff was tossed into the air with a long wooden fork, the chaff was carried away by the prevailing wind. Using small wicker screens as sieves, tiny bits of pottery and stone were sifted from the grain. The grain kernels were then swept up, collected, and a portion of them allocated to the people by the village elders. Another portion was ground into flour. The rest was stored in pottery jars or storage pits.

Once the raising and harvesting of the various food products was completed, an additional extensive period of time and labor was required to process them into forms that could be preserved to last beyond harvest times.

And then there were the many time-consuming routine chores. Houses, pens, terraces, and sheds needed to be built and maintained. Tools and implements had to be made and maintained. Cisterns hewed out. Basketry and ceramics produced. Wool and flax taken through many complex processes to produce clothing.

Religious Life

The religious life of these early Israelite settlers in Canaan centered around their relatively newfound deity Yahweh. It was he, after all, who had liberated them from Egyptian bondage and navigated them through a long, harrowing wilderness journey. Shiloh, Yahweh's tabernacle site, was the original ground zero for their religious practice. But as the people dispersed into their settlements, additional sanctuaries for Yahweh worship sprang up throughout the land.

Three times a year, following their three annual harvest seasons, the people made pilgrimages to these sanctuaries to participate in special religious festivals. Their farm-life rhythms of seasonal plantings and harvestings became occasions for also remembering and celebrating the key events in their history—the times when Yahweh had taken significant action to shape their identity: when he delivered them from Egypt, when he formed them into a covenant community at Mt Sinai, and when he provided for them during their wilderness journey.

The seven-day springtime Feast of Unleavened Bread (immediately following the celebration of Passover) introduced the new harvest season and often marked the end of a period of famine. It was an opportunity to express joy at the anticipated harvest. The first sheaves of grain were offered to Yahweh, and the newly baked bread from this harvest was eaten before him. Its lack of leavening distinguished it from their everyday food, reminding them of the unleavened bread eaten by their ancestors as they were being freed from Egyptian oppression.

During the next seven weeks, families offered their sacrifices and thank offerings of the first fruits. This concluded in early summer, at the end of the wheat harvest, with a one-day Feast of Weeks (later known as Pentecost). It involved remembering and celebrating Yahweh's giving them the Torah and drawing them into covenant with him at Mount Sinai.

The festal high point was the Feast of Tabernacles, which took place in the fall after the harvest of the fruit and grapes, when the work in the winepress and on the threshing floor had been completed. This was essentially a seven-day wine festival, an opportunity to celebrate Yahweh with music, singing, dancing, lavish sacrificial meals, and wine. Using leaves, vines, and palm branches, the people constructed temporary huts ("tabernacles") to live in for seven days. This was a reenactment of their ancestors' wilderness wanderings between Mount Sinai and the Promised Land. When shaken, their palm branches sounded like rain, reminding them of how Yahweh had provided them water amid its scarcity in the desert. Their temporary huts recalled for them how Yahweh had provided their ancestors much-needed shelter from the searing desert sun. Yahweh's protective presence among them, both then and now, called for celebration.

Their ancestors' formative desert experience provided lasting metaphors for portraying their relationship with Yahweh. Because he had demonstrated his ultimate superior power and authority over other ancient Middle Eastern deities, they pictured Yahweh as the overshadowing Most High God. This gave rise to the use of images of shade and shadow to depict Yahweh's protective care amid the deadly dangers of blistering desert heat. The book of Psalms would come to include references to finding refuge in "the shadow of Yahweh's wings" and in "the shadow of his hand."

And yet, below the surface of these outward expressions of Yahweh worship, all was not well. For one thing, the vestiges of a polytheistic mindset continued to linger among them. Many still clung to the household gods their ancestors had adopted back in Egypt. For another thing, the religious trend lines appeared to be headed in the wrong direction. They had no single national religious leader to keep them unified as they had during the days of Moses and Joshua. And they had become more scattered geographically. Consequently, their religious practice became more decentralized—and more diversified. Feeling free now to make their own local adaptations, regional variations of Yahweh worship emerged. The biblical account appropriately summarizes this era of the "judges" as a time when "everyone did what was right in their own eyes." It was this apparent spirit of religious autonomy and experimentation that probably also awakened their curiosity about the non-Yahweh religious practices of their new Canaanite neighbors.

The Canaanites, no less religious than these Israelite newcomers, had their own unique system of temples, altars, prayers, sacrifices, and rituals. In typical West Semitic fashion, they believed in the existence of a variety of deities. Chief among them was the god El, the head of a pantheon of gods. His wife Asherah was considered the mother goddess of seventy deities. The people envisioned El and Asherah as sitting in splendor on a remote mountain in the north.

Their son Baal was the most popular Canaanite deity. He was their water god, the one who controlled the rain, the dew, and thus the fertility of Canaanite soil. But those powers were dependent on his connection with two female goddesses. One was his own mother, Asherah. The other was the fertility goddess Ashtoreth. Since rainfall was considered to be Baal's soil-fertilizing semen, the Canaanites believed it would rain only if and when there had been prior sexual activity in the realm of the gods between Baal and one of these goddesses.

But how could Baal's followers be sure he was actually participating in that activity? They came up with an idea. They created multiple open-area religious sanctuaries in higher elevation locations—so-called high places—and furnished them with an altar and two symbols of divine presence. Fertility symbols. A cultic stone pillar representing Baal, and a cultic tree or post (literally an *ashera*) representing the female goddess. There was now one last thing left to do. Get Baal's attention. Have him watch as they themselves engaged in sexually explicit behaviors. Surely, he would then become inspired to do likewise. And produce the rainfall they so desperately depended on.

With the passing of time, Israel's settlers began intermingling with these Baal-worshipping Canaanites. They intermarried, formed tribal alliances, and adapted to aspects of their culture. As they observed Canaanite religious practice, they were intrigued. And they were enticed—to the point where they began incorporating some of its elements into their own religious practices.

What made these practices so irresistible? Surely there was the lure of religiously sanctioned sexual pleasure. But there was more. The Israelites, too, were consumed by concern with basic survival. And survival depended on being able to have children, maintain one's flocks, and produce crops. All in a setting that was extremely unfavorable to eking out a subsistence living. Infertility, poor soil conditions, drought, famine, blight, and disease—these were ever-present life-or-death perils. Threats that lie utterly beyond the reach of human control.

These were all forces that the deities were assumed to control. Yahweh had miraculously led them to this place. Certainly, he could now be trusted to provide what they needed to make it in this new homeland: offspring, fruitful harvests, fertile flocks, protection against the battering forces of nature. Or could he? Could they be sure? It's the universal human self-talk we've all uttered. The inner voice of fear, doubt, and mistrust that so quickly and naturally inundates our minds. The disquieting awareness that we lack ultimate sway over the things we most desperately wish to control.

Was there anything else they could do to ensure their success? Other than just passively sitting back waiting, hoping, and praying for Yahweh to spring into action? Even just some small control lever they could somehow maneuver? The Canaanites appeared to have one. Something the Israelites did not: a female mating partner for their male god Baal. There was no need to reject or abandon Yahweh. How about just substituting him for Baal? And supplementing him with Baal's female goddess mating partner. Let's use Canaanite ritual practices to manipulate Yahweh into giving us what we need.

What a brilliant idea! How could that not increase their odds of securing and enhancing the fertility of their land, their cattle, and their families? No harm, no foul. Or so they thought.

Sadly, history would prove them gravely mistaken. Pure Yahweh religious devotion had become poisoned by a corrupting Canaanite compromise, a melding of Asherah-centered rituals with a Yahweh-centered religion. It was a deep, severe self-inflicted wound that would yield devastating consequences for centuries to come.

Leadership Crisis

As the populations of the Israelite villages in the central hill country continued to grow, they began running out of room to expand. More land was needed to create additional settlements and raise more crops. Meanwhile, another immigrant people arriving from the Aegean Sea region had settled as newcomers along Canaan's southern Mediterranean coast. They were the "Sea Peoples," who became known as the Philistines. Having established their own confederation of city-states in southwestern Canaan, they too had a need for more land. Inevitably, the Philistines and Israelites came to blows in the border area between them. The Philistines seemed intent on bringing the people of Israel into subordination. Israel's very survival as a nation was seriously threatened.

Israel's tribal leaders became convinced that the only way they could stave off the Philistine threat was by making a change in Israel's national leadership. For the prior 250 years, the Israelites had lived without a monarch, and without soldiers. Facing the threat of annihilation at the hands of the Philistines, that was about to change.

Samuel, an itinerant priest, and the last of the series of judges, had gained the respect and loyalty of the tribal leaders.

They saw him as having the necessary religious authority to sanction their proposed change. So, they approached him with an urgent appeal: we need a "king" like the other nations have—a single "war chief," a strongman, who can marshal our tribes into a united military front against our enemy.

2

The Rise and Fall of a Nation

Road to Nationhood

The tribe of Benjamin was small. It occupied a dangerous area of about ten miles by ten miles in the valleys and hills between two antagonizing Canaanite populations. Jebusite-controlled Jerusalem lay to their east and the Philistine-occupied plain to their west. Through repeated skirmishes with these two adversaries over the years, the Benjaminites had developed a reputation as feared warriors. Not surprisingly, it was a Benjaminite that Samuel selected to be the first great war chief of the Israelite tribal coalition. His name was Saul. And he had the best fighting men in the entire confederation.

He achieved early military success against the Ammonites and the Philistines. And for a time, it even appeared he might be able to defeat the Philistines. Unable to win every battle, however, he began to lose support among the tribal leaders. Caught up in petty jealousies and feeling apprehensive about the loss of their own tribal autonomy, they grew increasingly skeptical about Saul's leadership.

Saul's gloomy, ruminating nature did not help. It led to a complete falling out with Samuel and a decision by the priests to choose Saul's replacement. When Saul and his three sons died in battle, the aged Samuel gave his blessing to a young man named David.

Israel was not yet formally a state. Its frayed confederation of tribal leaders was teetering on the brink of dissolution. The Philistines remained a menacing threat. But after a protracted, bloody, and sporadic border war between his "mighty warriors" and Saul's surviving loyalists, David gained the critical support of the elders of the rest of Israel's tribes. He soon leveraged his role as the Israelites' new warrior king into a position of recognized leadership, unified them into a nation, and transformed them into a regional empire.

This was a rare period in ancient Near Eastern history when there was no dominant outside empirical power exercising control over the land of Canaan. It allowed David to implement an ambitious strategy. He occupied, purchased, or conquered all the land he could to the west, south, and east of Israel's existing territory in the central hill country—amassing great wealth for himself in the process.

First up was the strategic city of Jerusalem, a long-standing Canaanite urban center that had remained occupied by the Jebusites. It was a walled citadel, about twelve acres in size, sitting atop steep canyons on three sides. David envisioned its potential as his own highly defensible military bastion. And since none of Israel's twelve tribes yet occupied it, he could claim it as his personal royal property from which to exercise his centralized power.

Next, David secured Israel's political control over large areas of Canaan and Transjordan, confiscating gold and jewels as he went. The Philistines were finally defeated once and for all. Gradually, Israel's old loyalties to tribe and clan were replaced by new loyalties to the Jerusalem capital and the king.

David initiated new national religious developments as well. He brought the ark of the covenant—Israel's most important religious symbol—to his new capital. He established and reinforced the worship of Yahweh throughout the land and began to draw up plans for the construction of a temple for Yahweh in his royal city.

David's son Solomon built onto his father's accomplishments. He oversaw the implementation of a genuine monarchical system consisting of redrawn political districts. He appointed bureaucrats to administer them, collect taxes, and provide work crews for public works and defense projects. Jerusalem emerged as a true administrative and religious center for all of Israel.

Using the enormous wealth left to him by his father, and the trained architects and building materials provided by the neighboring King Hiram of Tyre, Solomon constructed an ornate royal palace for himself and a lavish Canaanite-style temple for Yahweh. To ensure his royal control over this new national, temple-centered religious system, he cast aside the old traditional Levitical line of priests from their old tabernacle days. He installed his ally Zadok as the head of an entirely new line of priests.

Solomon's political and economic achievements were remarkable. Partnering with King Hiram of Tyre, he created one of the great commercial enterprises of history. He built a seaport town at Elath on the Red Sea, where Hiram's shipbuilders constructed an impressive fleet of cargo ships. A lucrative, monopolizing trading business with markets in Babylon and India was thereby established. His great wealth afforded him armies with thousands of chariots and tens of thousands of armor-clad mercenary soldiers. His stables at Megiddo were one of the wonders of the ancient world. Entire cities were built for the express purpose of storing wheat and barley. Travelers, diplomats, and kings from all over the world came to see the splendor of his royal court.

A small, new, economically expanding elite upper class had also emerged. They lived in the urban centers that sprang up on top of the ruins of older Canaanite cities and played an increasingly dominant socio-economic role. No longer farmers, they were involved in the burgeoning trade industry as merchants or manufacturers, were landowners or trained scribes, were involved in the military, or were government officials.

Economic Collateral Damage

But Israel's vast majority continued to subsist as agriculturalists in small, unwalled villages and towns. Most likely, my ancestors were among them. It was they who absorbed the repressive measures employed to fuel Israel's economic expansion: imposition of royal taxes on their flocks and produce; inducement into forced labor on government construction projects; and conscription into a standing army.

As economic burdens became increasingly difficult to bear, many resorted to taking out loans to sustain themselves. And that usually only made matters worse, thanks to the harsh system of credit they were subjected to. High interest rates were the norm. Significant financial pledges, which often involved giving the lender part of the next harvest, were demanded as security. In the event of an insufficient harvest, it meant being required to sell members of their family and finally even themselves into a specified period of slave labor to pay off the debt. Sometimes it came to selling off their land to a wealthy landowner. And then joining groups of bandits in the hills or migrating to the urban areas and resorting to gleaning harvest fields or working as day laborers in menial tasks. Large parts of the rural farming sector subsequently became a permanently impoverished underclass, driven to dependence on the wealthy urban upper class.

Religious Alterations

During Israel's early monarchy—the "united kingdom" years of the reigns of David and Solomon (1000–922 BC)—significant religious developments had unfolded as well. Power and influence had originally been diffused among the various tribes and clans. Now it was centralized in a single Israelite household: the "house of David." Jerusalem, having been converted by David into his family's privately owned estate, was not merely the new national capital. It also became the focal point of an emerging royalty-centered religious system.

Yahweh came to be seen by David and his succeeding royal family as having appointed their household to rule as Yahweh's vassal son. Yahweh's covenant with the corporate people of Israel was now understood to have been narrowed down to a covenant between Yahweh and the house of David. David and Solomon had strategically positioned the two embodiments of Yahweh's earthly presence, the ark of the covenant and the temple. In Jerusalem, David's city. The message was unmistakable. Yahweh himself had endorsed this new Davidic royal dynasty,

David and his heirs now stood able to exercise control over key aspects of Israel's religious expression. They established new national religious pilgrimage festivals at the Jerusalem temple. This was done to rival and replace local clan harvest celebrations. They imposed their kingly authority over the temple and its priests, essentially turning them into royal officials. The temple became effectively a national bank, a treasury for the royal state. Religious gifts and offerings, state-imposed taxes, and revenue generated through royal control of markets, all ended up lining the pockets of the royal family.

A Divided Kingdom

The days of Israel's international glory under Solomon ended with his death. Seeds of dissatisfaction had been growing for some time. His wide-open acceptance of foreign influence was viewed suspiciously. And the burden of his high taxes became deeply resented. As his son Rehoboam began his reign, tribal leaders sought more autonomy, a greater share in governance, and the lifting of their heavy taxation. But Rehoboam refused to compromise. With this, the ten tribal leaders of northern Israel rose in revolt. They divorced themselves from the house of David, acknowledging Jeroboam as their new king. Rehoboam was left holding only David's original kingdom—the tribal territory of Judah plus the city of Jerusalem.

Seeking to create a separate identity for his new northern kingdom, Jeroboam restored two old religious centers. The one in Dan at the extreme northern border of his kingdom and the one in Bethel at the extreme southern border. To symbolize the divine presence at these shrines, he installed images of golden bull calves. This harkened back to the time when Yahweh-worshiping Israelite settlers had incorporated cultic practices of their Baal-worshiping Canaanite neighbors. A new non-Levitical line of priests was placed in charge of these shrines. And, to deter people from attending the temple in Jerusalem, he set up a modified religious festival calendar that would draw worshipers to his shrines instead.

But Jeroboam and his successors were dogged by formidable challenges. Having no royal heritage to point to, their legitimacy was never fully accepted. They faced ongoing political instability. Political pressure from tribal leaders continued. The Levitical priestly community, whom he had excluded from the central shrines at Dan and Bethel, was angry.

Lacking a track record of smooth transitions in power, the pattern of succession to the throne often involved assassinations or military coups.

Voice of the Prophets

It was common in ancient Near Eastern culture for professional religious officials to consult the gods through divination. This became prevalent in Israel as well during the time of their divided kingdom. Israel's prophets were independent of, and often antithetical to, the royal and aristocratic power center in their society. There were two primary themes in the directives from Israel's prophets during this time: the importance of maintaining covenantal faithfulness by worshiping only Yahweh; and, equally crucial, ensuring social justice and equality among the rich and poor.

Three great prophets arose within the northern kingdom. The legendary Elijah contended for Yahweh against the wayward worship of Ashtoreth and the golden bull calves. Around 760 BC the literary prophet Amos, highlighting the righteousness of Yahweh, spoke out against the oppression of the poor. Fifteen to twenty years later, there was Hosea, who warned of their impending destruction by Assyria.

Among the major prophetic voices speaking out on behalf of Yahweh among the people of the southern kingdom of Judah were Isaiah, Habakkuk, and Jeremiah. Isaiah urged and supported King Hezekiah's efforts to rid the Jerusalem temple of the presence of vestiges of foreign religious idols. Habakkuk warned of the looming threat posed by the rising Babylonian kingdom. Jeremiah, acknowledging the inevitable invasion by the Babylonians, called upon the people of Judah not to oppose this act of Yahweh's judgment upon them.

In general, Israel's prophets portrayed Yahweh as desiring to distance himself from so much that he was displeased with among his people: the reliance on political and military power, the unjust economic order, the monarchy, and even the existing religious order. These things had all become impediments to the relationship he yearned to have with his covenant people.

This voice of opposition to the status quo, small and isolated as it appears to have been at times, did have an impact. It helped spur the reforms initiated in the southern kingdom of Judah by King Hezekiah at the end of the eighth century BC, and again by King Josiah in the seventh century. And after the collapse of the monarchy and the Jerusalem temple, the prophetic community would become the most important vehicle for maintaining official Yahweh religion during the time of the exile in Babylon.

Demise of the Northern Kingdom

Eventually, the deteriorating political situation in the northern kingdom hastened its demise. Two emerging superpowers were looking to expand into Israel's territory: Egypt and Assyria. Coming from the territory north and east of Israel in the eighth century BC, the Assyrian military mounted a ferocious onslaught. Forcing their way south and west to the Mediterranean coast, they ravaged large areas and massacred entire city populations. Their brutal style of warfare was accompanied by the ruthless psychological terror of impaling corpses on stakes, stacking severed heads in heaps, and skinning their captives alive. Initially, the northern kingdom of Israel became a vassal state under Assyria's harsh rule. Finally, in response to a revolt led by Israel's King Hoshea in 722 BC, the Assyrians destroyed the northern kingdom's capital at Samaria and deported a large segment of its population to remote areas in the Assyrian empire, never to return.

Kingdom of Judah

The southern kingdom of Judah continued to exist for another three hundred years beyond the time of Solomon, surviving nearly a century and a half past the end of the northern kingdom. But it was only a matter of time until the Assyrian threat would lead to Judah's own eventual demise as well.

It was during the reign of King Hezekiah (715–687 BC) that the kingdom of Judah began to feel the traumatic effect of the Assyrian menace. The destruction of the northern kingdom and sacking of its capital, Samaria, in 722 BC caused thousands of Israelites to flee south to safety in Judah. Those with political and religious responsibility in Judah were confronted by an alarming question. How will we be able to escape the same catastrophe? Hezekiah had an answer. A sweeping religious reform initiative was required. Non-Yahweh divine images and religious symbols, customarily in use until now, were eliminated from the temple and other sanctuaries. An unprecedented emphasis on the exclusivity of Yahweh in religious practice ensued.

But the Assyrian threat only grew more ominous. In 701 BC they attacked. The Assyrian King Sennacherib, in his annals, claimed to have laid siege to forty-six of Hezekiah's cities and to countless small villages in their vicinity. And that he drove out more than two hundred thousand people and countless animals—horses, mules, donkeys, camels, and cattle—and "considered them booty." As for Hezekiah himself, he reported, "I made [him] a prisoner in Jerusalem, his royal residence, like a bird in a cage."

For the next sixty years, Judah lived in political submission. A vassal state of an Assyrian empire whose control stretched from Mesopotamia to Egypt. Their soldiers, administrative officials, and merchants occupied the land. Judeans, especially those residing in Jerusalem, began to adopt aspects of these Assyrians' culture and religious practices. Once again, we see how susceptible Yahweh's followers seem to have been to incorporating elements of non-Yahweh culture and religion.

By the middle of the seventh century, though, Assyria's power had rapidly declined in the face of attacks by the Babylonians and Medes. They lost control of their vassals in the Palestine region. Judah now had an opportunity to make a new political beginning. A sweeping religious, social, and national renewal movement—the "Deuteronomic Reform"—was set in motion. A politically active group called "the people of the land" paved the way. These middle-class landowning farmers, allied with the royal house, helped orchestrate the ascension of the eight-year-old Josiah to the throne. A coalition of influential royal court officials trained in wisdom, a large part of the Jerusalem temple priesthood, individual prophets such as Jeremiah, and the royal house of David joined together to implement radical religious reforms.

Their primary purpose: secure nationwide adherence to the exclusive worship of Yahweh; and thereby restore the powers of the monarchy and of the Jerusalem priesthood. It began with a renovation of the Jerusalem temple, which led to the recovery of the "Book of the Law." This legal code stipulated that Jerusalem was to be the only true place of sacrifice and worship. And that all vestiges of Canaanite and Assyrian worship were to be eliminated. Thus, the various high places and local altars throughout the land were destroyed. The seasonal religious festivals became once again centered on Jerusalem. The activities of the Levitical priesthood became restricted to the confines of Jerusalem. Additionally, the Passover festival, which had not been kept during the time of the judges or since the beginning of the monarchy, was reinstituted. The nation's religious expression consequently became standardized and centralized around the worship of Yahweh at the Jerusalem temple.

But the movement was aimed at making some social reforms as well. Its proponents wished to stem the tide of growing impoverishment within their society and relieve the distress of the lower classes who by and large had lost their land and become debtor slaves.

Reform Movement Failure

Yet, the high hopes of achieving the radical national, social, and religious renewal envisioned by these reformers became shattered after the unexpected death of Josiah in 609 BC. In the face of Babylonia's rising power, Pharaoh Neco of Egypt allied himself with the Assyrians. As Neco's forces traveled through Palestine to assist the Assyrians, King Josiah and his forces engaged them in battle. Josiah was killed. With that, Egypt laid claim to Judah and the surrounding region. Substantial turmoil in Judah followed, expediting its eventual political downfall and destruction.

"The people of the land"—the assembly of Judean land-owning farmers who had earlier installed Josiah as king—bypassed the normal order of succession to Josiah's throne. They anointed his younger son, Johoahaz, believing he was the most likely to carry on his father's reform policies. But Pharaoh Neco of Egypt, looking to succeed Assyrian control of the Palestine region, opposed this move. Feeling threatened by the potential national renewal of Judah, he removed Jehoahaz after three months and installed Josiah's son Eliakim, the "rightful heir," as his puppet king. To reinforce Eliakim's status as Egypt's lackey, Neco changed his name to Jehoiakim. And once in power, Jehoiakim exacted a vengeful tax on the landowner farmers who had tried to bypass him.

The original coalition that initiated the Deuteronomic reform quickly fell apart, with diverging interests. The new king was obviously not on board, and in fact had no qualms about imposing forced labor on the people. Large segments of the aristocracy all too quickly reverted to oppressing the poorer groups in society. The Jerusalem priesthood had gotten what they wanted in the form of religious reform and had never been all that interested in social reform in the first place. The royal court officials who had played a key role now became divided into two rival groups: one fully supporting the new king's anti-social-reform policies, and the other unwilling to fall completely in line behind him. The upper- and middle-class landowners also became split into two opposing groups: one willing to remain committed to the Deuteronomic law, and the other more interested in seeking their own economic advantage. Not surprisingly, Jeremiah portrays a society that at this time had become frayed with rampant greed, deception, and violence.

End of the Davidic Monarchy

The final excruciating days of Judah's monarchy now ensued. In 605 BC, the Babylonians established their superiority over the region by defeating the Assyrians and their Egyptian allies. Shortly thereafter, they seized control of Judah from the Egyptians and made it their own vassal state. But Judah's monarchy refused to go down without further resistance. In 601, counting on assistance from Egypt, King Jehoiakim revolted. Babylon's king Nebuchadnezzar responded by laying siege to Jerusalem in 598, capturing the city, killing Jehoiakim, and taking his son Jehoiachin and a large part of Judah's ruling class—leaders and priests, including the priest/prophet Ezekiel—as hostages back to Babylon. He then installed the last remaining son of Josiah, Mattaniah, as his new puppet king in Judah and changed his name to Zedekiah.

After a nine-year period of relative quiet and acquiescence, Zedekiah initiated his own revolt against his Babylonian masters. Nebuchadnezzar responded this time in 587 BC with more drastic actions, tearing down the city walls of Jerusalem, destroying its buildings, including the magnificent temple, confiscating the temple's treasures, executing Zedekiah's sons in front of him, and then gouging out his eyes. Practically all the skilled and educated people of Judah, though constituting but a small minority of the overall population—the aristocracy, the priests, the craftsmen, the physicians—were deported to Babylon.

Left behind in the war-damaged valleys of the Judean hills were the majority of their compatriots—the farming and vine-growing peasant poor. Most likely among them were my own Judean ancestors. They continued working the land and raising families, slowly recovering a bleak agricultural daily life. Eking out a meager existence under the watchful eye of their Babylonian overlords. Many of the towns and villages that suffered considerable destruction remained under-occupied and impoverished for years to come. Neighboring non-Jewish tribes moved in and laid claim to parts of this territory.

The nation of Israel was no more. Reduced to a failed and decimated state. Its religious and cultural infrastructure was completely dismantled. Its people beaten, scattered, demoralized. Stunned by their abrupt arrival at the end of a dead-end road. Had Yahweh abandoned them? Had the gods of Babylon overpowered him? So much for Yahweh's promise to make Abraham's descendants into a "great nation" through which all the nations of the earth would be blessed. That plan, it seemed, had been completely shredded.

3

Ruled by Foreign Powers

Exiled to Babylon

The educated and skilled Judeans exiled to Babylon were not treated as prisoners of war. They were not enslaved. Nebuchadnezzar merely needed them relocated, so he could install his own superstructure atop the Judean government and economy. That way, he could exploit the production and exportation of Judea's two principal commodities: wine and olive oil. This was an economic windfall for Nebuchadnezzar's coffers.

The Judean deportees were a valuable imported commodity themselves. Babylon's booming economy, with Nebuchadnezzar's many building projects, had created a market demand for the services that Judah's educated and artisan class stood ready to supply. They were transported to ruined cities near Babylon, where they built houses and were provided with fruit trees and vineyards and land for farming. There, they were permitted to govern themselves under the sovereign authority of the Babylonian empire.

Nebuchadnezzar likely assumed these Jewish exiles would eventually become compliantly assimilated into his Babylonian culture. If so, he had badly miscalculated. They may have suddenly found themselves living in a veritable "land of opportunity," enjoying an economic prosperity beyond what was possible back in their homeland. But, clustering together in their own colonies and maintaining a certain level of isolation from their Babylonian neighbors, they stubbornly resisted becoming culturally assimilated.

This was much more than simply being removed from their Jewish homeland. It involved the trauma of being severed from the presence of Yahweh. His earthly dwelling, six hundred miles distant in Jerusalem, had been annihilated. Where was he now? Somewhere back in Jerusalem? Or had he invisibly accompanied them to this foreign land? And now what were they to do? Abandon their Jewish culture and religion, and move on without it?

They chose a different path. Convinced that Yahweh was still among them in their new surroundings, they adopted a new form of religious expression. One that could function independently from their old temple system. The consequences were monumental: they escaped cultural extinction and built a revitalized foundation for strengthening and advancing their Jewish religion.

It seems the seeds for this transformation may have been planted by Yahweh's prophets during the waning days of Judah's kingdom and in the wake of the Babylonian exile. Repeatedly, they had emphasized the pure expression of devotion to Yahweh; that religious rituals and temple sacrifices were of no value to Yahweh in and of themselves; that he was much more interested in their moral living and promotion of social justice. By so undermining the value of temple sacrifices, whether intending to or not, they had prepared the way for the Jews in exile to reconfigure their religious expression—in a way that was no longer temple- or priest-dependent.

One of their innovations was to begin canonizing their scriptures. Remember, these deportees were the highly educated religious experts of Jewish society—intellectuals, scribes, priests, prophets, and former royal court officials. And among the belongings they brought with them from Jerusalem was their literary treasure. Fragments of sacred writing—the oldest parts of the Torah, the chronicles, and works of the prophets. Not to mention the memories of oral legends and histories etched in their minds, and an apparent passion for preserving their heritage for future generations.

They appear to have created a kind of "editorial committee," which gathered together a full collection of the written materials they had brought with them: their oldest manuscripts; ancient clay tablets; scrolls of the books of Moses; the laws of Leviticus and Numbers; legends; historical accounts of battles; stories from their ancestors passed down through the centuries. A systematic assemblage of literature consequently came into being. An initial framework for what would eventually develop into the full Hebrew Scriptures: The Torah (the five books of Moses), books of history, prophecy, ethics, and poetry written in praise of Yahweh. Jewish religion was making a pivotal shift. What had previously been a temple/building-centered religion was now centering itself around the written word. Jewish exiles were becoming a people of the book.

They made one other significant innovation. They began holding religious gatherings on the Sabbath day. These revolved around praying, reading scripture, and listening to discourses. A group of non-priestly lay leaders, who would much later come to be called rabbis, emerged within these settings as well. The various Babylonian Jewish communities thereby became more religiously unified. And a historical foundation was laid for what would later become the Jewish synagogue system. It could be said that the response of those deported to Babylon was to become more intensely Jewish and Yahweh-focused than ever before.

Return From Exile

Around 550 BC, the Babylonian kingdom was defeated by Cyrus the Great and his rising Persian empire. When Cyrus allowed the Jewish exiles in Babylon to return to their homeland, many of them declined to go. They had apparently acclimated themselves comfortably to their new homeland. Babylon had provided new economic opportunities. Having brought wealth in gold and jewels with them to Babylon, and now living in a thriving economic center that provided avenues to Persia, India, and even China, many of them became traders, merchants, and bankers. Many became prosperous, and some became very rich. By the end of the exile period, many Jewish traders had penetrated deep into India and China. Eventually, Babylon would become one of the greatest centers of Jewish wealth and culture in the ancient world, the place where the monumental Jewish Talmud would one day be written.

Although only a small percentage of Jewish exiles did return to Judah, those who did played a pivotal role in Jewish history. They restored the historic Jewish identity of their Palestinian homeland and reestablished the historic connection of their Jewish religion to the Jerusalem temple and its associated religious functions. Inspired by the prophetic voices of Haggai and Zechariah, and led by two high-ranking Jewish officials in the Babylonian royal court, Ezra and Nehemiah, the city walls of Jerusalem and the temple itself were rebuilt.

But Ezra's and Nehemiah's mission expanded beyond a mere physical rebuilding project. Having discovered an unsatisfactory religious situation among the non-deported Jewish population of Judea, they were intent on bringing about religious reform as well. Observing how far these Judeans had strayed from their Jewish religious roots and practices over the past seventy years, Nehemiah couldn't help describing them as "foreigners."

Reform was driven by the scriptural writings—"the law"—brought back with them from Babylon. Though likely not yet the complete Pentateuch, Ezra and Nehemiah viewed it as having ultimate authority over Jewish life. Together, they summoned an extraordinary assembly of the people (the "Great Assembly" or "Men of the Great Synagogue") to pronounce the Torah as the official constitution of the newly re-emerging Judean vassal state. This was intended to blunt the religious authority asserted by the temple priests and the lay aristocracy who had resisted their reforms.

This assembly was soon converted into a central council or tribunal, whose members were selected based on their learning of the religious law and their piety, as opposed to their social status. They asserted their supreme religious and judicial authority as the rightful heir to the tribunal of Jerusalem that had been established by the Davidic dynasty in pre-exilic times. They saw themselves as the recipients of a clear chain of authoritative tradition that had been passed from Yahweh to Moses, from Moses to the prophets, and from the prophets to their tribunal. Thus, while the high priest of Jerusalem became the official political representative of the people as their intermediary with their Persian overlords, this new assembly asserted itself as the Jews' highest administrative body and court.

Ezra had done something unheard of. He called into question the religious supremacy of the priests. He considered them too lenient regarding the high moral standards of the Torah, whose religious authority he believed outranked that of the priesthood. This caused a significant fissure within the Jewish religious leadership circle that reshaped the course of Jewish history. There were now two rival camps, both claiming to be pursuing the preferred, most purely Jewish religious path. Ezra and his followers, emphasizing the study and spread of the Torah, gave rise to a religious camp that would become known as the Pharisees. Those who were supportive of the supreme authority of the priests, on the other hand, would become known as the Sadducees. Their rivalry and mutual antagonism would endure for the next six centuries.

Life in Post-Exile Judah

This is some of what we know about the province of Judea during the post-exilic period under Persian control (450–330 BC). It was a small, physically and economically isolated territory of about eight hundred square miles. It consisted of about thirty thousand inhabitants living mostly in the Judean hill country. Jerusalem was its only urban area with a few thousand residents at its largest. The vast majority lived in unwalled farming villages that were populated on average by less than three hundred people. In one of those villages, there likely resided some of my own ancestors.

The economy was largely agrarian. The bulk of the population engaged in subsistence farming using primitive, labor-intensive methods. Whatever small surplus they produced was extracted through taxation. Just two social classes existed. There were vast numbers of the peasant poor. And the tiny few making up the affluent upper class: the priests living very well off a religious tax, and the considerably wealthy landowning nobles.

A viable Jewish vassal state had been reestablished. It had a rebuilt and repopulated Jerusalem and a rebuilt, fully functioning temple. Once again, the temple had become the spiritual center for the Jewish people. Religious pilgrimages to Jerusalem had resumed. The high priest was back at his temple duties. Sacrifices were again being offered on the temple altar. Regular temple services, including singing and prayer, were taking place. For more than the next one hundred years, the people lived in peace under the friendly protection of the mighty Persian empire.

Then, suddenly, the seemingly indestructible Persian empire was no more, going the way all empires inevitably go. And a new actor appeared on the stage of human history to take its place—Alexander the Great.

Alexander the Great and Hellenization

In 336 BC, at the age of twenty, Alexander succeeded his father to the throne of the Greek state of Macedon. Motivated by the desire for revenge against the ruling Persians and equipped with an unstoppable innovative infantry formation—his father's Macedonian modification of the Greek phalanx—he launched a campaign to seize control of the Persian empire. After freeing the Greek city-states from Persian control and defeating Darius III's armies stationed in Macedonia, Alexander's forces steamrolled their way to victory after victory against Persian strongholds. With his thirty-two thousand infantrymen, he decimated an army that had millions of soldiers. By 323 BC, he had conquered the entire Middle East—Egypt, plus what is today Turkey, Syria, Lebanon, Israel, Jordan, Iran, Iraq, Saudi Arabia, and eastward to India.

Then he suddenly died, leaving no clear successor. So his generals sought to divide the empire among themselves. After many years of conflict, his general Seleucus gained control of the provinces of Asia and Asia Minor, while his general Ptolemy became ruler over Egypt, Syria, and Palestine. Jerusalem surrendered to Ptolemy without a battle, and Judea thereby became part of the Syrian-Palestinian province that the Greeks called "Lower Syria."

To the Jewish population of Judea, the Egyptian Greeks were just another in a rotating series of conquering superpowers. Tribute payments now merely went to the Greeks instead of the Persians. A century-and-a-half period of relative peace and stability ensued. Temple worship continued unhindered. Religious authority continued to be exercised by the high priest.

Alexander's conquering Macedonians viewed those living outside the Greek cultural environment with disdain. They considered their new oriental subjects to be inferior, uncultured "barbarians." To fortify their achievement of absolute military and political superiority over these "barbarians," transplanted Greek mercenaries, civil servants, and technicians took up residence among them. Within ten years, Alexander had built twenty-five new, distinctively Greek-styled cities ("polises") in the Middle East to accommodate them. These became enclaves of "superior" Greek-Hellenist culture.

Those Hellenist centers established in Palestine were limited to the strategic coastal region and to the east of the Jordan River. The small Judean hill-country area around Jerusalem was initially left untouched by any direct contact with Hellenist culture. But that would eventually change.

Alexander the Great's namesake city, Alexandria, Egypt, became a centerpiece of Greek culture in the Middle Eastern world. Jews who were living there during this time quickly adopted the Greek language and many elements of the Greek way of life. As some of them emigrated back to their Judean homeland, they took these Greek cultural influences with them. This unleashed a gradual process of "Hellenization," a blending of Greek and Jewish cultures, within Judea. A rancorous culture war between Jewish factions ensued. For the next five centuries, the course of Palestinian Jewish life—socially, religiously, politically, and culturally—was significantly affected.

What made Hellenist culture so uniquely different? It placed a high value on learning, scientific knowledge, philosophy, the arts, athleticism, entertainment, and the physical beauty of human shape and movement. Greek cities were designed with the intent to display and promote these values. They housed the fundamental Hellenist cultural institutions. The gymnasium, where young men over eighteen engaged in athletic training and educational endeavors. The stadium, where athletic contests were held. The hippodrome, where people could be entertained by horse races. The theater, where people could experience the dramatic arts. There was an element of charm and vitality about all of this that many non-Greek residents found attractive, as it opened up entirely new vistas.

Judean Jewish response to this foreign cultural encroachment was mixed. The vast rural peasant class was minimally affected. But the ruling aristocracy in Jerusalem—the wealthy priestly families—seemed eager to embrace it. They began adopting Greek manners and Greek names, started speaking Greek, wearing tunics, and participating in Greek cultural institutions. Their youth began attending the gymnasium (from the Greek *gymnos,* literally meaning 'nude'). There, in addition to working out and participating with Greek youth in various athletic contests (in the nude), they were educated in the Greek philosophers and poets. They attended the theater where they became swept up in the celebration of the values promoted there by Greek playwrights. All while barely blinking an eye at having to make sacrifices to Greek deities as part of the ritual of participation. From such venues, there extended a slippery slope that could potentially lead to the embrace of a prostitute in a pagan Greek temple.

Jewish intellectuals, whose previous reading and studying had been limited exclusively to Jewish thought, discovered that the Greeks, too, had a body of literature. Ideas. Philosophies. A specific way of picturing the gods and humanity. An alternative approach to the one they had been indoctrinated in at their synagogues. They were especially taken by the Epicurean philosophers, who idolized the pursuit of pleasure. Claiming that the gods don't really care about matters of morality and immorality, they taught that humanity is therefore free to pursue pleasure as their highest goal. And if that entails engaging in immorality, it doesn't matter. The gods don't care. There will be no divine consequences.

Most Jews, though, remained opposed to this intruding Hellenization—offended by its licentious elements. A group of men joined together in standing firmly against Hellenism. The Hasideans, or Pious Ones. They favored isolation over assimilation. Champions of Jewish law, they eagerly defended Jewish religious purity and cultural distinctiveness. As their membership increased, so too did their political voice and influence.

The Seleucids Take Control

The lands of Syria and Judea sat as a buffer zone between the Egyptian Greek Ptolemy-controlled territory to its south and the Greek Seleucid-controlled territory to its north. From day one, this area had been a bone of contention between these two regimes. Around 200 BC, the Seleucids, led by their king Antiochus, wrested it away from Egyptian control. This was part of Antiochus's grandiose plan to unify the entire former Alexandrian empire under his rule and defeat the Romans. He believed he would achieve that unity through an intense program of Hellenization, the erection of statues of Greek gods and of himself throughout his domain.

Palestine's Jews resisted his demand to erect these statues in their temple. Hadn't they already proved their loyalty by paying him taxes and bearing arms for him? Antiochus acquiesced and allowed a Jewish exception to his Hellenizing policy. But his son Antiochus Epiphanes, inheriting the throne in 176 BC, believed as a matter of principle that the Jews, too, should be subjected to this policy.

While the governors of provinces under Seleucid rule were customarily appointed by the Seleucid king, the Jews, by contrast, were self-governed under the office of high priest. In their case, the Seleucid king would usually appoint the high priest recommended to them by the Jews themselves. This set off a power struggle among the Jewish leaders. Who should they recommend as high priest? And who among them got to make this selection? Hellenized Jewish aristocrats wanted to help Antiochus Epiphanes in his plan to Hellenize Palestine. Through deception and bribery, they convinced him to appoint a leading Hellenizing priest in Palestine as high priest. His name was Jason. (He preferred this Greek form of his name to the Hebrew form, Joshua.)

Under Jason's high priesthood, Greek statues were brought into the temple sanctuary. Jewish priests presided at Greek cultic rites, dressed in Greek costumes. Naked Jewish young men participated in Greek games in the temple courts. A gymnasium was constructed in Jerusalem and enrolled Jewish youths. They donned the hat of Hemes, the patron god of Greek sports, and changed their Hebrew names to Greek forms. Anti-Hellenistic Jews bristled with anger and resentment. The ranks of the resistant Hasidean party grew. Tension mounted between Jewish Hellenizers and anti-Hellenizers.

A few years later, a man named Menelaus, having been sent by Jason to Antiochus to deliver Jason's annual tribute money to his Seleucid overlords, decided to make a power move for the high priest position for himself. He offered Antiochus a higher bid than Jason's and pledged an even more thorough policy of

Hellenization. Antiochus acceded, and Menelaus arrived back in Jerusalem as the new Seleucid-sanctioned high priest as Jason's replacement. Jason took refuge in Transjordan, awaiting an opportunity to strike back. His opportunity came a few years later when a rumor reached Jerusalem that Antiochus had died during his army's march against Egypt. With a force of one thousand men, Jason attacked Jerusalem and drove Menelaus into refuge in its citadel, massacring many innocent people in the process. Eventually, though, he was forced out of the city and back to the Transjordan.

Antiochus's Vengeful Response

But the rumor that Antiochus had died in Egypt proved false. Given an embarrassing ultimatum to leave Egypt and facing open rebellion against his authority in Palestine, Antiochus decided to vent his rage on the Jews. He marched his armies out of Egypt and into Jerusalem. Indiscriminately slaughtered ten thousand of its inhabitants. Installed a new set of pagan statues in the temple to replace the old ones that had been tossed over the temple wall and shattered on the ground below. Reinstated Menelaus as high priest, and, in Menelaus's presence, proceeded to defile the temple and plunder its treasures. He then departed, leaving the city under the charge of one of his Syrian military commanders.

A year later, following further unrest in Jerusalem, he sent his general Apollonius to deal with the matter. Apollonius arrived, pretending to have friendly and peaceful intentions. Waiting until the Sabbath, knowing the orthodox Jews would not fight on that day, his troops bolted into the city, took women and children as slaves, and killed many of its residents. They rampaged through the city, plundering, burning, and razing houses to the ground.

They fortified the citadel on the western hill opposite the temple and turned it into a fortress occupied by Syrian troops and Jewish Hellenist sympathizers. Dubbed the Akra, it essentially became a "Greek city" in and of itself, holding command over the subjugated city of Jerusalem. Newly empowered, the Hellenizing wealthy Jewish priestly and noble families imposed taxes on, and confiscated land from, the mass of people living in Jerusalem and the surrounding countryside. Syrian soldiers appropriated the Jewish temple for worshiping their own pagan gods, with no apparent objection from the Jewish priests. Finding these conditions too intolerable, a considerable number of Jewish residents fled the city.

Setting his sights on the distinctive expressions of the Jewish faith, Antiochus implemented a policy aimed at eradicating the Jewish religion altogether. He issued and then enforced a severe decree. It called for the destruction of all copies of the Torah. Prohibited the traditional Jewish temple sacrifices from being offered. Banned participation in customary Jewish religious festivals. Outlawed Sabbath observance and the circumcision of children. Violators were to be executed.

And he went even further. It became mandatory for all his subjects to participate in the official Greek religious cult. Pagan temples and idolatrous altars were set up throughout the land. There, on the penalty of death, Jews were required to offer unclean sacrifices and eat the flesh of swine in direct violation of their own religious law. Most offensive of all, the temple of Yahweh was converted to a house of worship for the Olympian god Zeus. In the holy of holies above the great altar of Yahweh, stood a new altar with a bearded image of Zeus. The altar of Yahweh now served as a mere pedestal for the altar of Zeus. The terrorizing symbolism of this image was unmistakable. Yahweh had been dethroned by a superior deity. Where exactly, in the midst of all this, was their sovereign Yahweh to be found? Could he not put a stop to this travesty?

A few Jews yielded to these coercive measures by renouncing their own religion and nationality. Others stubbornly resisted and paid with their lives. Hoping to escape harassment by Syrian agents, many left the Jewish cities for refuge in remote villages and surrounding mountain and desert regions. Among them were the members of the orthodox, anti-Hellenist Hasidean party. Withdrawing to the desert region, hiding in the caves and ravines of the Judean hills, they plotted to regain their religious and political freedom. Emerging occasionally from their hideouts and making their way undetected to various towns and villages, they inspired their fellow Jews to rise in resistance. This undercurrent of dissension would soon erupt into a major resistance uprising.

Battling for Freedom

That eruption burst to the surface in 165 BC in the village of Modein, seventeen miles northwest of Jerusalem. An elderly priest named Mattathias of the house of Hasmon had moved there with his five sons—John, Simon, Judas, Eleazar, and Jonathan. Syrian agents arrived one day to coerce the villagers into renouncing Yahweh and offering pagan sacrifices. As a recognized leader in the village, Mattathias was ordered to be the first to comply and set the example for his community. He refused and publicly declared his loyalty to Yahweh. Another villager volunteered to offer the mandated sacrifice instead. Mattathias, incensed at the prospect of this profanity, took the man's life on the altar. He then turned and murdered a Syrian officer standing nearby and destroyed the pagan altar. Imploring all those who were devoted to the Torah to join him, he and his supporters fled to the mountains in the Judean wilderness.

Joining forces there with the like-minded Hasideans, they took up tactics of guerrilla warfare. They went village to village tearing down altars. Forcibly circumcised uncircumcised children. Executed Jewish people who had participated in pagan sacrifices. Mattathias's third son, Judas, succeeded him as the leader of this subversive movement. He was tagged with the nickname "Maccabee" (meaning "hammer" or "hammer-headed"). Under his guidance, the group engaged in well-planned battles and full-scale warfare in what would come to be known as the Maccabean Revolt.

After winning some initial victories, he marched into Jerusalem, surrounded the Akra, and trapped the Syrian troops and Jewish Hellenist sympathizers inside it. Next, he proceeded to restore the Jewish temple. The detested altar to Zeus was destroyed. The sanctuary and temple interior were renovated. Exactly three years after its desecration by Antiochus Epiphanes, the temple and its altar were rededicated to their proper use. High defensive walls and towers were built around Jerusalem, stationed with armed protective troops.

Having secured the territory of Judea under his control, Judas now turned his attention beyond Judea's borders. Desiring to make the entire Palestinian area completely Jewish, he launched successful campaigns across the border to the south, east, and north. Unable to sustain permanent control in those areas, however, he brought Jewish residents living there back to Judea.

There was yet one outstanding issue for him to address. The despised symbol of terrorizing Syrian domination, the Akra, was still in enemy possession. A stark reminder that Antiochus IV's atrocious anti-Jewish decree was officially yet in effect. Judas initiated a blockade against it. Eventually a settlement was reached. The anti-Jewish decree was rescinded in exchange for the lifting of Judas's blockade.

Jewish *religious* freedom had at last been achieved. Yet, Judea remained under Syrian *political* control. Conflict between pro-Syrian and anti-Syrian elements within the Jewish power structure continued to fester. And Syrian efforts to leverage that internal conflict to their own advantage persisted.

To that end, the Syrians appointed a member of the Jews' pro-Syrian Hellenizing party named Alcimus as the new high priest. Judas rejected this appointment and prevented him from assuming his assignment in Jerusalem. Meanwhile a power struggle in Syria had resulted in the assumption of Demetrius I to its throne. In return for Alcimus's and his Jewish Hellenist supporters' pledge of support, Demetrius affirmed Alcimus as high priest. When Demetrius sent an army to Jerusalem to capture Judas and enforce Alcimus's appointment, it was defeated and Alcimus fled to safety in Syria. Demetrius then sent another more imposing army contingent to Jerusalem to engage Judas and his men in battle. Judas was killed. Some of his associates were apprehended, tortured, and executed. Many others fled into hiding in the Judean desert. Alcimus became high priest, with the Hellenists once again in control. Judas's younger brother Jonathan, meanwhile, assumed the mantel of Maccabean rebel leadership.

When Alcimus died a couple years later, no appropriate candidate was found to replace him. The office of high priest remained vacant for the next seven years. Jonathan and his followers seized this opportunity to increase their power and influence over Judean affairs. And a period of peace within Judea ensued.

But a time of internal conflict developed within Syria. And Jonathan exploited it. Alexander Balas, claiming to be the son of the deceased Antiochus Epiphanes, challenged Demetrius's right to the Syrian throne. The two men, acknowledging that Jonathan was now the de facto leader of Judea, attempted to outbid each other in wooing Jonathan's support with proposals favorable to the Jewish cause.

In the end, Jonathan achieved a scaling back of Syrian troop presence in Judea. He secured for himself the appointment as high priest and was made "general and governor of Judea." This essentially ended the Hellenist element's political influence in Judean affairs. He then set his sights on expanding the territory of the Judean state but met his untimely death before he could do so.

His brother Simon immediately succeeded him. Continuing to exploit internal Syrian strife, Simon achieved in 142 BC the objective that both his Maccabean brothers Judas and Jonathan had pursued. The Jewish nation was at last independent from Seleucid-Syrian rule. The Akra in Jerusalem, the last remaining Syrian stronghold in Judea and the symbol of Syrian domination for the past forty years, was finally captured. For the next seventy years (142–63 BC), the people of Judea would enjoy the independence which had been so relentlessly fought for and won. But then another, even greater, world power would emerge and wrest it away once more.

Hasmonean Rule

Having achieved his nation's political independence, Simon now sought to solidify his base of power and influence among his people. To his role as *political* leader of Judea, he added the pivotal role of highest *religious* authority—the high priest. Traditionally, this role had been filled by a member of the officially recognized high priestly family and was officially sanctioned by the Jewish religious council (Sanhedrin). The three previous high priests, however, had not been members of the traditional high priestly family and had been appointed by the Syrian king, not by the Jewish Council. So, Simon got the council to appoint himself—someone *not* from the high priestly family—as the new high priest. He also got them to designate his Hasmonean family as the new official high priestly family with hereditary rights to the office. Thus, Simon and his descendants had vested within them both priestly and political power.

In 134 BC, Simon and two of his sons were treacherously murdered in a coup attempt by his son-in-law. A third surviving son, John (Hyrcanus I), succeeded him as high priest and political ruler for the next thirty years. The Syrian-Seleucids were preoccupied at this time with internal strife and thereby rendered incapable of any longer interfering in the affairs of Judea. Hyrcanus consequently seized the opportunity to expand his borders. He invaded Idumea (Edom) to the south, forcibly circumcising many inhabitants in the process. In the Samaritan region to the north, he conquered Shechem, destroyed the Samaritan temple at Gerizim, and razed the Greek city of Samaria to the ground.

Sadducees Versus Pharisees

During Hyrcanus's time as national leader and high priest, two influential rivaling groups of national religious leaders gained increased prominence: the Sadducees and the Pharisees. Both were represented in the governing body known as the Sanhedrin. Both were wrestling with the same dilemma: what did it mean for them to be a Jewish nation? Did it mean, as the Pharisees believed, remaining primarily a *spiritual* nation, emphasizing Jewish religious purity and isolation from the non-Jewish world? Or did it mean, as the Sadducees believed, becoming another *political* nation like others around them, separating government from religion and adopting Hellenized concepts and practices of secular statehood?

The conflict between these two religious groups was multilayered. For one thing, they belonged to two different social classes. The Sadducees belonged to the influential, wealthy, aristocratic upper class of Jewish society. Many of them were priests, descendants of the ancient priestly family of Zadok, high priest of Israel during the time of David and Solomon. But there were also wealthy traders and high-ranking government officials among their ranks as well. The Pharisees, on the other hand, belonged to the middle class of society.

For another thing, there was a "clergy versus layman" dynamic at play between them. The Sadducees were mostly a priestly group, steeped in the tradition of special anointing for the high calling of temple service. They championed the observance of the temple ritual system. They were "people of the temple building." The Pharisees, by contrast (although some priests were included among their ranks), were primarily non-ordained laymen. They championed the intellectual and scholarly pursuit of studying and interpreting the Torah, and were passionate about pious, moral living. They were "people of the book."

Both parties acknowledged the supremacy of the Jewish Law. But one of their most fundamental differences had to do with what actually constituted that Law. The Sadducees considered the Torah (Pentateuch) alone to be the authoritative Law. And any interpretations to be made regarding it were considered the exclusive prerogative of the priests. Those seeking to obey the commands of God simply needed to follow the priests' interpretations of the Torah, along with the priestly dictates and practices found therein. The Torah was considered to have a narrow application to the temple and its rituals, not to the details of the people's everyday living.

The Pharisees, however, were the heirs of a long tradition of scribal writings whose purpose was to interpret the meaning of the Torah. They had, over time, developed an elaborate system of oral laws to bolster the Torah's authority with a protective "fence" around it. By applying the minute details of this oral law to their everyday life, the people could supposedly protect themselves from violating the stipulations of the Torah itself. They came to consider this legal tradition—their "tradition of elders"—to be just as authoritative and binding as the written Torah itself. And, unlike the Sadducees, they considered the sacred body of authoritative scriptures to include the Prophets and the Writings as well as the Torah.

One can well imagine the potential for animosity here. Middle-class non-ordained laymen were challenging the historical prerogative of upper-class ordained priests to be the official interpreters of the Torah. Not only that. They were also elevating their own oral scribal traditions to the same honored level as the sacred Scripture itself.

A Brewing Civil War

When Hyrcanus first began as leader and high priest, he was aligned with the Pharisee camp. It had at that time achieved considerable influence on the Jewish population. Their concept of the "tradition of the fathers" and the teachings derived from it had captured the hearts and minds of most of the Judean people. Soon, however, the Pharisees became disillusioned with what they perceived to be the increasing secularization and worldliness of the high priesthood. In their eyes, it had become profaned by political ambition and thirst for military might. They increasingly opposed the concentration of both secular and religious power in a single person, such as Hyrcanus, who was functioning as both king and high priest.

The Sadducees used this opposition to convince Hyrcanus to switch his loyalties to their camp. This did not sit well with the masses, however. It provoked a pro-Pharisee rebellion that Hyrcanus was compelled to subdue. But widespread pro-Pharisee sentiment persisted. And it became even more passionately inflamed under the reign of Hyrcanus's successor son, Alexander Jannaeus.

Jannaeus's ruthless character, his infatuation with being a warrior king, his impious, drunkard lifestyle, and his cavalier approach to the high priesthood did not go over well. The Pharisees, especially, became exasperated. And eventually became openly critical. His growing unpopularity came to a head on one occasion during the Feast of the Tabernacles, at which Jannaeus was presiding as high priest. Standing in front of the altar and preparing to offer the sacrifice, he flippantly poured a water libation over his own feet instead of on the altar as Pharisaic tradition required. In response, the people pelted him with citrons and launched insults at him, accusing him of being unfit to be their high priest. He became so enraged that he unleashed his mercenaries in a bloodbath, murdering six thousand people.

Civil unrest broke out in Jerusalem. Urged on by the Pharisees, the people rose in revolt. During the six years of civil war that followed, Jannaeus killed no fewer than fifty thousand of his fellow Jews. In desperation, the Pharisees turned to the Seleucid king Demetrius III for help. Defeated by Demetrius, Jannaeus and his mercenaries fled into hiding in the mountains. He was joined by six thousand loyalists. After regrouping, Jannaeus forced Demetrius to withdraw and unleashed his vengeance on his Pharisee enemies. He captured about eight hundred of them and brought them back to Jerusalem. There, while feasting and carousing with his concubines, he had their children slaughtered in front of them and then had them crucified. His remaining eight thousand Jewish enemies took flight by night and remained in exile for the remainder of Jannaeus's life.

When Jannaeus died at the age of forty-nine from a drinking-related illness, he handed control of his affairs to his widow, Salome Alexandra. This was because Jannaeus's oldest son and rightful heir to the throne, Hyrcanus II, was deemed unfit to serve as king. She thus became queen and ruled in his stead for the next nine years. But, being a woman and thereby disqualified from becoming high priest, she appointed Hyrcanus II to that position. This did not sit well with his younger brother Aristobulus II. He considered himself much more qualified, not only for being high priest but also for being king. This sibling rivalry shifted to a battlefield after the death of their mother. Hyrcanus surrendered and relinquished his role as king and high priest to Aristobulus.

At this time, a third prominent figure entered the Jewish political scene to complicate matters further. His name was Antipater, son of the Antipater whom Jannaeus had appointed governor of Idumea. He was none other than the father of the future Herod the Great. Antipater viewed the power struggle between Hyrcanus and Aristobulus as something he could leverage to gain power for himself. While pretending to be a mediator between the brothers, he worked behind the scenes, paving the way for the Romans to take over and place him in charge instead.

Arrival of the Romans

Meanwhile, Roman armies had arrived in Syria to snatch up its crumbling empire and head through Palestine on their conquest to the Euphrates River. Civil war in Judea would only hamper their larger plans. When the Roman general Pompey had reached Damascus in 65 BC, he was approached by three competing delegations of Jews seeking a deal. One was led by

Aristobulus II, who claimed his brother Hyrcanus II lacked the ability to be the Jewish leader. Another was led by Hyrcanus II, who asserted that as the older brother, he was the legitimate heir to the Jewish throne. A third was made up of Pharisees, requesting that these two brothers' Hasmonean house of rulership itself be abolished and the original high priestly family be reestablished.

Pompey took Hyrcanus's side and imprisoned Aristobulus. When he advanced his Roman army on Jerusalem in 63 BC, Hyrcanus's supporters capitulated and opened the city gates for them. But Aristobulus's followers had fortified themselves in the temple area, planning to resist. After a three-month assault, their position was overrun, and a massacre of twelve thousand Jewish lives ensued. Aristobulus, however, was spared and taken captive to Rome. Hyrcanus was reinstated as high priest, but his role as king was abolished.

And so, the Hasmonean era of Jewish political independence came to a bleak demise. Territory they had added to the Jewish kingdom was taken away. The Jewish nation was reduced to Judea and the districts of Galilee in the north, Idumea in the south, and Perea east of the Jordan. They were now merely an annex to the Roman province of Syria.

Futile attempts to regain this lost ground and restore the Hasmoneans to political power continued for the next twenty years. There was dissension among the people regarding this loss of freedom, and with the continuing high priesthood of Hyrcanus II. Aristobulus II, who had escaped capture in Rome and returned to Judea, attempted popular uprisings against Hyrcanus and his cohort Antipater.

Further developments on the Judean political scene became entangled with political developments in Rome. A growing rivalry between Julius Caesar and Pompey had by 49 BC erupted into civil war. Antipater and Hyrcanus sided with Caesar. So, when Pompey was murdered the following year, Caesar gladly rewarded them for their support. He appointed Hyrcanus as ethnarch of Judea—having both the role of religious and civil leader for the first time. He granted Roman citizenship to Antipater and had him appointed by the Roman Senate to the more senior role as procurator of Judea.

When Julius Caesar was murdered four years later by members of the Roman Senate, Antipater and Hyrcanus retained their positions by siding with Cassius, one of the conspirators against Caesar. As Roman procurator now of Judea, Antipater named his oldest son, Phasael, governor of Jerusalem with jurisdiction over Judea and Perea, and he placed his fifteen-or-so-year-old son Herod in charge of Galilee. In 42 BC, Antipater was poisoned to death by family members at a feast with his concubines, and Herod assumed headship of the family. One year later, Mark Anthony, having become the new Roman power in the East, appointed the two brothers Herod and Phasael joint tetrarchs of Judea.

The Parthians, however, were still vying with Rome for control of Syria. While Rome's Antony was tied up with military matters in Egypt, they made a play against Rome for control of Judea. They captured both the Rome-backed high priest Hyrcanus II and governor Phasael, and declared Aristobulus II's son, Antigonus III, to be Judea's new high priest and king. Phasael committed suicide while in prison by bashing his head on a rock. Hyrcanus's ears were cut off, making him legally disqualified to continue serving as high priest.

In 40 BC, Antigonus arrived in Jerusalem with a powerful Parthian army. Chased out of Jerusalem by these Parthian forces, Herod and his household fled by night for safety to the desert fortress of Masada near the Dead Sea. En route, just past Bethlehem, Herod's entourage was attacked by local Judeans. According to the first-century Jewish historian Josephus, Herod "slaughtered many of them." He would later memorialize this battle site and his butchery here through the construction of a grand fortress palace-tomb—the Herodion. His victims' families were thereby forever reminded of his vicious cruelty.

Herod escaped to Arabia, and, hoping to join up with his Roman ally Antony, made his way first to Egypt and then to Rome. There he was eminently acclaimed as Rome's ally against their Parthian enemies. Declared by the Roman Senate as the legitimate "King of the Judeans," he left the Senate meeting grandiosely strolling between the renowned Mark Antony and Caesar Augustus. He then returned to Judea to oust Antigonus and lay claim to his kingship.

Buttressed by Antony's army under the leadership of the Roman governor of Syria, Sossius, Herod and his forces, in 37 BC, captured Jerusalem. Large numbers of its residents were abused and massacred. Antigonus was seized, and, abhorrently, "treated as a woman" by Sossius, sent to Antony in Syria, and beheaded with an axe. The legendary Hasmonean family line was now finally extinguished. And Herod assumed the throne.

We will pick up the story of Herod and his reign of terror later in Chapter 5. But first, the story of the rise of Rome must be told. It will help us better understand the broader historical and political dynamics that shaped Palestinian Jewish life during the epic era of Jesus of Nazareth.

4
The Rise of Rome

Unremarkable Beginnings

Back when my Jewish ancestors were trapped in Egyptian bondage, other events were unfolding across the Mediterranean Sea from them. Fifteen hundred miles to their northwest, on the Italian peninsula, hundreds of tiny villages had sprouted—a hodgepodge of independent people groups with many different origins, languages, and cultural traditions.

Indistinguishable among the thousands of ordinary tiny settlements there, one had begun to form on a group of hilltops near the Tiber River in central Italy. Later, at about the same time that King David was establishing his monarchical dynasty in Jerusalem around 1000 BC, these little hilltop settlements coalesced into a single community of a few thousand wattle-and-daub-hut dwellers. Before long, an increasingly wealthy handful of elite families among them seized political control. To survive in a world of independent local warrior bands, they formed their own miniature monarchy with a war chief of their own. Eventually, this cluster of hilltop communities began envisioning itself as "Rome."

By the sixth century BC, around the time King Nebuchadnezzar was sacking Jerusalem and hauling away Judean exiles to Babylon, this settlement near the Tiber River had become a recognizable urban community with public buildings, temples, and a city center. With approximately twenty to thirty thousand inhabitants, it was substantially larger than its surrounding Latin settlements. Yet, though it had become a major player in the region, there was nothing uniquely different about it.

Early Roman Expansion

That changed during the 400s and early 300s BC. While Persia and Greece were duking it out for dominance of the eastern Mediterranean region in which my Palestinian Jewish ancestors resided, the city of Rome was dramatically expanding its influence and power throughout the Italian peninsula. What had been just an ordinary small town in 500 BC had, by 300 BC, become home to an extraordinary population of sixty to ninety thousand people. Rome now found itself in exclusive company—sharing the stage with a mere handful of the largest urban centers in the entire Mediterranean world.

Disputes between the independent villages and people groups inhabiting Italy at this time were inevitable. Violent force was typically used to settle them. The lucrative plundering of one's neighboring community was considered a legitimate source of income. Rome, too, became entangled in these turf battles. But as its annual warfare campaigns brought its warriors further and further away from home, they adopted a groundbreaking approach. Unlike any other ancient city before, they formed friendly alliances with their defeated foes. Offered them Roman citizenship, the unheard-of ability to be official citizens of two places at once—both of their hometown and of Rome. With this came the benefits of partnership in the profitable financial enterprise that Rome's conquests were producing: a stake in the ever-growing booty and glory garnered by Rome's continued expansion.

Only one obligation was imposed on them in return: the provision of troops for Rome's growing army. Each new conquered community consequently raised up, equipped, and helped command their own new recruits. Thus, without the use of occupying Roman forces or any Rome-imposed local government, newly defeated Italian territories were incorporated into Rome's growing military machine. This became a self-sustaining system for continued Roman expansion, an approach that no other ancient city had ever before taken. Accordingly, by 300 BC Rome controlled over half the Italian peninsula.

The Romans had discovered the key to military achievement during this era. It was not the use of superior tactics, or having stronger skills, or better equipment, or greater motivation. Success hinged, rather, on how many soldiers could be deployed. While Alexander the Great had had one hundred thousand troops available to defend against the Persian invasion of his Greek territory, and while he had later used around fifty thousand troops in his own victorious campaign in the eastern Mediterranean, the Romans at this time had amassed nearly an astounding five hundred thousand Italian soldiers.

Overseas Expansion

During the third and second centuries BC, while the Syrian Seleucid (Greek) rulers were imposing their will over the realm of my Jewish ancestors in Palestine, and as pressure was building there toward the eruption of the Jewish Maccabean Revolt, the Romans shifted to a new phase of military activity beyond the Italian peninsula. For twenty years, they battled the North African city of Carthage (in the First Punic War) to finally gain control of Sicily. A clash between Romans and

Carthaginians in Spain subsequently sparked the Second Punic War, during which the Carthaginian general Hannibal crossed the Alps into Italy from the north with his elephants and inflicted severe casualties. Anticipating support for Hannibal from the Macedonians in northern Greece, the Romans went on the offensive against them and gained control of mainland Greece. There were additional conflicts with the Gauls in far northern Italy. And they decisively defeated the Palestinian Jewish people's great nemesis, the repressive Seleucid king, Antiochus of Syria.

In 146 BC Roman armies utterly destroyed their oldest, wealthiest, and most powerful Mediterranean rivals: the North African city of Carthage and the city of Corinth in Greece. With that, they assumed control of almost the entire known world. Thousands upon thousands of slaves from all over the world, at a rate of eight thousand new captives each year, poured into Italy and Rome to work their fields, mills, and mines. Rome's economic growth and production skyrocketed.

The Roman people, with the staggering profits attained through all their conquests, became far and away the wealthiest of any in the known world. Their trophies of conquest—captured soldiers, newly conscripted slaves, and confiscated booty—were paraded through the city of Rome in a great triumphal procession after each new major victory. The one held in 167 BC in celebration of their defeat of the Macedonians included 250 truckloads of sculptures and paintings alone. It took three days to parade all the loot through the city. The impounded silver coins filled 750 large vessels, requiring three thousand men to cart them to the state treasury in the well-guarded basement of the temple of Saturn in the Forum. During another triumph celebrated in 61 BC, seventy-five million silver coins were paraded through Rome, an amount equivalent to the empire's entire annual tax revenue, enough cash to feed two million people for an entire year. Much of it, however, went toward the construction of a stone theater in Rome that had a stage wider than the length of a football field.

Government in Crisis

By the mid-first century BC, Rome had become an immense metropolis with more than a million residents. After two centuries of military aggression, warfare, and negotiation, it held sway over a vast Mediterranean empire. But the Roman Republic's five-hundred-year-old political system was ill-equipped to manage this new reality. It could barely govern the peninsula of Italy, let alone manage an empire that consisted of almost the entire known world.

Originally designed to ensure a balance of power and prevent the emergence of another monarchy, the Roman Republic's old system was complex and unwieldy. Its Senate consisted of hundreds of wealthy, highly influential aristocratic former magistrates. Although they did not legislate, they did control Rome's finances, its foreign policy, and its military affairs. There were various additional assemblies that gathered to pass laws, elect magistrates, and make key decisions. Among them was the Plebian Council representing the common citizens. It played a crucial role in balancing the aristocratic power of the Senate with a push for reforms that would be more favorable to the commoners. Executive power was held by two annually elected "consuls"—chief executives and military commanders who presided over the Senate and the assemblies.

These traditional political structures were now being strained to a breaking point. Part of the stress came from social conditions within Rome itself: massive disparities of wealth, widespread hunger, and exploitation of the poor. Efforts to bring about political reforms that would improve the lot of the poor were vehemently thwarted by groups of senators. The wealthy Senate members themselves were divided between those who favored the continuation of the status quo and those who sought popular support against the status quo.

Social unrest erupted into protests, riots, and crime waves—and there was no police force to prevent this from spilling into lethal political violence. The political process progressively degenerated as street violence became a go-to political tool. Swords and clubs were replacing the ballot box. Murder was becoming a political weapon of choice against one's opponent.

For generation after generation, the Senate had been monopolized by the same old aristocratic families. It had become a snobbishly exclusive "old boys" network resistant to admitting newcomers who were more competent. It had earned a widely perceived reputation for bribery and ineptitude.

The demands of defending, policing, and occasionally extending its widespread empire placed even more stress on Rome's struggling political infrastructure. To sustain its imperial enterprise, individual commanders were given enormous financial and military resources for years on end. These generals subsequently turned their legions into private militias centered around the personal interests of their generals instead of the interests of Rome. In exchange for a share in their commanders' booty and the offer of a lucrative retirement package of land at the end of their military service, soldiers were rendering absolute loyalty to their generals rather than to Rome.

Because of their immense power, wealth, and military backing, these commanders came to dominate the political scene as well. For it was the general population, through the vote of their assemblies—not the Senate—that determined who would command Rome's armies. To obtain approval for such an appointment and the vast resources to fund it, one had to persuade the assembly that he was the best candidate for the position. Roman governance thus became increasingly dependent on the abilities and efforts of a very few select politically-savvy military commanders.

A Temporary Solution

Around 60 BC, three of Rome's most powerful and wealthy men had become exasperated with Rome's gridlocked political process. All three were waiting on Senate action on their particular proposals. Tired of waiting any longer, they made an informal side deal among themselves to break the impasse. Pooling their finances and their influence, they came up with a way to fix the political process such that each of their own divergent personal interests could be served.

One of the three, Pompey, had recently carried out a successful military campaign in the eastern Mediterranean regions of Syria and Mesopotamia. He had been back in Rome now for the past two years, waiting for a procrastinating Senate to approve the new treaties and geographical re-structuring he had arranged there. He was also looking for land to provide to his forty thousand ex-soldiers in fulfillment of the retirement packages he had promised them.

Marcus Crassus, purportedly the wealthiest man in Rome, had been working with a struggling group of contractors who had put in a bid for the tax rights of the province of Asia. They had way overbid, and Crassus was now trying to get the Senate's permission for them to renegotiate a new bid.

Julius Caesar, the least wealthy and experienced of the three, was aiming to get elected to the consulship of 59 BC and then secure a major military command. After he was successfully elected consul for 59 BC, Caesar was able to implement the threesome's privately arranged plan. He sponsored the legislation that both Pompey and Crassus had been seeking. And he secured a ten-year military command for himself in southern Gaul with a contingent of forty thousand troops at his disposal.

During his decade of warfare in Gaul, Caesar added more territory to Rome's control than Pompey had added in the East— albeit slaughtering nearly a million people in the process. About the time that his ten-year assignment to Gaul was approaching its end, Rome's Senate, in 50 BC, voted 370–22 that both Caesar and Pompey were to immediately relinquish their commands. Pompey, residing in Rome at this time, simply ignored the Senate's wishes. Caesar attempted to negotiate with the Senate, but to no avail.

Caesar Seizes Control

The next year, Caesar and one of his legions fatefully stepped across the northern boundary of Italy, the babbling brook of the Rubicon, and began marching toward Rome to seize control. A contingent of his supporters in Rome hastily met up with him in northern Italy. Pompey, meanwhile, departed Italy, retreating to his power base in the East for the looming battle. Civil war between the two armies spread throughout the Mediterranean world. In 48 BC Caesar decisively defeated Pompey's forces in a battle in Greece. Pompey sought refuge in Egypt and was murdered there shortly after.

Over the next three years, a victorious Caesar further consolidated his grip on power by defeating additional internal adversaries in Africa and Spain. And then he turned his attention eastward to the Parthian Empire centered in present-day Iran. Not only did he have a personal score to settle with them. They also provided him with an attractive opportunity for achieving military glory. Something more than just the glory of defeating his own Roman enemies. He had his eye on the higher personal glory that would come with his defeat of a potent and threatening foreign enemy.

Just a few days before his scheduled departure for the East in 44 BC, his plans were suddenly interrupted. A group of about twenty disgruntled senators surrounded him in the Senate, pretending to have a petition they wished to hand him. One of them knelt to his feet and tugged on Caesar's toga—a prearranged cue for initiating Caesar's assassination. It was a nearly bungled attempt. The first sword strike missed Caesar entirely, allowing him to fight back with the sharp pen he was holding. Several assassins were injured in the friendly crossfire of inaccurate senatorial sword-wielding, but Caesar had no chance. The onlooking senators turned heel and rushed for the exits. Their quick escape was impeded by a crowd of thousands of spectators who were at that moment filing out of the Theater of Pompey next door at the end of a gladiatorial show.

What was behind this assassination plot? Fear. Fear of the changes Caesar had been promoting: a program of reforms he had pressured a compliant Senate to endorse; an ambitious plan to revamp Roman government; an apparent attempted takeover of the democratic process. And they feared what it seemed Caesar was ultimately aiming for: becoming a king—the very thing that had long been considered anathema to Roman Republic tradition.

There was plenty of evidence to justify their fear. In 49 BC and again in 48 BC Caesar had gotten the Senate to appoint him to the office of "dictator" for a year. In 46 BC, he was made dictator for ten years, and by 44 BC it was dictator for life. He was the only human to ever have his likeness placed on a coin while still living. His private home had been decorated with a triangular gable, suggesting its resemblance to a temple, the home of a god. His statue could be found inside every existing temple in Rome. He had purportedly been promised a temple and a priesthood to be dedicated in his honor. And during a religious festival just a month before his assassination, one of the consuls of the year, Mark Antony, had offered him a royal crown.

Despite Caesar's autocratic ambitions, most Roman citizens still preferred the reforms he had been promoting—support for the poor and occasional cash handouts to the common people. The popular mood was decidedly pro-Caesar, a sentiment that erupted into a riot at Caesar's own funeral in the Forum. His two primary opposing co-conspirators, Brutus and Cassius, wisely left Rome for safer environs but were able to retain their official positions as praetors. Cicero advised the Senate to adopt a compromise proposal that might quell further violence and reprisals. It subsequently ratified all Caesar's decisions, in return for amnesty for his assassins. Further violence was thereby avoided—but only temporarily.

Roman Civil War

Things changed when Caesar's heir-apparent, an eighteen-year-old Gaius Octavius, arrived back in Rome from across the Adriatic Sea, where he was helping prepare for Caesar's pending invasion of the Parthian Empire. Because Caesar had no recognized legitimate natural son, he had legally adopted his great-nephew Octavius as his son and had named him in his will as the main beneficiary of his fortune. Octavius was adamant that his father's assassins should be punished, and that none of his many possible rivals—primarily Mark Antony—should be allowed to fill Caesar's shoes.

While still alive, Caesar had made claims of having a divine ancestry. He traced his genealogy to the god Aeneas, son of Venus, whom he honored with the construction of the grand temple of Venus in Rome. Some, already during his lifetime, had considered Caesar to be divine. Not surprisingly, two years after

Caesar's death, the Senate formally declared that he had become a god, securing his position within the pantheon of Roman deities.

Conveniently, Octavius leveraged his status as Caesar's son to bolster his legitimacy. His claim to be the "son of a god" proved advantageous in rousing both troops and public support for the defeat of his rivals and the consolidation of his imperial power. He propagated this title across the empire on coins, monuments, and inscriptions.

It took more than a decade of civil war, however, before Octavius could secure his position as Caesar's successor. His two initial competitors—his father's principal assassins Brutus and Cassius—had already fled Italy to govern provinces in the East. That left him with just one remaining local rival, Mark Antony. After engaging each other militarily for a while in northern Italy, Octavius and Antony formed a three-way alliance with Lepidus in a "triumvirate for establishing government." It was a formal five-year agreement giving each of them power equivalent to that of a consul, the choice of which provinces they wished to be in charge over, and the ability to control Roman elections.

In 42 BC, this triumvirate's combined forces defeated Brutus and Cassius near the town of Phillipi in far northern Greece. Six years later, Lepidus was squeezed out of the coalition, leaving Octavius and Antony to battle it out between them for who was going to rule the Roman world. For much of the '30s BC, Octavius operated in the western part of the empire, doing away with any remaining enemies in Rome as well as those still at large elsewhere. Antony set up headquarters in Alexandria, Egypt, where he formed a military alliance and romantic relationship with Egypt's Queen Cleopatra. From his base in Egypt, Antony pursued high-profile military campaigns in the East against Parthia and Armenia, with limited success.

There was growing suspicion in Rome that Antony's loyalties had shifted from Rome to Alexandria. He had staged a ceremony there during which Cleopatra was pronounced Queen of Kings, and her son Caesarion (allegedly conceived with Julius Caesar) was declared King of Kings. The three children born through Antony and Cleopatra's affair were also given grandiose royal titles. This all appeared to be a transfer of eastern Roman territories into Greek hands. Attempting to exploit this apparent disloyalty to Rome, Octavius, in 33 BC, obtained a document that was said to be Antony's will and read out some incriminating sections of it before the Roman Senate. It spelled out Antony's plan to leave large territories and significant amounts of money to Cleopatra and her children, and his wish to be buried in Alexandria alongside Cleopatra. It sure sounded like Antony was planning to abandon Rome and make Alexandria the empire's new capital city.

Two years later, full-scale war broke out between Octavius and Antony. Antony, thanks to his partnership with Cleopatra, initially had substantially more cash and troops at his disposal. However, he and Cleopatra lost the first battle at sea near Actium in northern Greece, and they never recovered. Realizing that Octavius was gaining the upper hand, they quickly retreated to Egypt, abandoning most of their sailors and soldiers. A year later, Octavius went to Alexandria to finish the job. Thinking Cleopatra was already dead, Antony stabbed himself to death, living just long enough to discover she had not yet died. Her life was taken shortly thereafter, and so was that of her son Caesarion.

Caesar Augustus: The First Roman Emperor

Rome's longstanding tradition of power-sharing political leadership thus abruptly ended. It had slipped headlong into autocracy. Returning triumphantly to Rome from Egypt, eager to convey a new public image, Octavius gave himself a new name: Augustus. His old warlord notoriety now painted over with a fresh new coat, glistening with a self-declared aura of religious authority. Echoing the title of a group of Roman priests—the *augures*—it carried the connotation of "revered one." Its similarity to the title "reverend," used to distinguish modernity's Christian clergy from the laity, is notable. It was as if he had named himself "Reverend Caesar."

How was a mere eighteen-year-old Octavius, the adopted son of a just-assassinated dictator, with a résumé merely showing a brief stint as a military leader, able to pull this off? How did he create this new role of Roman emperor? Successfully serve in this capacity for the next forty years? And pave the way for fourteen successive emperors to seamlessly follow in his footsteps over the next few centuries? He had no carefully designed master plan. No one to mentor him. He had to figure it out on the fly, step by step. From day one, he faced a daunting challenge. How could he defuse his anti-Caesar opposition and avoid the fate of his father? How could he win the hearts and minds of Rome's citizens?

He soon revealed an intuitive political savviness. Acknowledging the Roman Republic's historical antipathy toward anything resembling a monarchy, he consciously avoided calling himself a "king." He also wisely made an elaborate display of rejecting the hot-button title "dictator" that Caesar had adopted. And he realized he couldn't just suddenly do away with Rome's longstanding political infrastructure. Instead, he cleverly commandeered it to advance his own cause. He grabbed multiple familiar leadership titles and offices from the existing system— tribune, consul, etc.—and affixed them to himself. By using these old, familiar political terms and titles, he made it look and sound like he was maintaining the traditional political structure.

He was not. It was all a facade, a gaming of the system to consolidate his singular superior power.

He also made sure no one else would easily be able to follow his own path to autocracy by raising a private army themselves, and then taking over the state. As the new first-ever commander in chief over the entire Roman military, he deprivatized it. He seized control of the soldiers' pension system, severed the links of loyalty and dependency between them and their individual commanders, thereby ensuring that Roman troops would now be loyal to him and him alone. No longer could an ambitious army general leverage the loyalty of his troops for personal political gain. That door was slammed shut.

On top of all this, he gradually did away with Rome's traditional popular elections. In past times, winning elections had been the tried-and-true path ambitious people used to gain political power. It necessitated drumming up popular support for one's cause. But what do ambitious people do when there are no elections to run for, and thus no personal payoff for going out and garnering public support? There was now only one way for them to advance themselves politically—to ingratiate themselves with Augustus instead.

Managing an Empire

It was one thing for Augustus, at the beginning of his reign, to secure sole possession of supreme Roman power. His astute maneuvering enabled him to eliminate his opposition and cut off all available pathways any future rival might use to rise up and take his place. But it was another thing, over the course of the next four decades, to successfully unify and manage a vast territory inhabited by fifty million people from a variety of different cultures. How did he do it?

The Romans were too few in number to be dispatched all across their vast territory to form and staff brand-new top-down governmental structures. Non-Roman local elites were already effectively governing most of the empire's numerous towns and cities. Why not let them continue? Except now as the instruments of Rome's central government. Augustus efficiently swept these existing local hierarchical governmental structures under the larger umbrella of Rome's "I'll scratch your back if you scratch mine" patronage system.

Patronage had been the Roman way for centuries. Like all the other ancient Mediterranean people, the Romans, too, instinctively "knew" that an invisible spiritual realm surrounded their earthly existence. Unseen beings, deities, gods somehow held sway over the circumstances of their everyday lives. Life could go well only so long as people were properly honoring them through temple offerings, prayers, and generous sacrifices. And since the gods had also superimposed a rigid hierarchical pyramid structure on Roman society, its people could flourish only so long as they showed proper honor to their socio-economic superiors—priests, rulers, patrons, fathers, husbands, those with more wealth and power. Society was segmented into clearly defined socio-economic levels. People at each level, in exchange for honoring those in the tier above them, received from them certain financial benefits and expressions of honor. It was an archaic version of trickle-down economics.

Augustus imposed this same patronage system on the rest of the Roman Empire, becoming the generous patron of local provincial and municipal elites. Through his inheritance from Caesar, his seizure of the exorbitant riches of Egypt upon his defeat of Antony and Cleopatra, and his occasional obscuring of the boundaries between the empire's funds and his own, Augustus had created an unprecedented stockpile of wealth. Realizing its potential for consolidating his grip on power, he made generosity his good friend, a self-serving tool to flaunt before his dazzled subjects' watching eyes. He offered his new patrons positions of honor—priesthoods and political offices. Set up profitable business arrangements with them. Provided them with certain benefits and protections related to Roman taxation. They, in turn, were expected to demonstrate their honor and loyalty by promoting the Roman state religion. Require their citizens to worship the goddess, Roma. Construct temples, set up altars, erect statues, and reproduce inscriptions that honored Rome and its emperor. Hold games and festivals, at local expense, to honor the divine Roma and the emperor. Ensure that Rome benefited from their city's wealth through adequate rendering of taxes.

Loyalty to Rome didn't end with these civic and provincial elites. They themselves became patrons, having clients under them. And those clients were patrons to still other clients underneath them. With everyone in the pyramid receiving the trickling down of benefits from Rome and actively demonstrating their loyalty to Rome in return, allegiance and devotion to Rome became widely and firmly entrenched.

Everywhere in Augustus's empire, new cities were founded, while existing ones were refurbished and expanded. New buildings appeared: public facilities, temples, and theaters. New aqueducts and roadways sprang to life. Economic activity flourished. Empire-wide trade blossomed and expanded. After the seemingly endless horrors of Roman civil war and regional military conflict, Augustus had ushered in an age of peace and prosperity—his legendary *Pax Romana* had taken hold.

Religion and Politics

Roman religious devotion was something that most of Rome's conquered populations could readily relate to. Almost every local community within its empire had inherited its own set of venerated deities from its distant ancestors. Altars of household gods stood in their homes. Temple gods dwelled among them in sacred public spaces. Their deities, too, were the objects of endless veneration, placation, appeasement, and sacrifice. Daily rituals of purification were to be performed before the religious images and altars in their homes. Slaughtered animals were to be regularly placed on sacrificial altars in local temples, gifts offered in hopes of appeasing their deities' ire and of gaining their continued favor. Every member of the community had a mandatory civic duty to do their part in keeping the local gods happy and staving off their retribution.

In addition to these countless local deities, there was a host of higher gods held in common across the empire's population. Already two thousand years before Christ, while the Jewish people's ancient ancestor Abraham was being introduced to a strange new desert deity named Yahweh, the ancient Greeks began weaving together a rich tapestry of stories reflecting their perception of the world of the gods. Passed down orally from generation to generation, they were eventually written down by Homer in his *Iliad* and *Odyssey*. This Greek mythology envisioned twelve primary deities existing at the heart of the divine world, all residing together as one family on top of Greece's Mount Olympus. According to Homer, these gods "take on many [human] forms as they wander through the cities in the guise of strangers from a distant place."

When, in the fifth century BC, the Romans were introduced to Greek mythology, they eagerly added these gods to their existing religious repertoire. What good would it do to appease just some of the gods? If there are other non-Roman gods out there who are not on our current list, we'd better make sure to cover all our bases and include them as well. But we will give them our own Roman names (with the exception of Apollo).

Thus, the Greeks' god Zeus, mightiest of all gods, became the Romans' Jupiter. His wife Hera became Juno. Apollo's twin sister Artemis was renamed Diana, Aphrodite renamed Venus, Hermes renamed Mercury, etc. And new Roman temple buildings were constructed to house them and provide the people with access to them.

Augustus took this inherent religious devotion of his new non-Roman subjects and, by superimposing the structure of Roman patronage on their cultures, effectively married Roman religion to Roman imperial politics. They became two sides of the same coin. But he went even a step further. He made religious devotion to the gods and political loyalty to Rome all about himself. He instituted the practice of emperor worship.

Emperor Worship

As mentioned earlier, when Augustus changed his name, he intended to create a sacral aura about himself. This didn't just happen out of nowhere. It was tied to a longstanding ancient Greek religious tradition that the Romans had inherited: hero worship. Deceased heroes in ancient Greece—those who had displayed unusual power and great achievements while living— were often venerated at their tombs or shrines with offerings and sacrifices after their death. While alive, they were believed to have been specially favored with divinely endowed abilities and accomplishments. Following their deaths, through their supposed continued connections with the divine, they were considered still able to provide protection and good fortune to the people who worshiped them.

In fifth-century BC Greece, a subtle shift occurred. The worship of deceased heroes was expanded to include the worship of living heroes—namely, the current rulers of Greek city-states such as Athens and Sparta, whose claims to fame had come through impressive military victories and political and economic achievements. When Alexander the Great later took over Greece and then conquered regions of the eastern Mediterranean, he and his successors extended this practice of Greek ruler worship there as well. And then, as the Romans gradually took over parts of Greece and Greece-ruled Asia Minor, the people there rather easily transferred the worship of their former Greek rulers to their new Roman rulers. Rome's superior military and political achievement, so they thought, was a convincing sign of divine favor. Old school hero worship had thus morphed into newfound emperor worship.

Yet, Augustus's subjects did not necessarily consider him to be one of their gods. Rather, they saw him as an intermediary between themselves and the gods. How else could he have arrived at the pinnacle of power if not for the gods having shown their favor upon him? As Augustus now basked in that divine favor, his subjects believed he could cause those divine favors to flow into their lives as well. They believed he possessed a special potent life force ("genius") that served as a two-way conduit. While their prayers and sacrifices passed through his genius on up to Rome's deities, the blessings of Rome's deities passed down through it for the benefit of the empire. Augustus threw himself into proving them right, bound and determined to be perceived as their great benefactor. When they could see with their own eyes the evidence of his benefactions in their communities—money, resources, buildings, urban development, peace, and prosperity—the legitimacy and sanctity of his rule would only become more self-evident. His new cult of the emperor proved to be an essential part of the stitchery Augustus used to bind together the patchwork of urban communities scattered across his empire.

Throughout the Mediterranean, these urban communities competed to outdo each other in sidling up to the Roman imperial order to prove their devotion and earn Augustus's favors. One way to compete was to build an imperial temple in honor of Augustus. Among such temples built throughout the empire were those erected among my Jewish ancestors in first-century BC Palestine—just a generation before the birth of Jesus—by its Rome-appointed ruler, Herod the Great. A temple of Augustus in 27 BC took its place atop a hill at the new Roman-built city of Sebaste in Samaria. A temple of Roma and Augustus, built in 23 BC stood prominently on a manufactured hill in the new Rome-constructed coastal city of Caesarea Maritime. Facing its harbor port, it could be seen from far out at sea. A third temple of Augustus was erected just north of Galilee in Banias—known in the time of Jesus as Caesarea Philippi—adjacent to the ancient sanctuary of the local pagan god Pan.

Each of them, nearly as large as a football field, towered over its surroundings, capturing the attention of local residents and passersby alike. The intended message was clear: this region belonged to an empire governed by a "son of god" (the "august" son of the man who became a god, Julius Caesar). First-century BC and AD Palestine, the longstanding ground zero for the Jewish people's worship of Yahweh, had become a center of worship for the Roman emperor as well.

The cult of Augustus spread as his portrait flooded the Mediterranean world, providing faraway populations a face-to-face encounter with their renowned ruler. It was seen stamped on the small change people carried in their pockets in distant Judea among my ancestors during the time of Jesus. People came eye to eye with him in the myriad life-size and larger bronze and marble statues that stood in the public squares and temples of their local communities. Miniature likenesses were engraved in rings and gems and embossed on dining room silverware. Through images portraying Augustus from a pious priest to a heroic conqueror, 250 statues have been recovered across Roman territories, from Spain to Turkey and beyond.

The Imperial Narrative

This was all part of a carefully crafted propaganda campaign aimed at disseminating a compelling narrative of Augustus's goodness and greatness. Before Augustus, so it was claimed, there had been chaos, turmoil, injustice, and scarcity. The deities of Rome had overseen the implementation of Augustus's reign. He had suppressed the chaos and ushered in a culminating moment in world history—the advent of peace, justice, abundance, and prosperity. The narrative Rome continually told itself and its subjects went like this. Our empire came to exist as a result of divine favor—favor bestowed on us because of our superior religious devotion and virtues. Our higher virtues of justice, courage, truth, mercy, modesty, and faithfulness displayed through our imperial system have blessed all the peoples under our rule. All who are living under the provision of our empire and who are faithful to it are experiencing the fruits of those virtues: peace, security, and prosperity.

This compelling story of the Roman Empire—the power of its military, the superiority of its culture, the justice of its laws, and the divine-like character of its emperor—was publicized across its realm with astonishing success. It was memorialized in vivid imagery on coins; through carvings on buildings and statues in public squares; through wall paintings hanging inside theaters, shops, and homes. It was celebrated during feasts and festivals. Sacrifices and praise for the emperor highlighted the beginning of every event in the theaters and the start of all meetings of local associations.

The narrative was indelibly inscribed in stone for all history to read. Two such inscriptions, dating back to the time of Christ, written in Greek, have been recovered in the ancient Greek city of Priene (located in present-day southwestern Turkey) along the Aegean coast of what was then Asia Minor/Galatia. One of the inscriptions is a formal decree praising the decision to redate the Asian calendar so that the new year (starting around 9 BC) would begin on Augustus's birthdate. The decree praises Augustus as the "savior" (*soter)* and describes "the birthday of the god" Augustus as the day that "began for the world the good news (*evangelion,* "gospel") that happened because of him." The other inscription was a tribute to Augustus recorded on a stone slab in Priene in AD 29 (at about the same time as the death of Jesus in Judea). It reads: "He brings war to an end; he orders peace; by manifesting himself, he surpasses the hopes of all who are looking for good news (*evangelion,* 'gospel')."

Forty years later, the earliest written account about Jesus of Nazareth surfaced. It was written in Greek and addressed to a Christian audience in Rome. It came to be known as the Gospel According to Mark. One cannot help noticing the similarities between the Priene descriptions of Augustus and Mark's description of Jesus in the opening sentence of his account: "[This is] the beginning of the gospel/good news (*evangelion*) about Jesus Christ, the Son of God."

5

Prelude to the Arrival of Jesus

Herod the Great

The writer of the Gospel According to Matthew, when recounting the stories available to him regarding the birth of Jesus, succinctly summarized its historical setting. It happened, he says, "in the days of Herod the king" (2:1). That is a loaded statement. He's not merely identifying for us the name of the guy who happened to be king at this time. Saying "the days of Herod" would be like saying "the days of covid." These were memorable days. Hard days. Scary days. Painful days. One of the most turbulent periods in all of Jewish history. In this chapter, we will try to capture the fuller picture of what life was like for my Palestinian Jewish ancestors during the tumultuous time leading up to the entrance of Jesus into their world.

Herod immediately sought to consolidate his power and gain the support of the people—objectives that were often at odds with each other. In typical autocratic fashion, he stripped the Sanhedrin of its political power, limiting its authority to strictly religious matters. Set up an alternate secular Hellenistic-style royal council and a centralized government bureaucracy. Replaced the old aristocracy with one whose wealth and position were now acquired directly from him. Degraded the office of high priest from a hereditary lifelong position to one occupied by whomever he wished to appoint, for a length of service that could be terminated at a moment's notice. Knowing that the Pharisees held great sway among the masses of commoners, he sought to appease them and gain their support by avoiding offense to their religious foibles. They, in turn, concentrated on religious rather than political affairs, while maintaining their suspicion of him and keeping their distance from him.

Through onerous taxation, Herod shrewdly funneled enormous wealth into his own coffers and skillfully leveraged that wealth into massive building projects. These initiatives appeared driven by his infatuation with grandiose architectural displays and his insatiable appetite for self-aggrandizement. Realizing his need to curry favor with his Roman overlords, he seemed intent on impressing them with his ability to bring their vaunted culture to "backward Judea." Entire new Hellenistic-style cities, including Judea's first Mediterranean seaport, Caesarea, were erected. Old cities were restored with all the typical Hellenistic features: temples, theaters, stadiums, gymnasiums, hippodromes, public baths, colonnaded streets, and ornate marketplaces. He facilitated the construction of Roman imperial cult temples—centers for Caesar-worship—at Sebaste in Samaria, in Caesarea Philippi to the north of Galilee, and in the coastal city of Caesarea Maritima. He built massive, lavish palaces for himself—not only the previously mentioned Herodion near Bethlehem, but also in Jerusalem, in Caesarea Maritima, in Jericho, and on top of Masada.

At the epicenter of his elaborate building frenzy was Jerusalem itself. A Roman-style theater was built in its city center. In honor of Emperor Augustus, a huge Greek-Olympiad-style amphitheater was constructed outside the city. His crowning architectural achievement, though, was his extravagant reconstruction of the Jewish temple, begun in 20 BC and completed some eighty years later.

All this glamorous construction and "cultural advancement," however, did nothing to win the favor of the masses of his Jewish subjects. Even their splendid new temple, built with the aim of gaining their admiration, failed to win him their confidence. He had, after all, also built temples to the Roman gods. His projected aura of Jewish religious piety had no credibility. And, the physical trappings of Hellenistic culture cropping up around them were so offensive to the moral and religious principles of most Judeans that they largely responded with the silent protest of non-engagement.

Herod's reign was dogged by pervasive widespread doubt regarding his legitimacy to be Judea's king. In the eyes of the general populace, he had none of the required credentials. Not only did he lack royal Davidic ancestry, but he was not even Judean. His Idumean father and Arabian mother had been forcibly "converted" to Judaism at the point of a Hasmonean-held sword, making him at best a mere half-Jew. His own claim to legitimacy rested merely on the authority of Rome and on his self-proclamation of having become king by "the will of God."

He was acutely aware of the overshadowing legacy of the historical house of David. He knew his Judean subjects were anticipating the return of one of David's descendants to become their king, and that many were expecting the true Messiah to arrive after the end of his own reign. His actions as king were largely driven by his consequent feelings of inferiority, insecurity, and paranoia.

His Herodion palace atop a man-made mountain overlooking nearby Bethlehem, the city of David and his descendants, was in large part a declaration of his kingly superiority over the house of David. In 10 BC he looted and desecrated David's tomb. The genealogical records of David's line, held in a Jerusalem archive, were destroyed in a fire for which Herod was blamed. Wanting his subjects to see him as the "anointed one," he had coins made which featured a jeweled crown with a superimposed Greek letter "chi,"—the first letter of "Christos," the anointed one.

The Urban Scene

For centuries, the vast majority of Judean Jews had lived a rural, agrarian, subsistence-level life. But then came the Greek invaders, with their jarringly alien Hellenistic ways. They had introduced a brand-new component amid Palestine's rustic landscape: the polis—a uniquely Greek-styled urban configuration. It featured majestic, sprawling, ornate, predominating new edifices: gymnasiums; theaters; stadiums; agoras. These were the brick-and-mortar embodiments of a civilization bent on dazzling its new non-Greek subjects with its supposed superior cultural ways.

All the accoutrements of the good life—knowledge, leisure, entertainment—could be found here. The gymnasium schooled young men in the Greek poets and philosophers and provided the amenities of a private workout or a bath at either the beginning or end of a workday. The stadium provided the spectacle of riveting athletic contests—wrestling matches, chariot races, foot races, and other Olympic events. The theater offered the amusement of dramatic live performances of Greek playwrights. Public bathhouses were frequented for socializing, business networking, exercising, and enjoying the indulgence of alternating hot and cold baths.

Urban public works projects provided employment for masons and other skilled workers. Urban industrial districts provided work in the large-scale manufacturing of woven cloth, leather goods, dyed material, metal utensils and implements, pottery, and weapons. Some rural village Jews were drawn to the city by such opportunities. An urban-based administrative civil service bureaucracy—necessary for collecting taxes, enforcing order, and the like—provided many Jews an opportunity for social and economic advancement. In fact, nearly all tax collectors, local judges, and civic officials in Judea by the time of Jesus were Jews.

Village Culture

Yet, the bulk of Palestine's Jewish contemporaries of Jesus continued to live in small, unwalled agricultural villages and in the countryside surrounding the urban centers. Village life centered around eking out a living by working small plots of land. With the passing of time, though, wealthy landowners mercilessly worked the system to their own advantage. They compelled increasing numbers of the landowning peasant class into landless dependency, forcing them now to make their livings toiling as tenant farmers and day laborers under the supervision of the wealthy landowners' stewards.

There were an estimated two hundred such Jewish villages in the areas of Judea and Galilee during the late first century BC and early first century AD. With an average village population of about five hundred people, there was an overall total of about one hundred thousand peasant Jewish villagers in Palestine when Jesus arrived on the scene. Somewhere, in one of those villages, my own ancestral family had a place they called home—and were likely eking out a meager tenant-farming living.

Village life remained resistant to the adoption of Hellenistic ways. Although Greek became the common language in the cities, Aramaic remained the common language in the villages. While city populations were a socially stratified mixture of

Greeks and Jews, villages consisted largely of a single, homogeneous peasant class of only Jews.

Village economies centered around raising crops and husbanding sheep and goats. They provided the supply chain of grain, meat, oil, and other farm products needed by people in the cities. Some villagers ran small shops out of their homes. Others produced household crafts through home-based cottage industries.

The typical rural village had at its center a public open area. It included the prominent presence of a synagogue, which functioned as the community's social and religious hub. Local matters continued to be decided by councils of elders. Social activities focused on family connections and seasonal religious festivals. Annual pilgrimages to Jerusalem for Passover and other major religious events provided villagers with additional social highpoints.

Religious Institutions

Jewish religious life during the time of Jesus revolved around two foundational institutions: the Jerusalem temple and the local synagogues. The temple was the official domain of the ordained priests. Their long-held traditional authority as teachers of the law was, as noted earlier, usurped by the rise of the lay Pharisee scribes. Priestly responsibilities thereby became increasingly confined to performing temple rituals and sacrifices. Ranked below the priests were a "minor clergy" group of Levites, whose task it was to serve in the choir and orchestra and carry out various menial temple tasks. These priests and Levites, numbering in the thousands, were divided into twenty-four teams. Each team served in the temple for a week at a time on a rotating basis.

Chief among the priests' routine religious rituals was the offering of daily sacrifices, one in the morning and one in mid-afternoon. The ceremony began with the recitation of the ten commandments, the burning of incense on the altar, and the priestly pronouncement of blessing over the gathered worshipers. Next, the animal sacrifice was burned on the altar, a meal-offering was made, and a drink offering was poured out. The Levitical choir, to the musical accompaniment of trumpets, cymbals, and wind and stringed instruments, sang the designated Psalm for the day. The people then prostrated themselves in worship.

The three major longstanding annual religious festivals discussed earlier in Chapter 1 were also still taking place at the temple. Passover (March–April) was the most popular and highly attended. On Passover Eve, each family group arrived in Jerusalem with a lamb or goat to use in making a temple sacrifice. Fanning out into the courtyards of the city, they roasted them over an open fire. While eating their lambs along with the unleavened bread and bitter herbs, they retold the story of the Exodus from Egypt.

During the Feast of Weeks (May–June), farmers arrived in procession, bringing baskets of newly harvested grain and first-fruit offerings. While handing them to the priest, they recited a litany thanking God for delivering them out of slavery in Egypt.

The most festive celebration, and main harvest festival, was the week-long Feast of Weeks (Feast of Tabernacles) in September–October at the beginning of the rainy season. Pilgrims gathered to acknowledge their dependence on Yahweh for abundant rain and a plentiful harvest for the coming season. They arrived carrying branches of palms, myrtles, and willows woven together, and a lemon-like citrus fruit called an etrog. They waved these in celebration, praying *"Hoshiana"* ("God save us"). Afterward, the etrogs were given to the children to eat.

There was an additional water-drawing ceremony in remembrance of Yahweh's provision of water for their ancestors during their desert wanderings. The priests drew a pitcher of water from Jerusalem's ancient spring, the Pool of Siloam. It was passed person to person through a long line of priests all the way up to the temple altar, where it was poured out as a drink offering. An all-night celebration followed until dawn of the next day.

The temple housed a treasury of great wealth. This was bolstered through the ongoing donations of Jewish pilgrims coming to Jerusalem from throughout the Greco-Roman empires. It was also funded through an annual half-shekel temple tax imposed on all adult Jewish males, including those living throughout the scattered Jewish communities beyond Palestine. (See map, *Diaspora Synagogues 1st -2nd Centuries CE*, p. ii). This made the temple the wealthiest institution in Palestine, and an attractive target for plundering by foreign invaders.

The origins of the Jewish synagogue (a Greek word meaning "assembly") are unclear. It did not exist during the Persian period. It arose sometime during the Greek period. It appears to have originated outside Palestine in the Jewish Diaspora. The earliest dated evidence for its existence is found in the second half of the third century BC. Egyptian records from that time refer to the dedication of a "house of prayer." This was around the same time that the original Hebrew-language version of the Torah was first translated into the Greek-language "Septuagint" version in Egypt.

A possible precursor in Palestine may have been the traditional Jewish city-gate, the historical setting for public gatherings and a variety of communal activities. The city-gate functioned also as a marketplace and as a venue where prophets would speak and rulers would hold court. The dawn of the Hellenistic era likely triggered a change in how villages and cities were fortified. Traditional Judean city-gate activities appear to have consequently shifted to an area inside the village. And, following the Hellenistic pattern, these open-air community venues were moved inside a (synagogue) building.

During the time of Jesus, synagogues were likely to be found in every Palestinian city and village where there resided the required quorum of ten males of Jewish birth. They had materialized through a weaving together of three separate institutions: prayer-houses, study-halls or schools, and community centers.

As community centers, they provided a focal point for cultural and social gatherings. This was where community-wide announcements were made, where discussions regarding community needs took place, and where funds for community purposes were raised.

As religious centers, they housed gatherings for public worship. Men, women, and children congregants, assembling there on Sabbaths, spent hours in prayer, reading the Torah, and listening to discourses on the Torah. Eventually, they accommodated daily and even multiple daily religious gatherings. Paralleling the morning and afternoon sacrifices in the temple and the burning of the leftover scraps from them in the evening, prayers were offered in the synagogue at the same three times each day.

Unlike temple worship, which was led by a hierarchical priesthood, synagogue worship was directed by lay people. The synagogue's chief officer, the "head of the assembly," oversaw its affairs. Those who led the congregation in prayer or in reading the Torah were not specially appointed to do so. Rather, they were chosen from among the worshipers present at the time. Various people were asked to read, and a short passage from the Law or the Prophets would be recited. An additional person would stand alongside the scripture reader to translate the Hebrew reading into the Aramaic vernacular of the congregants.

The typical synagogue Sabbath worship service began with the recitation of the traditional Jewish confession of faith, the "Shema" from Deuteronomy 6, "Hear, O Israel: the Lord our God, the Lord is one. Love the Lord your God with all your heart and with all your soul and with all your strength." This was recited within the framework of three brief prayers affirming God's goodness and love for his people. Then came the "Amidah" or "Standing (Prayer)," also known as the Eighteen Benedictions—something that eventually every Jew was expected to recite three times a day. The reading of the Law, occupying the central place in the service, then ensued. This was followed by a homily based on the reading, given by any competent member of the congregation. The service then concluded with a benediction.

Religious-Political Factions

The two primary religious factions of Jesus's day—the Pharisees and Sadducees—as was noted earlier, were longstanding rivals. They adopted contrasting postures toward Roman occupation as well. The wealthy landowning Sadducees were eager to maintain the lucrative income they received through their control of the temple financial system. Conflict with Rome could easily jeopardize this income. They were, therefore, self-interestedly eager to cooperate with Rome in governing the Jewish people.

The Pharisees, on the other hand, belonged to the middle class. They lived in the local towns among the people, working their occupations and attending the synagogues. Having no political power or economic influence of their own, they adopted a stance of political quietism. While acquiescing to Roman overlordship and Herodian rulership, they passionately pursued their agenda of religious activism. They believed that if they could pull off a renewed religious piety and obedience to the Torah among the people, Yahweh would reward them by sending them their Messiah. If only they could be pure enough, obedient enough, and Torah-keeping enough, then Yahweh's kingdom would surely be ushered in to rescue them from Roman oppression.

An Exploitative Economic System

Perhaps as much as 90 percent of Palestine's Jewish population during this time, likely including my own ancestors, belonged to an economically vulnerable peasant class. They lived at a subsistence level in an economic system that was stacked against them. Though their toil produced the goods of their agrarian society, the profits from their labor lined the pockets of others. Extracted through taxation, rental fees, governmental confiscations, tolls, and duties. Redistributed into the controlling hands of the Jewish upper class and Roman rulers. At the heart of this system was the temple itself, a hub of lucrative economic activity, the receptacle of tithes, offerings, and temple taxes delivered there throughout the year by pilgrims from all over the Jewish world.

Among the exploited were the urban skilled workers and the rural peasants who still possessed their own land. Yet, as poor and oppressed as they were living at a subsistence level and paying high taxes, they were still largely content with their lot— as long as they could live their traditional life and continue supporting their families.

Another group within the powerless, however, had grown restless and discontent—reaching the end of their rope. And understandably so. Among them were the landless peasants, displaced by wealthy estate owners who had snatched up their farmland and ensnared them in slave labor. Among them, too, were the unemployed urban poor. Out of desperation for survival, these marginalized lower classes often resorted to banditry. Raiding country estates and Roman garrisons, they exacted revenge against those who had forced them into landlessness and poverty. It was among this especially aggrieved population that the seeds of societal revolution would eventually sprout to life with the formation of rebel groups known as Zealots and the Sicarii.

This was thus an extremely distressing time for the Jews of Palestine. Roman and Herodian oppression was strangling them politically. Competing religious factions made for a contentious and confusing religious climate. And socio-economic conditions among the masses were becoming increasingly more excruciating. These turbulent societal undercurrents would soon converge into a swirling seismic sea wave that would come crashing toward shore.

A Focus on Religious Piety

What was the religious mindset of the people among whom Jesus came to live? They were passionately devoted to Yahweh, whom they considered to be the one true Most High God, and were confident in their calling as his specially chosen people. Their collection of sacred religious writings was believed to embody the very voice and authority of Yahweh himself. They were well-versed in its primary teachings: the high moral standards required of them by their holy and righteous God; that their inevitable failures to meet those standards could be atoned through temple sacrificial rituals; that despite their continued persistent lapses in faithfulness to Yahweh, his faithfulness to them would endure through all their generations.

Driven by a fervent desire to please Yahweh and honor the authority of his Torah, the Jews of Jesus's time displayed a highly regimented and ritualistic outward religious expression. This can be seen in their emphasis on proper Sabbath observance. From sundown Friday until sundown Saturday, they ceased from engaging in many of their daily routines. No work, or anything that might be construed to be a form of work by the Torah and Pharisaic interpretation. No traveling, no lighting fires, no buying and selling. And there was a whole host of other specifically forbidden routines as well.

An equally notable aspect of Jewish piety was their fixation on maintaining ritual purity. To enter the temple precinct and approach the presence of their pure and holy God, they first needed to cleanse themselves of all "impurity." Eating unkosher food, certain skin diseases and bodily fluids, contact with a dead body or carcass of an unclean animal, for example, made a person impure. One could avoid impurity by avoiding direct contact with these impure sources. But one could never be sure that an impurity may have been inadvertently passed along to them indirectly, secondhand, without one even knowing it.

The solution to this pesky problem was mikvah—full immersion in a body of "living" (naturally flowing, and thus Yahweh-sourced) water. Because Palestine had very few perennial sources of water, artificial pools were developed for year-round use for this purpose. Local Jewish villages typically had up to a half-dozen or so of such ritual bathing pools. Many were used communally. Clusters of such ritual baths were located around the Temple Mount in Jerusalem and along the principal pilgrimage routes leading to Jerusalem. After immersing oneself to make sure the water reached one's entire body, one would wash one's clothes and then wait until nightfall to be considered ritually clean.

Herod's Reign Ends

Herod's reign was plagued by threats of insurrection, both real and imagined. At one point, a group of ten men tried to kill him. Caught by a spy, they were tortured to death. When their supporters killed the spy, Herod rounded them up along with their entire families and had them all killed. Having fathered multiple children with ten different wives, there were many sons who could potentially compete to become Herod's successor. Within his court of five hundred people—family members, attendants, officials, bureaucrats, slaves, and bodyguards—there was much palace intrigue, suspicion, and finger-pointing. Herod soon resorted to torturing and murdering members of his household staff to snuff out any hint of insurrection. Eight years into his reign, for example, he executed his second wife, Mariamme (granddaughter of the Hasmonean high priest Hyrcanus) for suspected treason.

While Mariamme's two oldest sons, Alexander and Aristobulus, were in Rome being educated in Caesar's palace, Herod's favor turned toward the oldest son of his first wife Doris—Antipater. Seeing an opening for his own advancement, Antipater began maligning Alexander and Aristobulus. Unsurprisingly, after Alexander and Aristobulus returned from Rome, a forged letter implicated them in a plot to kill Herod. A royal court decided they should be executed. Taken to Sebaste in Samaria, they were strangled to death. Antipater then traveled to Rome to present himself to Augustus as the rightful heir to Judea's throne.

Nearing the age of seventy, an aging Herod became even more paranoid about conspiracies and death threats, ready to torture anyone—family or friend—to ferret them out. He pinpointed the wife of his brother Pheroras (tetrarch of Perea) as the instigator of one plot against him. She and Pheroras fled to

Perea, where Pheroras soon took ill. Herod, feigning brotherly love, went to visit him. Pheroras, subsequently, suddenly died. It was rumored that Herod had poisoned him.

As Herod continued torturing members of his court, he came to suspect his favored son Antipater of a treasonous plot. Unsuspectingly, Antipater returned home from Rome to encounter a furiously enraged Herod. First-century Jewish chronicler Josephus reported that palace intrigue had spread widely among Herod's subjects: "every city now was full of the talk about Antipater." Herod assembled a council of friends and relatives over which he and the new Roman governor of Syria, P. Quinctilius Varus, who happened to be visiting Herod's palace in Jerusalem from Antioch, presided. Antipater was shackled. Varus sent off a full report to Augustus, seeking his judgment, and then departed for Antioch the next day. Once again, Herod changed his will, naming a son of his Samaritan wife, Malthrace, Antipas, as his heir to the throne.

Word began spreading that Herod was dying. Two very popular leading Jerusalem scholars with a substantial following of young students, Judas son of Sepphoraeus and Matthias son of Margalas, were especially emboldened by this news. They directed their students' attention to the repulsive, majestic golden eagle that Herod had installed over the "great gate" of the temple. It symbolized the Romans' sky god Jupiter, the king of their gods (known to the Greeks as Zeus). Noting how this violated Yahweh's forbiddance of graven images, they challenged their students to muster the courage to go knock it down. At noon one day, while there was a large gathering of people in the temple, some of the students sprang into action. Armed with hatchets, they swung themselves down from the roof by rope and began hacking the eagle to pieces. Royal troops stepped in, arrested about forty young men, and hauled them before Herod at his winter palace in Jericho. After denouncing the two scholars and forty students before an assembly of Jericho's leading men, Herod had them burned alive, while others who had been arrested were killed by other means.

Meanwhile, leaders from towns and villages throughout Judea had come to Jericho to hear Herod's verdict regarding these insurrectionists. Believing Herod was near death, they remained in Jericho after the students' executions, waiting for him to die. But Herod lingered. A still-enraged Herod ordered that, upon his death, all these out-of-town leaders hanging on for his death should be herded into the Jericho hippodrome and massacred by his soldiers. That way, his Judean subjects would be unable to celebrate his death with a festival.

A letter then arrived from the Emperor Augustus with his judgment regarding Antipater's alleged plot against Herod. Augustus had deferred to Herod's discretion—he could either banish him or execute him. Herod ordered his guards to kill him on the spot. Small wonder that Augustus, having authorized the execution of multiple sons of Herod, once quipped: "I would rather be Herod's pig [because Jews don't butcher pigs] than his son." Once again, Herod changed his will, now naming Archelaus (another son of Malthace, Antipas's brother) as heir to his throne. In 4 BC, Herod died. But when Herod's army in Jericho went to place the deceased Herod's crown on Archelaus, he refused to accept it until Augustus ratified his kingship.

After Herod was buried in his towering Herodion edifice, and following seven days of decreed public mourning, Archelaus went to Jerusalem to offer a sacrifice at the temple. There, he attempted to strike a conciliatory note, announcing his goodwill toward his new subjects. Met by protests and outcries for the release of prisoners and the reduction of taxes, he apparently agreed to their demands.

However, the fallout from all the evil and injustice that had characterized Herod's reign—his lack of traditional kingly qualifications, his persistent loyalty to Rome, religious phoniness, economic oppression, his hideous execution of Judas, Matthias, and their students—had ignited an enormous backlash among his Judean subjects. Their fury could no longer be held back. Among the masses of pilgrims that converged on Jerusalem for Passover after Herod's death was a group of political agitators who organized a rowdy demonstration in the temple. There, on Passover Eve, they held a massive protest rally. They were not only expressing their exasperation with Herod's reign of terror. They were also feeling inspired by renewed hopes and expectations for a new era of political liberation from the oppressive house of Herod. Archelaus initially sent representatives to appease the crowd, but they were greeted with a flurry of hurling stones, causing them to scatter. The rally continued on into Passover day, growing larger as many recently arrived Jewish pilgrims joined in.

Finally losing his patience, Archelaus sent in one thousand soldiers to arrest the ringleaders. The crowd pelted them with stones and killed many of them. Archelaus then sent in his entire infantry and cavalry, which stormed the temple and killed nearly three thousand protesters. Leaving his brother Philip in charge, Archelaus then departed for Rome to be confirmed as Judea's new king.

The Rome-appointed legate of neighboring Syria, Publius Quinctilius Varus, filling in during Archelaus's absence, subsequently arrived in Jerusalem from Antioch with fifteen thousand troops. He sent Phillip off to Rome also, and installed Sabinus, procurator of the province of Syria, in Herod's Jerusalem palace with command over all Herod's palace fortresses.

While Herod's prospective heirs were in Rome disputing their succession before Augustus, with Judea now under the direct control of Rome, open rebellion burst out. At the Feast of

Pentecost, seven weeks following the Passover slaughter of three thousand Jews, Judean fighters—"tens of thousands" of them, according to Josephus—assembled at the temple. Spreading out and surrounding the five thousand Roman legionnaires stationed nearby, they attacked. Under the Romans' counterattack, the Judean warriors retreated to the temple. The Romans set the temple porticoes ablaze, burning many of the Judeans to death, and then plundered the temple treasury.

Hearing this news, Judean fighters elsewhere became even more incensed and inspired to join the battle. Bolstered by defections of large numbers of Herod's troops to their cause, they successfully surrounded the royal palace in Jerusalem. While their occupation of Jerusalem continued, revolts aimed at liberating Judea erupted elsewhere as well. A man named Judas, son of Hezekiah, amassed rebel fighters around the town of Sepphoris in Galilee, located just four miles north of Nazareth, where a young boy Jesus and his parents had likely just recently arrived to take up residence. The rebels, likely including men from neighboring Nazareth, stormed Sepphoris's royal Roman palace and broke into its arsenal. The crushing Roman response, led by Varus, was swift and brutal. Burning Sepphoris to the ground, they rampaged on into Samaria, torching various villages there as they went. Residents of Nazareth, including Jesus and his parents, almost certainly had witnessed the billowing smoke in the distance as Sepphoris was going up in flames.

Varus's troops continued on to Jerusalem, converging outside the city with additional armies led by other Roman client-kings. Seeing the overpowering might of Rome's forces, the Judean rebels in control of Jerusalem fled. Varus hunted them down, imprisoned many, and, according to Josephus, crucified two thousand of them.

Archelaus returned to Jerusalem from Rome to take up his position as Herod's officially sanctioned successor. His ten-year reign (4 BC to AD 6) was no less harsh than his father's. His building projects required levels of exorbitant taxation similar to Herod's. Josephus tells us he treated his Samaritan and Judean subjects "savagely." It was so bad that a contingent of Judean and Samaritan elders, accompanied by Archelaus's own brothers, traveled to Rome to complain to Augustus about his abuses. Augustus subsequently summoned him to Rome for trial, removed him from his post, and banished him to Gaul. Once again, hopes among Palestine's Jewish population for possible independence were rekindled.

Judea was then turned into a province under Syria and its Roman governor, Publius Quirinius. Quirinius immediately implemented a wide-scale census to form the basis of Roman taxation. (This was his second census, not to be confused with his first one that had resulted in Joseph's and Mary's reported trip to Bethlehem just prior to Jesus's birth.)

A Galilean named Judas of Gamla—it is unclear if this was the same Judas who led the Sepphoris insurrection ten years earlier—led a group of followers who, fearing higher taxes and forced labor, rose in armed opposition. Believing that only Yahweh should be ruling them, through a priestly hierarchy administering Jewish religious law, their rallying cry was: "No king but God." They believed the Jewish people should be living autonomously, not under the jurisdiction of some foreign political power. These rebels considered it cowardly for the Jews to accept paying tribute to Rome. Similar uprisings occurred in Judea, driven by the same patriotic resentment and passion for the political freedom of their people.

From AD 6–41, six different Roman governors or procurators ruled Judea with a suppressive iron hand. It was not so much the Jewish threat that concerned Rome. It was more the menace posed by developments happening to the east of Judea. There, remnants of the former Babylonian, Assyrian, and Persian kingdoms were coalescing into a new Parthian Empire. Although the Romans had won skirmish after skirmish with them, they had never been able to decisively defeat them. If there were any place the Parthians might attempt a breakthrough against the Roman Empire, it would be through Judea. By keeping Judea strongly garrisoned and firmly governed, Rome believed it could hold the Parthians at bay. Their paranoia, however, led to repressively excessive measures against the Jews.

The primary responsibility of Rome's appointed rulers over Judea was to collect and deliver the annual tax to the Roman Empire. Because they were allowed to keep whatever taxes they could raise above the required quota, they often imposed confiscatory taxes on the Jewish people. Just as infuriating, they also took over the appointment of the high priest, who increasingly was drawn from the ranks of Jews who collaborated with the Romans. And, they were responsible for maintaining order with the ever-present Roman military they had at their disposal. During festivals at the temple, for example, the soldiers would leave their barracks and occupy the military stronghold that surrounded the temple, turning this defensive structure into a perch for surveilling the Jews at the temple. Intended as a way to keep "order" and prevent popular revolt, this tactic only led to further resentment by those being "spied on" and often provoked clashes with the Jewish people rather than preventing them.

As the time of Christ approached, the specter of violence and bloodshed became increasingly prevalent. And it was only going to intensify. The one-hundred-year period from the time of Herod the Great, thirty years prior to the birth of Jesus, until seventy years following his birth, was replete with Jewish carnage. Astoundingly, no fewer than two hundred thousand Palestinian Jews lost their lives through political disturbances, clashes and uprisings against the authorities, and massacres by Herod and his successors. By the grace of God, my direct ancestors were not among them.

Messianic Hope and Expectations

There was one other important aspect to the Jewish religious mindset at this time. It had to do with this pressing existential question: What should they now expect from Yahweh for their future as his chosen nation? Given all the ups and downs of their long journey through history with this God of Abraham. In light of all that he had revealed to them about himself along the way. And, especially, given their current dismal circumstances under Herodian and Roman rule.

Think of what they knew, or at least had been taught through their sacred writings to believe. Yahweh had promised to make their patriarch Abraham into a great nation—his chosen kingdom on earth. Under Kings David and Solomon, they had become just such a great nation. And while David was serving as their king, Yahweh had promised that there would continue to be a descendant from David's royal family sitting on his throne continuously, forever. But during the latter period of the Davidic monarchy, their ancestors had essentially turned their backs on Yahweh. Their kingdom, their Jerusalem, and their temple were consequently demolished, and a vital segment of their population was deported from their homeland.

Amid this disciplinary judgment and punishment, Yahweh had sent them prophets bearing a message of hope and restoration. Yes, so they heard, they were receiving the punishment they deserved. But, as they also heard, there would be a day coming beyond this when there would be a restoration. A return from exile. A rebuilding of Jerusalem. A restoration of the temple. And . . . the reestablishment of Israel's Davidic kingship. Such promises would certainly have been heard as recognizably consistent with Yahweh's demonstrated character. Repeatedly, he had been described to them in their oral tradition and scriptures as one who, above all else, had promised them his unfailing love and his never-ending faithfulness.

Thankfully, that unfailing love and enduring faithfulness came through for them. Exiles to Babylon returned. The walls of Jerusalem and the temple were rebuilt. However—and this had to have been a huge source of doubt within their Jewish religious faith—the expected reestablishment of an independent kingdom of Israel with its own king had *never materialized*. Instead, for four hundred of the past five hundred years, they had been living under the dominion of various foreign empires. And at one point in 167 BC, Syria's Antiochus IV had imposed the *death penalty* for obeying the Torah *in their own land*. Nothing in their tradition had prepared them to cope with living as aliens in their own land, under the rulership of idolaters. No prophet had ever predicted anything like this would happen.

Even the brief interlude of Jewish independence under the rule of the Hasmoneans (167–63 BC) never developed into the reestablishment of the Davidic kingdom. They had belonged to the priestly clan of Levi, not to the royal family of David. That brief interlude, though, likely helped people realize that the emergence of an autonomous Jewish kingdom might just be possible. Yet, given the formidable grip of Roman power over them, that appeared highly unlikely to happen anytime soon. And so, the question remained: Why this continued delay in the fulfillment of God's promises?

This disconnect, between what the divine prophetic promises had led the people to expect and what they were living through under foreign oppression, appears to have created significant cognitive dissonance. Jewish biblical scholars were driven back to the drawing boards to figure out an explanation for this perplexing incongruity. Knowing that the writers of the prophetic scriptures of the seventh and eighth centuries BC had also dealt with the crisis of foreign oppression, they pored through those biblical writings once again, looking for clues.

They found that all those writings voiced a belief that "the end" was fast approaching, that Yahweh's final restoration of his covenant people, Israel, was at hand. As they reflected on these teachings and on their own historical circumstances, they began, around 150 years before Christ, to produce a whole new set of Jewish religious writings. This was a brand-new literary genre: apocalyptic literature. These writings envisioned a specific scenario playing out among them in the near future. Yahweh was going to establish his kingdom, restore Jerusalem and the temple to its rightful functions, gather in Israel's long-scattered exiles, punish the unrighteous, crush idolatry, and replace the Jews' suffering and distress with everlasting peace. At the core of this apocalyptic message was the same conviction that had inspired the prophets. Regardless of how hopeless things looked, God's covenant with Israel was everlasting, and he would therefore surely redeem and restore his people.

As these apocalyptic writers revisited the historical events described by the prophets—the Exile, the return from Babylon, the anticipation of a king descended from David retaking Israel's throne—they added a new interpretive twist. They concluded that all the prophets' talk about Israel's "restoration" was not referring to things that would be happening *within* Israel's history, but rather at the *end* of world history. At that culminating climax of human history, on "The Day of the Lord," Yahweh will finally seize active control of things. Either he himself will lead the battle against the forces of evil, or else he will send his prophet Elijah to anoint his messiah to lead his army. Or perhaps he might send the messiah directly himself, or even hand the battle's leadership to a nonhuman hero figure (a

"Son of Man"). Led by Yahweh, through his messiah, the forces of good would utterly defeat the hostile powers of evil, and the kingdom of God would finally be established.

Three explicitly apocalyptic works mention the future coming of a "Son of Man" figure. Daniel 7 mentions "one like a Son of Man," who was someone or something in human form. A later writing, 2 Esdras, drawing on the book of Daniel, mentions a Son of Man who is a nonhuman, supernatural redeemer but resembles a human being. The author of Enoch identifies Daniel's Son of Man figure as the heavenly Enoch who is mentioned in the book of Genesis and who was seated on God's throne of glory.

Apocalyptic literature of this time also talked about a "messiah" ("anointed one") figure. Although "messiah" occurs thirty-nine times in the Hebrew scriptures, it is never used there in reference to a *future* figure. The word was most commonly understood to be specifically connected with Israel's legendary warrior king David. Intertestamental Jewish apocalyptic writings thus envisioned a future messiah as a David-like figure. Like David (who was renowned for slaying Philistines by the tens of thousands), he would be a dreaded man of war. Someone able to strike fear into oppressive foreign powers and inflict final defeat on the forces of evil. A prince epitomizing David's legendary valor, piety, courage, wisdom, justice, and knowledge of the Torah. He would commence history's final drama: execute judgment, defeat Yahweh's enemies, become enthroned over a restored nation of Israel, and establish a never-ending peace.

6

The Jesus Archives

A Consequential Moment in History

My Jewish ancestors' passage through history can neither be recounted nor understood in isolation from a larger overshadowing storyline—that of their first-century Jewish contemporary, Jesus of Nazareth. His birth marked the consequential moment when human history was bifurcated into a decisive before-and-after. The movement he initiated sent endless reverberations rippling across the world and down through millennia. The trajectory of my ancestors' journey, indeed the course of world history itself, was subsequently forever altered.

First-century Palestinian Jews were confronted by a fateful quandary: what to make of this Jesus? Some concluded he was Yahweh's promised "anointed one"—the Messiah. Others became convinced he was not. Who was right? My own ancestors appear to have been among the majority of Jesus's contemporaries who ultimately remained unconvinced. Over the next several centuries, while cloistered in their Jewish enclaves, continuing in their traditional religious and cultural ways, the fleeting story of a Jesus of Nazareth from the distant past gradually faded from their corporate memory.

But the story of Jesus had, of course, lived on. First, among a small group of Jesus's personal acquaintances, which subsequently grew into a full-fledged, Jerusalem-based, Jewish Jesus movement. Then, it spilled over among non-Jewish people outside of Judea into places like Syria, spread further westward mainly among Gentiles in the Roman Mediterranean world, and led to the emergence of what we've come to know as early Christianity. The story of Jesus continued to endure as Christianity, during the 300s, became sanctioned as the official religion of the Roman Empire. Partnered now with the empire's governing elite, the Roman Church was positioned to play a predominant role in shaping the course of Western society into the Middle Ages and beyond.

While this church-state governmental system of Christendom was overseeing the emergence of a Christian European society, my Jewish ancestors were making their migratory journey from Palestine to Italy and then on into Germany. Little did they know what was awaiting them as a tiny immigrant, social, racial, cultural, and religious minority group amid a Christian-dominated European population. Especially when, after the year 1100, the cultural environment surrounding them took a dark and dangerous turn, precipitated by a grotesque medieval distortion of the ancient Jesus movement. Anti-Jewish resentment, disdain, and animosity dramatically intensified, erupting to the surface in outbreaks of violence, destruction, torture, and massacres—all in what its perpetrators believed to be the cause of Jesus.

The life and enduring legacy of Jesus of Nazareth, looming so large over the trajectory of my Jewish ancestors' path through history, thus warrants our further examination. Who exactly was he? What was his life really all about? How did his Palestinian Jewish contemporaries—including my own ancestors—view him? What did they know about him? What had they thought of him? Why did some choose to follow him, while others did not? These and other questions will be addressed in the next chapter.

But first, there are other, more preliminary questions to consider. What can we possibly know about Jesus as we look back from our perspective 2,000 years after the fact? What are the sources that provide us access to any such knowledge? And are those sources historically reliable?

The Gospel Artifacts

Fortunately, historical evidence of Jesus has survived. During the decades after he lived, his defining identity was remembered and conveyed among his earliest followers. They purposefully retained and preserved these memories, convinced of both their truth and significance. Further efforts to preserve them resulted in their commitment to writing. Documents were composed and left behind as historical artifacts. Literary works embodying firsthand eyewitness testimony, the personal reports of things people saw and heard while in the presence of Jesus. We have come to know them as the four New Testament "Gospels."

Did you realize, however, that it wasn't until forty years after Jesus's death that the first of these four was actually written? Think back to forty years ago when Ronald Reagan was president. What if nothing had ever been written about his presidency until just this year? Would you not be a bit skeptical about the historical reliability of such a long-delayed account? Such skepticism among some biblical scholars regarding the historical reliability of the Gospels is certainly understandable. But the basis for such skepticism begins to erode upon a closer examination of the actual process that, in all probability, led to the creation of the Gospel accounts.

That process began already during Jesus's own lifetime. It didn't take long for his own contemporaries to discover that he was no ordinary first-century Galilean. His notoriety spread quickly and widely. Here was an unusually wise and authoritative teacher. A worker of miracles. A healer of diseases. An attractor of large crowds. A sharp critic of the Jewish religious establishment. An empathizer with the poor and socio-economically disadvantaged masses.

Eyewitnesses

He had eyewitnesses. People who saw him with their own eyes and heard him with their own ears. Lots of them. The entire Galilean region of his day likely had two hundred thousand inhabitants. They were mostly concentrated in the densely populated area around the Sea of Galilee, where Jesus spent most of his time. Without traveling any great distance, Jesus was probably able to teach and perform miracles in front of thousands of people. In addition, there were those who knew him up close and personally. His parents. His siblings. His neighbors. Fellow villagers. His handpicked twelve disciples. His casual acquaintances. Those who experienced his healing touch or his release from demonic bondage. Countless mental video and audio recordings had been transcribed—unalterably and inerasably—inside the memory banks of those who had encountered him face to face.

Eyewitness Stories and Testimonies

There was an astounding supernatural dimension evident in much of what these witnesses saw and heard. The kinds of experiences that would be impossible to keep to oneself: "You're not going to believe what I just saw happen today . . .! I have got to tell you this . . .!" These eyewitness accounts spread in the only way possible back then—by word of mouth, from one person to the next. Think of all the people, thousands or more of them, who potentially had such stories to tell. Who, in turn, probably told at least dozens more, and they in turn likely told still dozens more. Galilean towns and villages must have been abuzz with the continuous telling and repeated retellings of the observed actions and teachings of Jesus. And this was just during the three years of his public ministry.

Imagine the impact that his reported death, resurrection, and ascension had on this ongoing dissemination of personal stories and testimonies. We all know what typically happens when a popular, charismatic, inspiring, heroic, emerging young leader is suddenly gunned down in the prime of life. Their legendary persona grows even larger in people's memories. Now, on top of everything else Jesus had been heard saying and seen doing, there were even more spectacular personal eyewitness reports about his death and resurrection circulating through Galilean and Judean communities. Through the next three or four decades, and for the remainder of their lives, these eyewitnesses continued to be readily accessible. They became the trusted go-to authoritative historical sources, able to vouch for the things they had reported seeing and hearing regarding their personal interactions with Jesus.

Initial Formulation and Transmission of Jesus's Teachings

Aside from the educated elite and the professional scribes and copyists, more than 90 percent of first-century Jewish Palestinians could neither read nor write. How does one function without the use of notebooks, to-do lists, memo pads, or sticky notes? Nearly everything they needed to remember had to be inscribed in their minds. Unable to read even their own Hebrew scriptures, the vast majority had to train themselves to be attentive listeners to, and astute memorizers of, what they heard read to them.

Since learning was therefore boiled down to memorization, Jewish wisdom teachers and rabbis had to use special techniques to help their non-reading students remember what they were teaching them. These included carefully crafted, memorable aphorisms and narrative parables. Literary techniques such as parallelism, alliteration, assonance, rhyme, rhythm, and wordplay helped make their teachings easier to recall. Jesus most likely employed a similar teaching style with his twelve disciples. It wasn't that his memorable sayings just happened to stick in their memories. Rather, his disciples understood that he intended for them to deliberately commit to memory the things he was teaching them. That's what was expected of disciples of Jewish rabbis in Jesus's day.

For three years, Jesus's disciples sat under his intense discipleship, listening, asking questions, observing, comparing mental notes, internalizing, memorizing, and reciting their learnings to others. We can reasonably expect that after three years, they would have accumulated and committed to memory a formulated set of Jesus's core foundational sayings, parables, and teachings. These memorable summations of Jesus's ministry are what the disciples then most likely continued sharing orally, in their native Aramaic language, with a growing body of Jesus-followers in the wake of his death and resurrection. An authentic, authoritative, eyewitness-based oral "Jesus tradition" was thus spawned. It served to keep alive their memories of his teachings and activities as they had personally witnessed them. This was the seed that, beginning some forty years later, would sprout into the written Gospel accounts.

In the predominantly oral culture of Jesus's day, writing was often used to supplement and support the oral forms of teaching and remembering. Already during Jesus's ministry, some of this oral Jesus tradition could well have begun to be converted to written records and circulated as such among his disciples. Rabbis were known to have used private notebooks to store notes as aids in remembering the material they wanted to orally transmit to their disciples. There were undoubtedly some among Jesus's earliest followers who could write. It is highly unlikely that none of them would have jotted down portions of the oral Jesus traditions in their notebooks for their own private use as Christian teachers.

Of central significance to the early Jesus movement was the nucleus of first-generation Christians who comprised the church in Jerusalem. Most of those who had been Jesus's personal disciples were based here, along with other eyewitnesses whose personal testimony to the life of Jesus was highly valued. Among this community were some who had studied the Hebrew scriptures and were capable writers. Some rather sophisticated scribal activity appears to have been occurring here as well. Greek-speaking Jews from the diaspora also became prominent within this early Jerusalem Christian community. It was most likely here that the Aramaic oral and written Jesus traditions were first translated into Greek (the language used by the Gospel writers). Scholars have thus envisaged Jerusalem as the key place where the eyewitness-based Jesus traditions of primarily the Twelve were carefully compiled and formulated into a unified collection, which they then authorized as an official body of witness about Jesus.

We know from the apostle Paul that already within the first year following Jesus's death, such a pre-formed oral tradition existed. He describes having received a set of teachings about Jesus in Damascus after his conversion. His likely instructor there was the Jesus-following Damascus resident, Ananias. And what Ananias had "handed over" to Paul (Saul) was something recently formulated in Jerusalem by the disciples. In Paul's first letter to the Corinthians (15:1–3), he summarizes what the core of that transmitted Jesus tradition was. "What I received [in Damascus from Ananias via the Jerusalem apostles] I passed on to you: that Christ died for our sins . . . that he was buried, that he was raised on the third day . . . and that he appeared to Peter and then to the Twelve." By the time the apostle Paul began writing his epistles around AD 50, it would still be another twenty years before the New Testament Gospels would begin to appear. Yet it is apparent from Paul's early writings that a collection or multiple collections of the teachings of Jesus already existed in oral form by about AD 50.

From Jesus Traditions to Gospel Writings

Why was it during the particular time frame of the late first century that the four Gospel accounts emerged? The story of Papias (c.60–c.130), the bishop of Hierapolis (an ancient Roman city located in present-day western Turkey), is instructive. His city of Hierapolis was a major crossroad for early Christian leaders traveling from Jerusalem and Antioch in the east to the new church startup in Ephesus to its west. It was also a crossroad for Christian leaders traveling between various towns in Asia Minor where other new church plantings existed. Papias was strategically positioned to have personal interactions with many of these traveling early church leaders. He appears to have made it his personal mission to talk to as many of them as he could and collect from them as many of the stories about Jesus as he possibly could.

Papias was especially interested in hearing the stories of those who had personally known Jesus and his original twelve disciples. Two daughters of Philip the evangelist, a key leader in the early Jerusalem church mentioned in the Book of Acts, lived in Hierapolis. They told Papias some of the stories they knew through their father's association with the original apostles back in Jerusalem. Papias also had conversations with two men who had been personal disciples of Jesus but were not part of the original twelve. One was named Aristion. The other was named John, who Papias referred to as John "the Elder" to distinguish him from the John who had been one of the Twelve. They were both prominent Christian leaders in Asia Minor while Papias was bishop of Hierapolis. Papias took all his collected stories and, near the end of the first century, turned them into a five-volume work, *Exposition of the Sayings of the Lord.*

Why was Papias so passionate about collecting and writing down all these stories? It appears that as he went about seeking eyewitness reminiscences about Jesus, it dawned on him that there were very few people with such remembrances still living. The original twelve had all died. The two living eyewitnesses to whom he had access, Aristion and John the Elder, were very old. The day was about to dawn when there would no longer be what Papias described as "a living and surviving voice"—the literal voice of an informant—to tell the stories of Jesus. The oral eyewitness-based Jesus traditions were about to die along with the eyewitnesses themselves. Someone needed to do something to keep that voice alive past their deaths—gather them together and put them in writing. And so that's what he did. Disappointingly, only a couple dozen fragments of Papias's *Exposition* survived for the early church historian Eusebius, bishop of Caesarea, to read and tell us about. But it was enough to help us capture the essence of what he was trying to accomplish.

The motivation behind Papias's writing of his *Exposition* appears to have similarly been behind the compositions of four other works that were written during the same general time frame as Papias's: Matthew, Mark, Luke, and John. The composers of these accounts, too, seem to have sensed an urgency to go to the eyewitnesses of Jesus, or to the most reliable sources with direct personal links with those eyewitnesses, while there was still time to do so. They, too, felt compelled to collect their stories and compile them together into a unified whole. They, too, realized the imperative need for their fellow Jesus-followers to have a written document summarizing for them the essence of Jesus's life and ministry and its significance for how they were to live their lives as his followers.

A Brand-New Genre

Around AD 70, an anonymous Greek-speaking Jewish Christian wrote what later became titled *According to Mark*. It spread quickly and widely among various early Christian communities throughout the Mediterranean world. Papias of Hierapolis claimed to have been informed by John the Elder (one of the two elderly personal disciples of Jesus he was able to interview) that it was written by John Mark, the apostle Peter's close companion and Greek interpreter in Rome. Peter had been teaching the oral traditions about Jesus in Rome—presumably using the unified body of material the Twelve had first formulated together earlier in Jerusalem. It was believed that, following Peter's martyrdom, Mark used these teachings he had personally heard Peter giving in Rome as the basis for his composition.

Mark chose the word "gospel" to encapsulate his narrative. The apostle Paul had already incorporated this word into early Christianity's vocabulary when he began writing his epistles twenty years before this. Likely echoing what he'd been taught by his mentors as a new convert to Jesus, Paul considered Jesus's orally-reported saving death and resurrection to be the essence of this "good news." Mark now sat down to put that same good-news passion story of Jesus's suffering, death, and resurrection—as told to him by the eyewitness Peter—in writing. This was thus a landmark historical development. What had primarily existed for the previous forty years (AD 30–70) as *oral* gospel accounts was, for the first time, transposed into a *written* Gospel account.

Mark introduced an additional innovative twist. He began his account by saying: "[This is] the beginning of the gospel/good news about Jesus Christ the Son of God." The *beginning* of the gospel? It appears to have occurred to Mark that if he was going to recount the climactic good news story of Jesus's death and resurrection, he first needed to provide its backstory. The *beginning* of that story—Jesus's three-year public career preceding his crucifixion—had to be written up as well. So Mark attached an extended introduction to it, and thereby reformatted the very concept of "the gospel." Thanks to Mark's pioneering work, the "gospel" came to be understood as more than merely the good news of Jesus's death and resurrection. It was, rather, the good news of *the entire life and ministry* of Jesus.

This "Gospel format"—the story of Jesus's passion, preceded by an extended introduction—soon became the established way of conceptualizing the story of Jesus's mission. Among those who read and studied Mark's account were two people whose own subsequent Gospel compositions also came to be included in the canonical New Testament: the anonymous author who wrote Matthew in the mid-80s (he was most likely *not* the tax collector Matthew/Levi who was one of the Twelve); and Paul's associate, Luke (who most probably wrote his Gospel between 80 and 90).

Both share substantial identical wording with Mark's account. The writer of Matthew replicates 90 percent of Mark's material, while Luke duplicates 50 percent of it. Scholars who have examined those parts of Matthew and Luke that were not lifted from Mark have discovered considerable overlap between Matthew's and Luke's non-Markan material. It appears they may both have, independently of each other, used an identical second source that had been making the rounds (but now lost to history) alongside Mark's account. Or, perhaps Luke had Matthew's Gospel in front of him while he was crafting his account and decided to include parts of it in his own composition. The writers of both Matthew and Luke thus felt free to pick and choose from available source materials, and to make minor editorial additions and revisions. Matthew, for example, inserted a narrative about Jesus's birth that reflects his father Joseph's perspective—an oral tradition that had likely filtered down through Jesus's siblings from Joseph himself. Luke replaced Matthew's birth narrative with one that reflects Jesus's mother Mary's perspective—an oral tradition that had likely filtered down to him through Jesus's siblings from their mother.

Variations in their accounts would be expected given that they were written by three different people, each with a unique background and writing style. They were composed in varying geographical locations and were intended to reach different audiences. Mark was most likely composed in Rome by a Greek-speaking Jewish Christian. He appears intent on defending the legitimacy of placing one's faith in a crucified Messiah, asserting the superior authority of Jesus over the imperial power of Rome, and encouraging his readers to persevere as followers of Jesus under opposition to his mission.

Many scholars believe Matthew was written in a Greek-speaking urban center in Syria—perhaps Antioch. It appears to have arisen out of an environment in which Jewish Christians and their Gentile converts wanted to stay connected with their Jewish roots in the broader Jewish synagogue community. But they were facing growing pressure to be expelled, which may have already begun to happen. The author presents to his mixed

Jewish-Gentile Christian community—and before their surrounding Jewish neighbors—a distinctively Jewish take on the story of Jesus. He presents it as the fulfillment of the Jews' ancient religious heritage. And he affirms that following Jesus is the truest expression of loyalty to the Jewish people's ancestral calling and hopes.

Luke's composition is the first part of a two-volume work dedicated to a man of notable social stature named Theophilus. Some scholars speculate he may have been Luke's patron, the sponsor of his literary endeavors, or perhaps a Gentile whom Luke is mentoring in the Christian faith. He tells Theophilus, and his broader non-Jewish Greco-Roman audience, a "Jewish" story of Jesus. Jesus is the fulfillment of the story of Israel's history. His life embodies the Jewish message of salvation for a pagan world.

What came to be called the Gospel of John was written independently of the other three (Synoptic) Gospels, probably in Ephesus around the year 70. Its anonymous author testifies to being the primary witness to the things he's included in his account. He never identifies himself by name but does portray himself as "the disciple whom Jesus loved." According to tradition, this was assumed to be John, son of Zebedee, one of the Twelve. But there is compelling evidence that its author was a different John—the disciple of Jesus whom Papias referred to as John "the Elder." The work seems intent on convincing both Jews and Gentiles that Jesus is the divine Messiah, and that both groups are legitimate inheritors of the heritage and promises of ancient Israel.

Evangelists

The Gospel writers were neither biographers nor historians. While their works display similarities to the genre of ancient biography, providing a detailed "life of Jesus" public-interest story was not their intent. Rather, they were self-described "evangelists"—intent on conveying a "good news" message centered around the historic, transformative impact Jesus had made. They all delivered the same central "gospel" message, which went something like this: through Jesus, the creator God, Yahweh, had become a king on earth as in heaven; the Hebrew scriptures had been pointing ahead to him all along; this is how the arrival of that kingdom took place; this is now the reality you Jesus-followers hearing/reading this account are consequently living in; and this is how that new reality is to shape your Jesus-following journey through life.

The Gospel compositions do, though, share striking similarities with the genre of ancient Greco-Roman and Jewish historical writings. Historians during this time believed that true history could be written only while the events they were recording were still recent enough to be within living memory. They were expected to document their accounts with the oral reports of direct eyewitnesses whom they could question themselves. The witnesses' ability to have seen the events of history with their own eyes, not just to have heard about them from someone else, was considered paramount. All four Gospels appear to deliberately follow this approach in their reporting. They all tell the "story of Jesus" using the story/testimony of witnesses who were participants in that story from beginning to end. Scholars have noted, additionally, that when these authors name specific individuals as characters in their accounts, they are likely footnoting for their readers the identity of their original eyewitness sources.

In summary, the objective of all four writers was both to preserve and convey the story of Jesus's ministry. Each engaged in an interpretative act of selecting and arranging their source material of eyewitness testimony and formed it into a uniquely styled literary account with specific audiences in mind. They thereby transmitted to all of subsequent history the story of Jesus as he was remembered by those who knew him best—the Jesus of testimony.

7

The Remembered Jesus

T he birth, ministry, and death of Jesus spawned a controversial new messianic sect within first-century Judaism. Responses varied. While a minority embraced him as their promised Messiah, many greeted his new movement with indifference. Still others—considering it blasphemous—angrily sought to stamp it out. Yet, while most first-century Jews took a pass on joining it, the early Jesus movement took firm root on Palestinian soil.

As mentioned earlier, my Jewish ancestors' journey through history can neither be recounted nor understood in isolation from this larger overshadowing story of Jesus of Nazareth. We've seen how that story, as remembered by personal eyewitnesses, came to be preserved and conveyed through the Gospel narratives. In this chapter, we will explore the main contours of that story. What do the eyewitness Gospel testimonies reveal to us about Jesus? And what do they disclose to us about the experience of Palestinian Jews during this momentous first-century era?

First-Century Galilee

When the Assyrians invaded the northern kingdom of Israel back in 733 BC, hauling away its population as captives, the vacated region of Galilee they left behind was resettled by Gentiles. Not until the time of the Jewish Hasmonean ruler John Hyrcanus (134–104 BC) was this territory reconquered and resettled by Jewish residents. Yet there remained in Galilee during the time of Jesus a number of Gentiles and a substantial presence of Hellenistic culture, surrounded as it was by Greek city-states and principalities.

Josephus had extensive knowledge of this region, based on information he had access to as the military commander of Galilean rebel fighters during their uprising against Rome in AD 67–68. He estimated its total population to be more than three million people. (He himself had mustered up to one hundred thousand fighters in the struggle against Rome.) He reported that its territory spanned forty-two miles from north to south and thirty miles from east to west at its widest point. Archaeologists have verified the reliability of his claim that Galilee was very densely populated with 204 cities and villages, which he described as being "close-packed." While recruiting rebel fighters, Josephus also discovered Galileans to be a "warriorlike" culture. Its boys and young men were well-versed in the basic survival skills of various fighting methods—the use of daggers, swords, and other weapons.

Its well-watered, fertile land made for a prosperous production of various crops: olives, fruits, vines, flax, and grain. Its large lake, the Sea of Galilee, sustained a flourishing fishing industry. Galilee was thus a lucrative region to be in control of. Herod Antipas, its Rome-appointed tetrarch, with his elite inner circle, was positioned at the top of a pyramidical socio-economic structure. Just beneath them was a privileged class of royal attendants, tax officials, bureaucrats, and military personnel. Below them was a small class of property owners—artisans, fishermen, and self-employed farmers.

At the base of this pyramid were the multitudinous members of the landless peasant class. Their properties, subjected to overly burdensome layers of taxation, had been confiscated and absorbed into the holdings of an expanding privileged class of estate owners. As Jews, they had to pay the annual half-shekel temple tax, plus the required tithes that supported the temple priests. Additionally, land taxes and custom tolls were levied by Herod Antipas to fund his extensive building projects. And on top of that, tribute payments were imposed by Rome. Altogether, the total tax burden on Galilean Jews during the first century typically amounted to one-third or more of all one's annual produce and income. A mood of social disorientation and unrest had taken root among this vast landless class. They sensed their traditional Jewish way of life was being ravaged by an oppressive economic system.

His Nazareth Roots

Nazareth was a small Jewish peasant hill-town in lower Galilee. It was established in the late second century/early first century BC on a ruined site from the eighth century BC. The Jews who initially settled there during the Maccabean era would typically have selected a tribal-related name for their new village. Interestingly, there is a striking similarity between "Nazareth" and the Hebrew word *netzer* ("branch"), which is used in Isaiah 11:1 to refer to a "branch" sprouting from "the stump of Jesse [King David's father]." This linguistic link suggests these settlers consciously self-identified as members of a Davidic clan. If true, then by the time of Jesus, the majority of

Nazareth's residents could be assumed to have shared in this Davidic ancestry.

According to Christian historian Julius Africanus of the late second century and early third century, Nazareth was a town where people who were recognized as descendants of David lived. His descendants from other places had relocated there as well—including refugees from Bethlehem, the "city of David." Jesus's own parents, Joseph and Mary, were among these refugees. They had fled to Egypt with a newborn Jesus to escape Herod's slaughter of newborn Bethlehem males. When it was safe for their return to Palestine, however, they did not return to Joseph's hometown of Bethlehem. Instead, as descendants of David, they relocated to the Davidic city of Nazareth in Galilee, a town of sixteen hundred to two thousand people.

Scholars point to a rekindling of Jewish national and religious identity that had recently spread through Galilee. The people of Nazareth, including Jesus's own family, were likely swept up in this resurgence as well. Clinging tenaciously to the foundations of their Jewish piety, these Galileans were living as fervent observant Jews: observing the Sabbath; practicing circumcision; attending the synagogue; and keeping the kosher food laws. They felt a deep and enduring affection for the symbols of Jerusalem and the temple, making regular religious pilgrimages there. And they sensed an intensified longing for the restoration of the nation of Israel in all its glory.

The importance of Jesus's Davidic lineage—being a "son of David"—would certainly have been impressed upon him at an early age by his father Joseph. He would also have learned his father's trade as a *tekton*—an artisan working with hard building materials of stone, metal, or lumber. It can be assumed that he worked with his father in this trade, building and repairing houses and furniture in and around Nazareth. He would typically have been trained in the Hebrew scriptures by his father and by a synagogue attendant. Already at the age of five, he would have begun his education in the synagogue. He would have spoken in the everyday language of Aramaic. Followed the traditional religious practices of his pious Jewish family. Participated in the communal life of his synagogue community and the regular pilgrimages to religious festivals at the Jerusalem temple.

A Public Unveiling

After living for thirty years in apparent relative obscurity, Jesus's unremarkable existence in Nazareth abruptly ended as he began a public outreach to his fellow Palestinian Jews. The Gospel writers associate this "going public" with his journey to the Judean desert region of the Jordan River valley southeast of Jerusalem, and his encounter there with a John the Baptizer. Something about this John, his message, and his baptizing activity in the desert attracted Jesus's attention.

As the only son of a priest, it was John the Baptist's traditional family duty to continue his family's priestly line by serving in the Jerusalem temple. Instead, apparently disenchanted with the temple and its ritual system, he became an anti-establishment prophet. Many of his fellow priests, feeling much the same, had formed an anti-temple Essene separatist group in the desert at Qumran. John was convinced that Yahweh had become deeply disturbed by the current state of religious affairs among his Israelite people. Like the Qumranites, he believed that a renewal movement was urgently needed. And for such a spiritual reboot to happen, Yahweh's people would need to experience a reconnection with the desert origins of their relationship with him. Making that reconnection would require a literal journey to the Jordan River, the edge of the desert. There they'd be able to visualize their ancestors faithfully following

Yahweh as he led them from the desert, across the Jordan, into the Promised Land.

The entire people of Israel—even the "holiest" among them—were, in John's view, living in violation of Yahweh's moral standards. His righteous judgment, therefore, was about to be unleashed. John's fellow Jews needed to be awakened to this imminent danger. There was only one way for them to avert this looming calamity. They needed to acknowledge their individual and corporate guilt. Journey to the Jordan River to receive a unique, once-for-all ritual immersive cleansing in its flowing waters. And repent—turn their lives back around again toward Yahweh.

To those who arrived at the Jordan for his ritual cleansing, he made an additional announcement. A far superior, "stronger" baptizer than himself would soon follow in his wake. As urgent as it was for them to be baptized now by him, this was merely a foreshadowing of that greater impending baptismal cleansing. That purification, said John, would not be done using mere water. It would instead be accomplished directly by Yahweh's "Holy Spirit." And it would bring to fruition what the ancient Hebrew prophets had envisioned happening in the "last days." Yahweh's Spirit would be poured out on the true people of Israel.

The Gospels report that among the many Jews who responded to John's call for national repentance, and who flocked to the Jordan for the protection of John's baptism, was Jesus. The implications seem quite clear. Jesus was not only acknowledging John's prophetic authority but was apparently also embracing and affirming John's message. John had it right. The end of Israel's history was fast approaching. Israel had gone astray and was in danger of being consumed by Yahweh's judgment. The only escape was through a basic change of heart and mind that was reflected in the way Yahweh's people lived their everyday lives. That Jesus appears to have chosen this venue as the springboard for his own ministry reveals something of his intentions for his own soon-to-be-unveiled ministry. It would be an urgent call to all Israel for a radical spiritual transformation of their minds, their hearts, and the conduct of their lives.

Decades later, when the Gospel authors were formulating their written accounts of the remembrances of Jesus's time among them, they directed their readers' attention to this encounter with John. They all recalled a startling incident as Jesus was being baptized by John. As Jesus emerged from the water, a dove landed and rested on him. They understood this as symbolizing the descent of Yahweh's Spirit to "anoint" him for his impending mission. And the unmistakable voice of Yahweh from heaven was heard pronouncing Jesus to be his Son. All the Gospel writers had thus become convinced, through eyewitness testimony, that the Jesus who had lived among them had been none other than Yahweh's royal Messiah, the Son of God. And they all pointed back to this seminal event at the Jordan River as the moment when his true identity as Yahweh's anointed Son was initially revealed.

His Mission

Promptly thereafter, Jesus's public mission began to unfold among the commoners in his native Galilee. He appeared among the fishermen, peasants, and artisans in the small villages of the northwest shore region of the Sea of Galilee. The lakeshore town of Capernaum, one of Galilee's larger villages of about six hundred to fifteen hundred residents, became his base of operations. It was probably the main fishing village of the area. Located on the road running to the northeast across the Jordan to Damascus, it was the last village in Herod Antipas's Galilean territory before crossing the border into Herod Philip's Gaulanitis territory. It thus served as a post for collecting customs on the passage of goods in and out of the area. As for why Jesus picked Capernaum, it may have been that one of his earliest followers provided him a room to stay in there. It did offer him quick access to Jewish settlements in the Golan region to the north, as well as the Galilean heartland to the west and south. It was also conveniently situated on the edge of Antipas's territory, allowing Jesus the option of slipping out of his jurisdiction, should the need suddenly arise. Given that Antipas had already ordered the beheading of John the Baptist, there was no telling what he might decide to do if he were to feel similarly threatened by Jesus.

He went about teaching in various local synagogues, where his audiences "were deeply moved by his teaching, for he taught them as one who possessed authority" (Mark 1:22). But the prophetic tone of his teaching proved to be a bit too unsettling to the Pharisee faction. As a result, the doors of the synagogues were soon closed to him. He resorted instead to teaching out in the fields and along the lakeshore. He attracted large, often enthusiastic crowds of curious and sympathetic onlookers as he performed miracles, healings, and exorcisms. Most people in those crowds, however, never became committed adherents. Those few who did often left behind families, possessions, and livelihoods to devotedly follow him on his teaching tours around Palestine. They listened to his parables, observed his miracles, and showed him their loyalty and devotion by offering him hospitality. Yet all the while, they failed to understand at the time what it was that he was actually up to.

Among his followers, of course, were the twelve men he handpicked as his close-knit inner circle of students. The number twelve sent an unmistakable message regarding the meaning and purpose of his mission. The original full and complete ancient nation of Israel had consisted of twelve patriarchal tribes. Centuries had now passed, though, since ten of those tribes had essentially vanished, having been driven out of this very Galilean northern territory of Israel. And yet there were lingering hopes and expectations that Yahweh would someday end their enduring exile. There just might yet be a reassembling and reconstituting of all twelve of his original tribes! Jesus, it seems, was sending a not-so-subtle message: through his selection of the Twelve, he intended to restore Yahweh's Israel of the past to its true and full end-time completeness.

The central message Jesus spread through both his words and actions was simply this: "the kingdom of God is now here." Interestingly, "the kingdom of God" was not a commonly used phrase among the Jews of Jesus's day. It never occurred in the Hebrew scriptures. It is noticeably absent in most of the other Jewish religious writings prior to Jesus's time. Which raises some provocative questions. Why did Jesus choose to use this almost unheard-of phrase to describe the essence of what his teachings and actions were all about? Why do we never hear him defining the meaning of that rarely used phrase? And why do we never hear his listeners perplexedly asking him to explain what he is referring to?

Perhaps the reason is this. Even though the phrase had an obscure ring to it in the ears of Jesus's listeners, it evoked a particular *imagery* that they could immediately visualize. Their memorized Hebrew scriptures had provided them with evocative mental images of Yahweh's power and authority as he had led them on their journey through history. From Egyptian bondage to freedom. From desert wanderings to the land of promise. From a vulnerable, fledgling clan of tribes to the formidable nation of Israel under Kings David and Solomon. Their book of Psalms repeatedly visualized for them mental images of Yahweh powerfully ruling over his creation as the eternal Sovereign King.

Their Hebrew scriptures had also primed them for a coming Day of the Lord when Yahweh would establish—through his people Israel—an earthly kingly rule over all the nations. However, having lived now for centuries under the rule of foreign nations, the people of Jesus's day had an especially hard time believing that would ever happen. They had largely lowered their expectations, now anticipating its arrival sometime in the faraway future at the end of history.

But this charismatic teacher and healer, Jesus, was confidently announcing that it had arrived now at this very moment of history. This was a stunning development in first-century Palestine. Here was a man who spoke and acted with what appeared to be divine authority. There was something fascinating and attractive about his message. Yahweh had arrived on Palestine's soil to assume his long-awaited role as the people's King. This was truly good news. The story of Israel would no longer feel like it was being suspended in air with an indefinitely delayed ending. The days of endless futile waiting for Yahweh to show up as their King were now suddenly over! He had arrived back among his people to finish their story and establish his kingdom—as he had always promised to.

Amazingly, the reality of this newly arrived kingdom was being enacted before their very eyes. A significant reversal of the status quo was taking place. Diseases and deformities were being healed. Demons were being purged. Sins were being declared forgiven. Lives were being transformed.

Paradoxically, however, there was, according to Jesus, a future aspect to this arrival of Yahweh's kingly reign still waiting to kick in later. Even though he had announced and demonstrated that Yahweh's kingdom was now here, he still taught his disciples to pray, asking Yahweh to yet make "his kingdom come on earth as it is in heaven."

The "already come" and "yet to come" dimensions of Yahweh's kingly rule on earth contrasted sharply with the typical Jewish concept regarding present and future realities. They traditionally thought in terms of two separate, contrasting, sequential ages. The present *evil* age would, at its end point, be followed by a future *good* age. But according to Jesus, that anticipated future good age the Jews were expecting was, in this very moment, being superimposed onto their present evil age. The present evil age of life under Roman tyranny had not yet ended. But a parallel reality—the future good age—had now also arrived. Though its arrival did not bring with it a sudden end to the present evil age (e.g., Roman oppression), a titanic shift had occurred. The reversal of its powerful grip on humanity had begun. The "yet to come" had indeed broken through onto the stage of human history. But there was a more thorough and final "yet to come" that would still be arriving later.

Jesus sought to elicit a very specific response from those hearing his announcement of the kingdom's arrival. First, they were to *metanoeó*. "Repent," "convert," "change their minds," "turn back around." He reiterated the often-repeated calls of the Hebrew prophets to "turn back" to Yahweh from a life lived in violation of Yahweh's moral standards. Second, they were to "believe"—place their trust and reliance in the power of Yahweh. And finally, Jesus challenged them to "follow" him, as a learning community, in order to receive more of his teaching. This personal "calling" to handpicked individuals to "follow after" their leader stands out as unique to Jesus and the Twelve in the first-century rabbinic world. Implicit within this chosen-ness of the Twelve was Jesus's intention for them to assist with and share in his mission.

Who Did He Think He Was?

Undoubtedly, Jesus thought of himself as a "son of David." That reality had almost certainly been impressed on him already at a young age growing up in the Davidic clan village of Nazareth. Did he think of himself, though, as *the* long-anticipated son of David who was to retake the royal throne over the nation of Israel? There is no documented remembrance of his ever explicitly making that claim. Yet, there are multiple occasions in his remembered teachings when, interestingly, he alluded to having such an identity by comparing himself to David and Solomon.

Did he consider himself to be the "Son of God?" Once again, nowhere in the written record of the remembrances of those whom Jesus lived among was he ever cited as explicitly ascribing to himself the title "Son of God." There are, however, recorded remembrances of Jesus having heard the voice of God publicly affirming him as his Son upon his emergence from his baptism in the Jordan River. Additionally, the gospels recount his use of "father" in addressing Yahweh in his prayers. They also record him making frequent references to Yahweh as his "father in heaven" in his discourses. The implication seems quite clear. People had observed Jesus revealing a uniquely immediate and intimate father-son relationship between him and Yahweh.

Consistent with this enigmatic approach to revealing his true self-identity, Jesus was also never remembered as having made any outright verbal claim to be the anticipated Jewish royal Messiah ("anointed one," "the Christ"). Given that first-century Jews lacked consensus on any single uniform messianic concept, this should come as no surprise. There were many diverse opinions about what type of figure the expected "anointed one" was actually going to be. Jesus's seeming reluctance to hastily apply this title to himself is thus understandable. Using such a loaded title would likely have created even more confusion and misunderstanding about his true role. People would likely have simply projected their own preconceived messianic notions onto him, based strictly on who they had been imagining the "anointed one" would be.

So rather than simply going around and stating outright, "I am the Messiah," Jesus seems to have preferred taking a different approach. Instead, he made veiled, yet unmistakable intimations of his messiahship, allowing his actions in many cases to speak louder than his words. This enabled him to "control the narrative" about the purpose of his mission. While that narrative remained a bit of a riddle to his disciples during Jesus's time with them, it became clearer as various pieces of the puzzle of his true identity began fitting together for them following his execution.

Jesus frequently referred to himself in the third person using the peculiar phrase "the Son of Man." This was a common non-religious Aramaic idiom simply meaning "this man." But it also, notably, happened to have been used in the book of Daniel. Daniel described a vision in which he saw a mysterious "one like a son of man" who had been given "authority, glory, and sovereign power," whose "dominion is an everlasting dominion" and whose "kingdom is one that will never be destroyed" (Dan. 7:13–14).

Jesus's apparent allusion to and association with this royal figure in Daniel seems more than coincidental. It appears to have been an intentional effort to connect his role with that of Daniel's envisioned figure. This was a subtle way to communicate what he saw as his role: the heavenly agent sent not only to embody Yahweh's kingly power and authority, but also to implement its earthly presence among the first-century people of Israel.

Jesus took specific actions, especially near the end of his life, whereby he appeared to be deliberately acting out a messianic role. He rode into Jerusalem on a donkey—the very thing the prophet Zechariah had predicted Yahweh's future anointed king would do—with the people shouting, "Hosanna to the son of David." He entered the Jerusalem temple and, seeming to claim royal authority over it, warned of its imminent destruction. He then predicted its rebuilding, something considered to be a messianic task. He ended up on trial before the Jewish High Priest on a messianic charge. And when asked point-blank a messianic question, he responded with an evasive, yet confirmatory response. He was executed on the charge of being a messianic impostor, and was mocked in his death as a Jewish king. All these occurrences make little sense apart from there having been at least some indications that Jesus had espoused what were interpreted to be royal claims and aspirations.

Further insight into Jesus's self-perceived messianic role is provided by a major motif that was expressed in the exilic and post-exilic Hebrew biblical writings. Those writings indicated that after the geographic return of Judean exiles from Babylon, Yahweh would return to take up residence once again in "Zion" (Jerusalem). This scriptural theme continued to be maintained in the Jewish post-biblical writings as well. Moreover, this expectation remained central to Jewish thought during the time of Jesus.

Interestingly, the Gospel accounts seem to portray Jesus's final journey to Jerusalem as intentionally symbolizing and embodying this long-awaited return of Yahweh to Zion. The implication is that he made his final entrance into Jerusalem not just as Israel's Messiah, but also as Israel's returning God. He was thus not merely *announcing* Yahweh's return to Zion but *personifying* that climactic event as well. He "cleansed" the temple, warned of its forthcoming destruction, and claimed authority over it. The implication: He was somehow its personal replacement as the new place of meeting between Yahweh and his people.

When asked by the High Priest Caiaphas at his trial if he was "the Messiah, the Son of the Blessed One," he responded, "I am, and you will see the Son of Man sitting at the right hand of the Mighty One." By thus identifying himself with the enthroned figure in Daniel's vision, he was making an astounding claim. He was on the cusp of being enthroned alongside the one sovereign God of Israel. Here was a Jewish human being placing himself within the sphere of the divine sovereignty of almighty Yahweh. Claiming to share Yahweh's throne as Israel's God.

The Climactic Culmination

Toward the end of Jesus's time, a couple of noticeable shifts began to unfold. For one thing, Jesus began broaching with his disciples the unsettling prospect of his looming suffering and death. They were perplexed and put off by such talk. It was an outcome that did not fit with their preconceived paradigm for the role of Israel's Messiah and the inauguration of Yahweh's kingdom among them.

The night before his execution, Jesus shared with them a "last supper," where he sought to explain what his impending death was all about. It was full of prophetic symbolism intended to illustrate *how* Yahweh's kingdom would come on earth as it is in heaven. As a Passover meal, it evoked the story of Israel's divine rescue from past tyranny. But it also pointed forward to the future restoration of Israel, her still-anticipated full and complete return from exile. At that time, they would rest assured knowing they had at last attained Yahweh's forgiveness for the sin of Israel that had precipitated their exile in the first place.

Using the bread and wine he was serving, Jesus merged his story, his kingdom agenda, and his approaching death into that larger story of Israel's restoration. By means of the breaking of his own body (bread) and pouring out of his own blood (wine), he indicated he would become the sacrificial Passover lamb through which Yahweh would be returning to fully redeem and restore his beloved Israel.

Another shift that occurred toward the end of Jesus's ministry was the intensification of anger and hostility toward him by the Pharisees, the Jewish high priestly families, and temple authorities. Already early on, Jesus's public teachings and actions had aroused suspicion. His signs and wonders had led to speculation that he was a false prophet in league with Satan, aiming to lead the Jewish people astray. The religious authorities had become increasingly wary of his unconventional ways and teachings, and his seemingly messianic overtones. There was increasing concern that, although he was not advocating for any revolutionary activity against Rome, he could become a dangerous political liability if he were to say or do something that might elicit an anti-Jewish reaction from Rome.

With his final trip into Jerusalem, Jesus seems to have deliberately set himself on a collision course with the ruling priests, stoking their antagonism and fury to the boiling point. Provocatively "cleansing" the temple, he confronted the temple leaders, insinuating that through their corrupt and oppressive leadership, they had failed to live up to their God-ordained task. They were deeply offended by his stark warning about the temple's coming judgment and destruction.

Such anti-temple talk and action could only be interpreted by the temple leadership as being blasphemously offensive to Yahweh. It was a direct assault not just against the legitimacy of their religious leadership, but against the essence of their Jewish religion itself. Jesus's public put-down of the temple was a gut-punch against the central symbol of Yahweh's presence among his people. Caiaphas, the high priest, became livid. Something drastic needed to be done to silence this man as soon as possible.

Lacking the legal authority to execute Jesus themselves, the priests had to become creative. Any issuance of a death penalty had to come through the official auspices of Rome. In order to achieve such a conviction, they would need to concoct a charge against Jesus that would be deemed offensive to Rome's authority. Conveniently, the Rome-appointed governor of Judea, Pontius Pilate, happened to be in Jerusalem at that very time for Passover. Since he would soon be returning home to Caesarea, however, time was of the essence. So, while he was still in town, they needed to quickly find a way to manipulate him into convicting Jesus of insurrection against Rome.

The first step was for Caiaphas to have Jesus taken into his custody. Since he had religious authority over temple affairs, and since Jesus had threatened to destroy the temple, he had the legal religious grounds for arresting Jesus. The second step was to cross-examine Jesus under oath in such a way that he would incriminate himself for having engaged in seditious activity—not against the Jewish temple, but against the Roman government. The third step was to take Jesus's self-incriminating confession before Pilate and prove to him that Jesus had indeed committed a capital offense against Rome.

Jesus's interrogation by Caiaphas and the religious authorities eventually reached a successful breakthrough. Caiaphas—apparently based on rumors about Jesus's purported messianic identity—finally asked Jesus point-blank if he was the Messiah, the Son of the Blessed One (Yahweh). His affirmative answer was exactly the foolproof evidence they believed they needed. A claim to being the Messiah was a claim to being the "king of the Jews"—a claim to royal authority over the Jewish people independent from and in direct defiance against the sovereign authority of Rome.

When Pilate, in turn, interrogated Jesus, he became highly skeptical of the Jewish leaders' charges. He seems to have sensed the disingenuousness of their tactics. He saw their political charge of sedition as merely a front for their underlying religious reasons for getting rid of Jesus. So, he scornfully refused their request. But when it was pointed out to him that by not executing a would-be rebel king, he himself would be seen as being disloyal to Caesar, he yielded to his own self-interest and handed Jesus over to be crucified as a rebel against Rome.

Jesus's arrest, trial, and humiliating execution immediately left his followers feeling dumbfounded and despondent. The movement he had been initiating among them had seemingly ended in a disheartening failure, having died with its leader.

Astoundingly, however, within a few days of his death, they began to experience personal encounters with a Jesus who had come back to them from the dead. Over a period of the next five to six weeks, multiple such encounters were reported to have occurred. There were appearances to the eleven apostles, a personal appearance to his own brother James, and an appearance to more than five hundred followers at one time that likely occurred in Galilee.

These interactions with a bodily resurrected Jesus triggered a transformation of the disciples' previous perception of him and his mission. Already prior to his death, they had apparently reached the conclusion that Jesus was the Messiah, son of David. There is a recorded remembrance in the Gospels of Jesus having point-blank asked the Twelve who they thought he was, and of Peter having responded as their spokesman, "You are the Messiah."

But never had they ever envisioned the Messiah as someone who would end up dead, let alone as someone who would come back from his grave alive. These new realities of death and resurrection now forced them to rethink the whole concept of Messiah. Just how much the post-resurrection Jesus may have directly instructed them in this rethinking process cannot be determined. Luke informs us in his book of Acts that the resurrected Jesus did "speak about the kingdom of God" to them during this time. We can ascertain, though, something about how their rethinking process likely unfolded. John's Gospel account relates that after Jesus's resurrection, the disciples recalled some of the Hebrew scriptures Jesus had cited as having been fulfilled in his messianic mission. And based on some of the public speeches of the apostles recorded in the book of Acts, it seems they came up with additional Hebrew scripture passages which they also now considered to have been fulfilled through the death and resurrection of Jesus Messiah.

Jesus's disciples had experienced the stunning reality of his resurrection from death. They had recalled and revisited various Hebrew scriptures that they could now see as messianic references to Jesus. Their concept of the Messiah was redefined. They were now convinced. Jesus was, in fact, the Messiah. And the Messiah was indeed someone who needed to suffer and die. All of this had been confirmed for them by the reality of Jesus having been raised from the dead. It was their conviction about these two realities—that Jesus was the Christ (Messiah) and that Yahweh had raised him from the dead—that provided the impetus for the rise of what would become the Christian movement.

8

The Emerging Jesus Movement

A Galilean Nucleus in Jerusalem

Jesus's prophetic activity and teaching in the villages of Galilee for two to three years had made an enduring impact. Not inconsequentially, he had sent some of his followers in pairs to various villages to extend his message. Yahweh's kingdom had come, and the renewal of Israel was at hand. Small responsive enclaves of friends and relatives appear to have materialized from those efforts. After the devastating news of Jesus's execution, these groups apparently continued to exist and developed an even more intensive community life.

There had been a contingent of such Galilean Jesus-followers, in addition to the Twelve, who had accompanied him on his final trip to Jerusalem for the Passover celebration. Following the confusing and disheartening end of Jesus's life there, some likely returned home to Galilee, refusing to suddenly abandon his memory. Others of them apparently stayed on in Jerusalem.

In the wake of Jesus's resurrection appearances and his eventual mysterious ascension into the skies, there remained a nucleus of about 120 Galilean Jesus-followers in the city of Jerusalem. Jesus had specifically instructed them to remain there in a kind of spiritual holding pattern awaiting an impending "gift my Father promised." This would be the experience of being "baptized with the Holy Spirit" that John the notorious water-baptizer in the Judean desert had predicted. Their home base was the "upper room" where Jesus and the Twelve had met for Passover the evening before his death. This was likely the upper part of a large house, whose obviously wealthy owner had provided as a space where they could congregate as necessary.

Day of Pentecost

Ten days after Jesus's ascension, during the Jewish harvest festival in Jerusalem known as the Feast of Weeks (or, in the Greek language, as Pentecost), a seismic event rocked the city. It propelled the Jerusalem followers of Jesus into bold new activity that would alter the very course of human history. A dramatic display of supernatural phenomena led Jesus's apostles to an inescapable conclusion. The actual Spirit of Yahweh had just been "poured out" on them—the precise event the ancient Israelite prophets had long envisioned! An exciting, overwhelming realization set in: A new age had dawned for the people of Israel. Yahweh's final purposes for them as his chosen people and for his entire creation were at this moment being fulfilled before their very eyes.

Newly emboldened, inspired, impassioned, and empowered, followers of Jesus began publicly announcing and explaining among fellow Jews in Jerusalem what they perceived to have just taken place. These mysterious phenomena, they explained, were in fact all part of, and indeed a dramatic culmination to, the life and mission of Jesus, the Israelites' resurrected Messiah.

Their audience consisted not only of local Jerusalemites but also of religious pilgrims from throughout the Mediterranean Jewish diaspora who were in Jerusalem for the Pentecost festival. They are described in Luke's account in his Book of Acts as having been "cut to the heart" by what they heard. The recently crucified Jesus, these apostles passionately explained, was none other than the man Yahweh had made "Lord (royal sovereign) and Messiah." Many listeners became deeply unsettled. Had this man Jesus really been Yahweh's anointed Israelite king? If so, they were in a perilous place with Yahweh. They had not acknowledged his anointed king. No wonder their response was a desperate-sounding, "What shall we do?!"

The lead apostle Peter's answer to this urgent question was simple and straightforward. They needed to do the same thing the Hebrew prophets had urged their ancestors to do. The same thing that John the Baptist had insisted the people do in the Judean desert. The same thing Jesus himself had personally implored Peter and the rest of the Twelve to do. "Repent." Turn back to Yahweh. And then, as a part of that repentance, Peter— just as John the Baptist had—exhorted them to "be baptized." Only this baptism would be different. It would be done "in the name of Jesus Messiah for the forgiveness of your sins."

The people's response was astounding. About three thousand Israelites were baptized. Most of them were probably diaspora Jews who would soon be returning to their countries of origin. They likely arrived home eager to share what they had just witnessed. The exaltation of Yahweh's Messiah Jesus had been accomplished. Those among these new Jesus-followers who were permanent residents of Jerusalem were added to the local core of 120 devotees.

A Messianic Faction Within Judaism

This now-expanded contingent of Jerusalem's Jesus-followers did not suddenly stop practicing their Jewish religion. They continued participating in temple worship. Observing the Torah. Attending their synagogues. The temple was still a focal point in their life, as they gathered regularly within its precincts at Solomon's Colonnade—the place where Jesus himself had taught. But they now assembled there to be led and instructed by Jesus's apostles. They did not see themselves as abandoning their Jewish faith in favor of some new and different religion. Rather, they believed they were merely initiating a new faction within the broader Judaism of their day. Understanding themselves to be Yahweh's "new" Israel, their focus had shifted. It was now fixed on the central focus of Jesus's own ministry: bringing about the full restoration, renewal, and redemption of their fellow Israelites.

What was new about this fledgling "Jewish sect" was, of course, their messianic take on their teacher and leader, Jesus. They considered him to be Israel's exalted royal Messiah enthroned alongside Yahweh, having been raised by him from the dead. It was to his ultimate authority that they now submitted themselves. And they began calling their fellow Jews to follow their lead.

One Community, Two Subcultures

Interestingly, Jesus's original core of Galilean devotees chose not to return home. They remained in Jerusalem instead. Why? Likely for "theological" reasons. Their Hebrew scriptures had long associated Israel's king with the place called Zion—the idealized Holy City of Jerusalem. Jesus had talked of returning soon for the final consummation of Yahweh's kingdom. Where else would that happen but in Jerusalem/Zion? They should stay and wait for him here. Jerusalem thus became ground zero for the emergence of Jesus's messianic community.

The dynamics within that early community were complicated. Although being a single collection of people, they came from two contrasting Jewish subcultures and linguistic backgrounds. Luke, in the Book of Acts, distinguishes

"Hebrews" and "Hellenists" among them. These were pejorative terms suggesting some mutual suspicion and perhaps even underlying hostility between them.

The "Hebrews" were the 120-plus Jewish transplants from Galilee associated with Jerusalem's upper room community. Many had had personal connections with Jesus during his time in Galilee. They were stereotypical country bumpkins, seemingly just hanging out in Jerusalem. They spoke Aramaic. The more cosmopolitan-oriented "Hellenists" likely viewed them as a bit too parochial and traditionalist for their taste.

The "Hellenists" were Jewish people who had relocated to Jerusalem from various places outside Palestine, where they had adopted some of the Greek cultural ways. They accounted for a substantial number of the one hundred thousand Jews living in Jerusalem at the time. They spoke Greek. They met in their own Greek-speaking synagogues to hear the reading of the Septuagint/Greek translation of the Hebrew scriptures, and to pray in Greek. A significant number of the estimated 390 synagogues in Jerusalem at this time likely consisted of such Hellenist Jews.

Some of these Hellenists heard the apostles' preaching about Jesus, affirmed him as Messiah, were baptized, and joined the fledgling Jesus movement in Jerusalem. But the cultural and language barrier between them and the Galilean "Hebrews" prevented them from being fully assimilated into the Galileans' upper room community. Instead, they continued meeting elsewhere in the city in their own Greek-speaking homes and synagogues with their fellow Greek-speaking diaspora transplants.

Eventually, the underlying tension between them rose to the surface. It revolved around the poor financial condition of the widows among them. Lacking the resources to obtain daily food, these women relied on charitable distributions from the rest of the Jesus community. The Hellenist widows were especially dependent on this charity as they usually had few, if any, local relatives to assist them. Sensing they were not getting their fair share, they complained.

To the credit of the apostle leaders, their complaint was heard and addressed. They appointed seven "deacons" (literally "table-waiters") to ensure their needs would be met. Interestingly, these seven men all had Greek names, indicating that they themselves were probably all part of the Greek-speaking Hellenist group. That Greek-speaking believers were assigned to oversee the needs of the Greek-speaking widows lends further credence to the presumption that Jerusalem's Greek-speaking believers were meeting, separately from its Aramaic-speaking believers, in Greek-speaking homes.

How did the apostles come up with the number seven? And why these seven men in particular? It is noteworthy that Luke at one point refers to them as "the seven," implying that they provided a parallel leadership to that of "the Twelve." It is also striking that these men eventually emerged as vigorous leaders in the expansion of the Jesus movement beyond Jerusalem. It seems these seven men were viewed by the Twelve as already-existing representative leaders of the Hellenist contingent. They may in fact have been the leaders of seven Greek-speaking messianic house groups/congregations ("churches") in Jerusalem.

A further contrast eventually emerged between these Hebrew and Hellenist groups. The "Hebrew" apostles seem to have embraced a neutral posture toward their Jewish temple. They continued attending services and engaging in teaching there. It appears that temple priests quite seamlessly embraced the apostles' messianic message and joined their community. This influx of priests likely reinforced the Hebrews' generally pro-temple attitude.

However, as the seven Hellenist deacons spread the message of Jesus within Jerusalem's various Greek-speaking synagogues, a contrasting perspective emerged. One of "the seven," Stephen, communicated the message about Jesus in anti-temple terms. This not only stirred up lively debate but also prompted a violent backlash.

Stephen

Stephen had somehow come to grasp an insight regarding Jesus that had apparently not yet sunk in for the Galilean Hebrew apostles. It seems he was captivated by the connection Jesus had drawn, just before his death, between his fate and that of Yahweh's Jerusalem temple. Stephen surmised that Jesus's death had consequently secured the "death" of the Jewish temple and its whole sacrificial religious system. And, by means of his resurrection, Jesus had brought about the temple's "resurrection." In Stephen's thinking, the temple had been transformed from a physical building "made by men" into a new community of Yahweh founded on the Twelve. It was now possible for the Jewish people to relate directly to Yahweh and his Messiah King Jesus independently of the Holy City of Jerusalem and its temple building. Therefore, continued loyalty to and participation in the temple system was no longer necessary for followers of Messiah Jesus.

It was in the Greek-speaking synagogues where Stephen and the rest of the seven had affiliations that Stephen began disseminating his anti-temple rhetoric. It was a recipe for disaster, as his audiences there were Jews who had forsaken their life in the diaspora for the express purpose of living near their revered temple. Stephen's disparagement of the temple, and by implication the Torah—two sacred symbols of the Jewish religious heritage—was considered a treacherous assault against

Yahweh himself. His teaching stirred up fierce resistance. Those who argued against him became enraged. Before long, a mob mentality took over and, in the end, he became the victim of a religious lynching by stoning.

Saul the Persecutor

Luke's account in the Book of Acts notes the presence of an approving silent bystander at Stephen's execution, a certain Saul of Tarsus. A diaspora Hellenist Jew himself, Saul had apparently come from Cilicia (present-day southern Turkey) to Jerusalem as a youth to study and teach the Torah. As a zealous young Pharisee, in his mid- to late-twenties, he appears to have been a rabbi in the Hellenist synagogues of Jerusalem, where he directly encountered Stephen's new teaching. He was likely front and center in engaging Stephen in dialogue, debate, and disputation. The more knowledgeable he became of Stephen's teaching, it seems, the more outraged he felt about what he was hearing. And the more urgent he believed it was to squelch the emerging Jesus movement.

Saul himself, in his writings later as the converted apostle Paul, attributed his earlier negative reaction to his "zeal" as a devoted Israelite. He was steeped in a deep-seated, ancient Jewish tradition of vehement passion for holiness, purity, separation, and an often-violent hatred of paganism. His hopes for the coming kingdom of God were dependent on strict adherence to the Torah and an impassioned attachment to the temple. If views such as Stephen's were to catch on, the long-awaited implementation of Yahweh's divine purposes could be delayed or even sidelined. Saul seems to have considered these ideas to be such an affront against Israel's holiness and such a perversion of the worship of Yahweh that he felt duty-bound to stop their spread by all possible means.

That Saul's vengeful response was aimed not only against Stephen and the Hellenist Greek-speaking Jesus-followers, but also against the Hebrew, pro-temple, Aramaic-speaking Jesus-believers as well, is telling. It indicates there was more than merely Stephen's rejection of the temple that moved Saul to action. Apparently, as he pursued his interrogations of Jesus's followers, his discovery of their underlying messianic claims about Jesus is what especially alarmed him.

What needed to be rooted out, Saul realized, was that which was the driving force behind Stephen's radicalism—the spread of the teaching that Jesus had been the Messiah. The adoration of a crucified man (of all things!) as Messiah and Lord was downright offensive to the Jewish religious tradition. People were increasingly buying into the lie of a false Messiah. Simply getting rid of Stephen was not going to put an end to this hoax. The entire movement needed to be expunged from the Jewish community.

Dispersed Beyond Jerusalem

Saul's assault against the Jerusalem messianic community in AD 34 drove both the Hellenist and Hebrew groups (except for the apostles) out of Jerusalem. Unnamed Hebrews, fleeing for refuge to Aramaic-speaking places in Judea and Galilee, spread the message of Messiah Jesus in synagogues and established "churches" in those places. These were not churches as they are typically pictured through one's twenty-first-century lenses. The Greek word used to refer to them was *ekklesia*, which simply denotes an "assembly." These first-century "churches" were essentially informal household-based assemblies, groupings, or communities of Jesus-followers. Later, Peter left Jerusalem and, with the assistance of the apostle John, helped to consolidate many of these Jesus-believing communities during his various travels throughout Palestine.

The Hellenist believers, on the other hand, scattered mostly to places beyond Judea and Palestine. Many of them likely returned to the places in the diaspora that they had come from. Philip, one of the seven, went spreading the message of Jesus to Samaria and Caesarea—where non-Jewish people made up the majority of the population. Others went eastward to Damascus, Syria. Some went northward along the Mediterranean coast, settling along the way in Phoenicia or offshore in Cyprus, or ended up in the Syrian metropolis of Antioch. They preached the message of Jesus to fellow Jews in the various synagogues.

This expansion broke new ground in Antioch in the early thirties. There, for the first time, the message of Jesus was reported to have crossed over the Jewish ethnic line into the non-Jewish, ethnically-Greek community. They were likely "God-fearers," as opposed to outright "pagans." These were Gentiles who had previously been drawn to the Jewish religion and synagogue life but had declined to submit to circumcision and full conversion to Judaism. Local authorities in Antioch noted this blending of two cultural streams into a new cultural-religious entity. Apparently sensing the need for a new category for identifying them, they coined a new term: "Christians" (literally "Christ-adherents"). Thus, what had begun as a culturally inward-focused Jewish sect in Jerusalem started shifting to a more outward-focused missionary movement among the Gentiles.

Paul the Missionary

While traveling to Damascus to hunt down and arrest any Jesus-followers who had fled there from Jerusalem, Saul experienced what he later described as a face-to-face encounter with the bodily resurrected Jesus. It resulted in a 180-degree turn in the direction and mission of his life—from Saul, the antagonist of Jesus, to Paul, the apostle of Jesus. Viewing this from our twenty-first-century vantage point might cause us to miss what really happened here. This was not simply a matter of Paul "changing religions," abandoning Judaism and adopting "Christianity" in its place. More precisely, Paul made a subtle, yet radical shift from a Pharisaic "brand" of Judaism to an alternative messianic one.

The reason he had gone to Damascus to arrest Jesus-followers there in the first place was that he was convinced they were committed to a false messiah. After meeting the resurrected Jesus on his way there, however, he realized that Jesus's resurrection was living proof that Yahweh had vindicated Jesus against the accusation of being an impostor messiah. The fact that Jesus was alive from the dead meant that Yahweh really had declared him to be "his Son," Yahweh's anointed, Israel's Messiah. And Paul seems to have perceived at once that if Jesus indeed was Israel's Messiah, then he must also be the world's true *kyrios* ("lord," "master"), the one before whom all humanity, including Gentiles, should bow their knees.

His vision of the God of Israel, whom he had been so zealously serving until now, was transformed. The messianic community he was out to destroy was actually the fulfillment of Yahweh's promises to Israel. More than that, it was also the instrument of his ongoing redemptive work among Jews and non-Jews alike. Paul's zeal for Yahweh, his people Israel, and his divine purposes did not let up. Rather, it became redirected toward serving Yahweh now as a newly enlisted envoy of his emerging messianic community.

Damascus became Paul's home base for the next few years, where he taught in synagogue gatherings that Jesus was the Son of God. Jews there who were not adherents of Jesus felt so threatened by Paul's messages that he was forced to flee due to plots against his life. So, he traveled to Jerusalem, where he became acquainted with the apostles Peter and James. His bold preaching of Jesus the Messiah there among non-Jesus-following Hellenist Jews so antagonized them that they tried to kill him. Consequently, he boarded a ship in Caesarea and traveled back to his hometown of Tarsus, where he spent the whole next decade.

Eventually, he was invited to join the Jesus community in Antioch. There, he became one of its teachers and leaders. Later, during the mid- to late-forties, he and his associate Barnabas traveled through Cyprus and southern Asia (the Roman province of Galatia), having been sent as missionaries by the Antioch church. Their efforts were centered in the various Jewish synagogues of the region. Their audiences were typically a mixture of Jews and non-Jewish God-fearers who had been attracted to Judaism, but whose males were unwilling to fully convert, as they did not want to be circumcised. While the message of Jesus being the Messiah, Son of God, and Lord was generally not well-accepted by Jewish recipients, it was welcomed among non-Jewish God-fearing hearers. They were attracted to this new "brand" of Judaism that no longer required them to be circumcised in order to be fully included, nor to be bound by all the restrictions imposed by the Jewish Torah.

Paul's evangelistic and church-planting ministry throughout the region of the Aegean Sea, in Asia Minor and Greece, continued until his execution in Rome in the early sixties AD. It resulted in the planting of Gentile-majority churches in several major urban areas. And it provided a prevailing impetus to the pivotal transition of the Jesus movement from a minor Jewish sect into a largely Gentile religious and cultural entity in the Greco-Roman world.

The Gentile Issue

That transition, though, did not occur without a struggle between two conflicting mindsets. The apostolic leadership base in Jerusalem had a Jewish-centric mindset regarding the expansion of the Jesus movement. Living among an all-Jewish population at Judaism's ground zero, they likely had never thought through the possibility of non-Jewish people joining their movement. It was assumed that Jesus Messiah had come for the Jewish people, which meant that the route into Jesus's community for a non-Jew would necessitate first becoming a Jewish proselyte.

A challenge to this Jerusalem mindset occurred already in the late thirties when Peter felt divinely led to go to the Gentile city of Caesarea. Once there, he found himself being divinely prompted to set aside his Jewish scruples about associating with "unclean" Gentiles. He was led to the home of a Gentile God-fearer named Cornelius. Stepping way out of his religious comfort zone, Peter not only agreed to meet with him, but, irrepressibly, shared the message of Jesus with him and a large gathering inside his home. He then baptized them all in the name of Jesus Messiah as his new followers. Once back in Jerusalem, Peter caught flak. But after relating the whole story of how it all happened beyond his own control, his critics were silenced by the surprising realization that the redeeming work of Jesus was apparently meant for Gentiles as well as Jews. This was a major first crack in the wall of resistance to the inclusion of Gentiles in the Jesus community.

Eventually, word got back to the Jerusalem church about additional questionable happenings in other scattered areas. They heard about the "open table" policy between believing Jews and believing Gentiles in the Antioch church. They heard how, through Paul's work in Galatia, people had been baptized as new

Gentile followers of Jesus without first being required to be circumcised. In response, a traditionalist element within the Jerusalem church sent representatives to Antioch and Galatia who insisted that Gentile converts to Jesus there should first become proselytes to Judaism through circumcision and observance of the Torah.

Around the year AD 49, a meeting of key leaders—Peter, James the brother of Jesus (primary leader of the Jerusalem church), and Paul—took place in Jerusalem to iron out a solution to this divisive problem. James convincingly offered a compromise that all agreed to. On the one hand, Gentile converts to Jesus should not be required to first become circumcised. On the other hand, they should be required to observe a handful of basic stipulations of the Torah that would not be considered too burdensome for them.

Continued Developments in Jerusalem

The original community of Jesus-followers in Jerusalem, as noted earlier, had formed around the inner circle of Jesus's twelve disciples. Three members of that inner circle, Peter and the two brothers John and James (sons of Zebedee), emerged as that community's initial leaders in the early thirties. As also mentioned earlier, many of its adherents, both Hellenists and Hebrews, had fled Saul's persecution, leaving behind the apostles and an increasingly Hebrew Jerusalem church. Using Jerusalem as their home base, Peter and John took frequent subsequent trips away from Jerusalem to help consolidate some of the scattered Palestinian church communities, while James remained in Jerusalem providing leadership to the Jesus-believers there.

Another serious threat to the survival of the Jerusalem church arose in the early forties at the instigation of Herod

Agrippa I, King of Judea (grandson of Herod the Great). Although educated in Rome and most likely a Gentile at heart, Agrippa, hoping to win the acceptance of his Judean subjects, attempted to pass himself off as an observant Jew. Peter's baptism of Gentiles in Caesarea had apparently created a perception among the broader Jewish community in Jerusalem that the Jesus-followers and their leaders were inappropriately pro-Gentile. Agrippa opportunistically and pretentiously seized on that perception by persecuting this minority group as supposed traitors to the Jewish nation's holy cause. Attempting to demonstrate his pro-Jewish credentials, he had James (brother of John) beheaded. He had Peter arrested, intending the same outcome for him. Due to a miraculous release from prison, however, Peter was able to escape from Jerusalem and went to stay, presumably, in his Galilean homeland until after Agrippa's death a few years later.

Interestingly, an additional key leader had emerged by this time among the Jesus-believers in Jerusalem. One who had not been among the original twelve disciples of Jesus: Jesus's own brother James. He had been an outsider to Jesus's original group of followers. Someone who had been less than impressed with Jesus and had even opposed him during his public ministry. Surprisingly, he emerged as the primary leader and spokesperson for the "mother church" in Jerusalem after Peter's departure. Apparently, when Jesus made a resurrection appearance individually to James, something happened that brought James fully on board with Jesus's movement. Equally surprising was his ability to remain in Jerusalem and avoid the same fate that had befallen James (son of Zebedee) and Peter at the hands of Agrippa, not to mention that of his own brother Jesus. In fact, he continued to effectively lead the Jerusalem church for more than twenty years until temple authorities had him stoned to death in AD 62.

His durability in Jerusalem was a significant accomplishment given the difficult terrain of Jerusalem's Jewish politics. It required walking a fine line between two competing pressures. On the one hand, there was pressure coming from within the Jesus community in various places at a distance—Caesarea, Antioch, Galatia, etc.—to fully include Gentiles into their membership without requiring them to first become Jews. On the other hand, there was pressure coming from the general Jewish population in Jerusalem, increasingly a hotbed of Jewish nationalism, to be stridently pro-Jewish.

In view of this prevailing Jewish nationalist mood, James was careful to prevent the Jerusalem church from being perceived as insufficiently Jewish. To survive in such an environment, the mother church could hardly be anything other than conservatively Jewish, increasingly taking on the character of a strictly law-observant, "Judaizing" community. It consequently became the center of a traditionalist conservative wing of Jesus's messianic movement, while the non-traditionalist wing continued expanding elsewhere among primarily non-Jewish people through the missions of Peter, John, and Paul.

After the stoning of Jesus's brother James and some of his friends in AD 62, things went from bad to worse for the Jerusalem Christ-followers. Declining to join the revolt against Rome in AD 66, they were further ostracized and persecuted by their fellow countrymen. According to the early church historian Eusebius, just prior to the revolt, the Jerusalem Christians received an oracle that ordered them to flee across the Jordan River to the city of Pella in Perea. The more fiercely nationalistic among them remained behind instead to fight in the war. They lost their lives in the dreadful siege and destruction of Jerusalem. The majority, though, fled while an escape from Jerusalem was still permitted.

Many who fled likely took up permanent residence in Transjordan, with their descendants gradually evolving there over the next few centuries into Jewish-Christian sects. Others returned later to the ruins of Judea and Jerusalem to pick up the pieces and restore some sense of a Christian presence in Palestine. An organized presence of Jewish Christians did continue in or near the ruined city and also in Galilee (most likely under the continued leadership of members of Jesus's family) until the Bar Kokhba revolt in the second century. But their presence had been significantly reduced and had lost much of its prior influence. (This will be discussed further in the next chapter.)

The Westward Shift

The Jesus movement, begun in Palestine among devout Jews, became, one hundred years later, a divergent religious community scattered across the Roman Empire, consisting almost entirely of Gentile converts from pagan religions.

What accounts for this fascinating turn of events? For one thing, the religious situation within the mid-first-century Mediterranean world was conducive to the Jesus movement's ability to take root. It was a dominantly Gentile, Roman-paganistic population. Yet, scattered throughout this region were various pockets of Jewish diaspora settlements, whose residents were practicing their traditional, synagogue-centered Jewish religion.

Some within the Gentile pagan population were drawn to elements of Judaism: its highly unusual monotheism, its strong ethical code, its worship and religious practices, and the status of its special role in history as depicted in their Jewish Scriptures. Consequently, Gentile "God-fearers" began affiliating with Jewish synagogues without fully converting to Judaism. They balked at submitting to circumcision, observing the Sabbath and other Jewish holy days, following Jewish dietary restrictions, and abstaining from many pagan ceremonies. The Jesus movement, perceived as a new Jewish sect, thus had an already-receptive audience among these Gentile God-fearers.

A second contributing factor to this westward shift was the unique role played by the apostle Paul. Using the various Jewish synagogues along his journeys as his base of operation, he proclaimed there the message of Jesus as Messiah/Christ, Son of God, and Lord. He was met with a mixed reaction. Synagogue leaders generally opposed his message and his use of their synagogue to promote what they considered to be a disruptive, unorthodox message. Gentile God-fearers, by contrast, seeking greater spiritual truth, were often attracted to Paul's teachings.

Paul allowed Gentiles desiring to become Jesus-followers to do so without taking on the unwanted burdensome Jewish trappings of circumcision, Sabbath observance, and following Mosaic Law requirements. The Jewish community, however, generally saw this as totally unacceptable, an abandonment of their Israelite heritage. This resistance eventually made it impossible for Paul to continue using the synagogues for promoting his teachings.

Small household-based assemblies (ekklesia)—house churches, essentially—were consequently formed as a synagogue alternative. They consisted mostly of Gentile God-fearing converts and a small minority of Jewish converts to Jesus Messiah. At first, there was significant overlap between these church and synagogue communities. Some Jewish converts to Jesus continued worshiping in their synagogue, celebrating Passover, and observing the Sabbath. There were Gentile God-fearing converts who belonged to both house church and synagogue. But by the year AD 100, these two enclaves, church and synagogue, were separating into two distinct and mutually exclusive groups. The Jesus movement was transitioning into an increasingly Gentile house church phenomenon.

A third major factor was the formative influence of the "Jesus tradition" in shaping both the content and the dispersion of the movement's message. As mentioned earlier, an oral tradition regarding Jesus's life and teachings had begun to take shape already during Jesus's lifetime. As also noted earlier, within a year after Jesus's death, a pre-formulated oral Jesus tradition circulating among his original disciples had been handed on to the apostle Paul, which subsequently became the core of his message to the Gentile world. In fact, for the first twenty to thirty years after the death of Jesus, everything that had been known, remembered, and communicated to others about Jesus existed almost exclusively in oral form. Eventually, as has also already been noted, the oral Jesus tradition was encapsulated in written form through the Gospel narratives.

This whole process of formulating and passing on what was at first an oral and then increasingly a written tradition about Jesus played a pivotal role in the expansion of the Jesus community in the Gentile world. It became the principal instrument through which the mission of Jesus continued to impact subsequent generations. Oral tradition was an especially vital resource for early church communities, given the typically high percentage of illiteracy and the vividness of communication that is possible through word of mouth and personal testimony. Even after copies of the written Gospels had begun circulating, most people were dependent on having them read aloud to them. Consequently, the Jesus tradition, whether in oral or written forms, continued to be communicated orally well into the second century. Yet as the second century progressed, it seems that reliance on oral tradition gradually decreased as the written Gospels became more extensively known and influential.

Gentile Christianity and Judaism – A Widening Rift

The relationship between the Jesus movement and its Judaism birth mother was fraught with tension from the beginning. Early Jewish followers of Jesus did not abandon their Judaism. They merely joined a new messianic sub-circle within Judaism. But this made for a sometimes fuzzy and fluid line of demarcation between them and their broader fellow-Jewish community. There was a built-in fault line between them, which was exposed and exacerbated as the Jesus movement spread westward from the mid-first century on and became an increasingly Gentile phenomenon. As Gentile Christianity progressed into the second century and beyond, Jews and Christians found it more and more necessary to define themselves over against each other. And as they did, the fault line between them became an irreconcilable gaping fissure that led ultimately to an antagonistic and acrimonious division.

To understand how that rift came about, it is instructive to examine how these two religious camps perceived each other. First, what was the Jewish perspective on Gentile Christianity? When the Jesus movement first took root within Jewish enclaves on Gentile soil, there were things that generally did not sit well within the broader Jewish communities. They viewed Jewish-Christian evangelization of Gentiles as too leniently downplaying the requirements of the Torah, a clear breach of proper Jewish proselytism. Also, their deification of Jesus was an obvious violation of the strict Jewish monotheism dictated by Yahweh's ancient first commandment.

Additional factors added fuel to their estrangement. With a rapid growth in the number of Gentile adherents, the predominating Jewish ethnicity of the early Jesus movement shifted dramatically to non-Jewish ethnicity. This created a socio-cultural barrier to the entry of additional new Jewish converts. Also, a growing Jewish nationalism led some Christian Jews to abandon the Christian community in order to remain loyal to their synagogue's Jewish roots. Facing the pressure to choose between faith in Jesus and allegiance to their Jewish heritage, loyalty to their Jewish nationality often won out.

Beneath all these factors, however, there was a deep-seated sticking point for many Jews. The Jesus movement's confident proclamation that Jesus had been Yahweh's promised Messiah for his people, Israel, seemed inherently problematic. As mentioned earlier, the Judaism of late antiquity had envisioned the coming Messiah as someone who would restore the nation of Israel and initiate a long and successful reign as her anointed King. The fact that Jesus had died, had never really begun his earthly reign over Israel, and in fact had allowed the nation to remain under subjugation to Rome, seemingly flew in the face of his messianic claim. His rejection by Jerusalem's religious authorities and his execution at the hands of Rome were viewed as convincing evidence of his prophetic failure and his political defeat.

Christ followers persistently tried to persuade Jews that Jesus really was Israel's Messiah. They provided a Hebrew scriptural explanation for his rejection by the religious authorities and his political defeat by the Romans. But their arguments were ultimately unable to persuade a significant number of Jews. Jesus's apparent defeat, the seeming failure of his promised kingdom to materialize, and his failure to return as his original followers had expected, simply created too many misgivings for them to be able to trust Jesus's purported messiahship.

There eventually came a point, though, when even the message of Jesus's messiahship itself seems to have receded in its relevance to a Jewish audience. Before and during the Jews' revolts against Rome, messianic expectations were at a heightened state. There was an eagerness then to latch onto any messianic movement that might be the means by which Rome could be overthrown. But after their near-annihilation by Rome, further Jewish interest in messianic beliefs plummeted.

On the flip side, what was the Gentile Christian perspective on Judaism that contributed to this antagonistic rift? What Jews considered to be their fidelity to Yahweh and faithfulness to Israel's holy traditions was often interpreted by Gentile Christians as an expression of Jewish conceit and stubbornness. Exasperated by this perceived recalcitrance, Christian leaders searched the Hebrew scriptures to understand more clearly: what was their distinct new Christian identity over against that of the Jews? They concluded that their faith in Jesus was indeed supported by those scriptures. While they initially saw themselves as a continuation of the biblical people of Israel, they soon came to believe, instead, that they were its replacement—the true fulfillment of what Yahweh had originally intended Israel to be.

By the middle of the second century, as the Christian movement was sweeping the Roman Empire, church and synagogue were disconnecting into two distinct, mutually exclusive bodies. Both had become convinced that the other had rejected the true God and was contorting the Hebrew scriptures. As Jewish synagogues held firm in rejecting the idea that Jesus was Israel's messiah, Christian leaders realized they were reaching an impasse. Synagogue communities were never going to change their minds. So church and synagogue split, each going its separate way. But the conflict between them continued. It made for a messy divorce.

The writings of mid-second-century church fathers reveal a "de-Judaizing" impulse. It wasn't just the synagogues that they wished to leave behind. They wanted to sever ties with their Jewish roots altogether. What better way to formulate and justify their own unique Christian identity than by using the Jewish religion that birthed them as their foil? "We are not them! In fact, we have superseded them as God's chosen people." Their polemical anti-Jewish sermons, diatribes, and dialogues display a bitter, incensed effort to overpower their Jewish opponents with every possible evidence that Judaism was a legalistic and dead religion.

Second- and third-century Christian literature—Cyprian's Three Books of Testimonies Against the Jews, Hippolytus's Expository Treatise Against the Jews, the writings of Irenaeus and others—betray a general contempt and ridicule of Jews and Judaism. The calamitous failure of the Jewish revolt against Rome in AD 70—the fall of Jerusalem, the temple's destruction, the consequent deaths, exile, and enslavement of thousands of Jews—provided them with lethal ammunition. Was this not proof positive of God's chastisement, his rejection and abandonment of his once-chosen people? And by the way, wasn't this also clearly a punishment for the crime of crucifying Jesus? Such suffering and ostracism are what happen to those who, in their ignorance and apostasy, reveal themselves to be a reprobate people. "These calamities they have suffered," wrote Origen, "because they were a most wicked nation, which, although guilty of many other sins, yet has been punished so severely for none, as for those that were committed against our Jesus." This antisemitic vindictiveness was taken even one step further: the Jews' unfaithfulness, they asserted, had tainted them with a collective guilt that subjugated them to a permanent, eternal curse by God.

While the early church fathers were bent on trashing Judaism and the Jewish people, they were unwilling to go so far as to ditch the Hebrew scriptures. Those scriptures presented them with an intriguing dilemma, however. If they were to fully accept those Jewish writings at face value, it would be tantamount to granting the Jewish people a measure of historical validity and legitimacy—a risk they were reluctant to take. Yet, those same writings provided the church with its own reason and purpose for existence. Besides, they supplied a gold mine of hundreds of prophetic texts that supported their messianic claims about Jesus. Irenaeus, Origen, Augustine, and others came up with a creative workaround to this quandary. Using a unique system of interpretation, they transformed the Old Testament into a purely "Christian" document. Rather than interpreting the Old Testament text in the light of its historical Jewish context, they made it out to be an allegory about Jesus and the church. It was now their story, not the Jewish people's story.

Sadly, the legacy of the early church fathers' anti-Judaism vitriol lived on within the Western church for centuries to come. In the wake of Constantine's acknowledgment of Christianity as the official religion of the Roman Empire in the fourth century, the Jewish people experienced a further wave of discrimination and persecution. They were prohibited from living in Jerusalem and from seeking converts. In 339, it became a criminal offense for someone to convert to Judaism. The Synod of Laodicea, decades later, ruled that Christians who feasted with Jews were to be considered heretics. Ambrose, bishop of Milan, praised the burning of a synagogue as a God-pleasing act. John Chrysostom, bishop of Antioch, penned a series of Eight Homilies Against the Jews. He describes the synagogue as "a brothel," "a den of robbers and a lodging for wild beasts," "a dwelling of demons." The Jews, he proclaimed, "know but one thing: to fill their bellies and be drunk."

Fifteen hundred years later, these two diverging, seemingly irreconcilable, streams of cultural and religious history reconverged - within my own family's ancestry. In seventeenth-century northern Germany a man of Jewish descent married a Gentile Christian woman, from whom I am a tenth-generation descendant. (That Christian woman's intriguing ancestral story remains to be told in a forthcoming book.)

9

Near-Annihilation by Rome

While the Jesus movement was giving impetus to an emerging Christian religion in the western world, Jewish religion and culture in Palestine was careening toward a near decapitation. A fierce Jewish revolt against Roman subjugation was about to elicit a bludgeoning response. Yet somehow a reconfigured Judaism arose from the rubble. And an inevitable parting of the ways between a fledgling Christianity and a newly reconstituted Judaism ensued.

Revolutionary Ferment

Popular unrest and revolutionary agitation among first-century Palestinian Jews intensified under the escalating weight of political and religious oppression. Rome's persistent promotion of its pagan religious ways was a constant aggravation. The Roman Emperor Caligula, in AD 39, turned the cult of emperor worship, started by Augustus, into a mandatory ritual of Roman state religion. The Jews stubbornly rejected this repugnant requirement. This only strengthened Rome's resolve to maintain a tight grip on political control.

The Jewish resistance movement consisted of two main elements. One was a group of freedom fighters in Galilee that came to be known as the Zealots. This was a "left-wing" offshoot within Pharisaism that had formed about ten years after Herod's death. Focusing on the Pharisees' core tenet of the kingship of God, they adopted a radicalized reinterpretation that ruled out any legitimate role for any secular rulership over the Jewish people. With this understanding of divine kingship, they justified active military resistance that amounted to political terrorism. Members of the exploited lower classes were especially attracted by the Zealots' radical appeal.

The other resistance bloc was an urban guerrilla-style terrorist group operating primarily in Jerusalem called the Sicarii. Their name derived from the concealed weapons—*sicae* or short daggers—they bore under their cloaks. Convinced that their fellow Jews needed to be physically intimidated into fighting for their freedom, they functioned as a literal "cloak and dagger" assassination unit. Their primary target was the moderate, "palace-loving" Jerusalem higher and middle social classes.

Rome's procurators during this time were outright hostile toward the Jewish population, often resorting to acts of brutality. Their ruthlessness reached a crescendo after Gessius Florus became procurator in the year 64. Using his position as a vehicle for achieving personal financial gain, Florus plundered entire villages and even the temple treasury. He often provoked uprisings in order to justify his anti-Jewish cruelty to his Roman overseers.

Two major acts of anti-Roman defiance erupted in the year 66, plunging the Jewish community headlong into open revolt. One was a change in high priestly policy initiated by a zealot element in Jerusalem. Under the coercion of Rome, Jewish priests were compelled to accept religious sacrifices made in honor of the Roman emperor from non-Jewish people. One day, the high priest refused to do so and slaughtered Florus's Roman garrison. This was tantamount to a declaration of war against Rome. The peace-loving anti-rebellion element among the Jews—many of the priests and Pharisees, who feared Roman retaliation—asked for the support of Roman troops to help restore peace and order. Three thousand Roman horsemen were consequently detached to Jerusalem.

Outbreak of Civil War

This precipitated a tragic civil war among the Jews, further complicating the Jewish revolt against Rome. The Roman military detachment, along with the Jewish peace-loving element, fortified themselves in the Upper City area of Jerusalem. The Zealots, meanwhile, took control of the Temple Hill and the Lower City area of Jerusalem.

A second major act of Jewish defiance soon spilled out. The rebel Sicarii leader Menahem and his followers captured the Roman military fortress at Masada in the Dead Sea area. After massacring the seven hundred Roman troops there and ransacking their arsenal, they set off for Jerusalem. By mingling with a group of pilgrims who were on their way to the temple, they infiltrated the city unnoticed. Once inside, they joined up with the Zealots. Together, they were able to free Jerusalem of Roman troops and gain the upper hand over the aristocratic peace-loving contingent.

A fight then broke out among the victorious rebels, pitting the Zealots and the Sicarii against each other. The Zealots were put off by what they considered to be excessive Sicarii brutality and the dictatorial ambitions of their leader Menahem. So they turned on the Sicarii, killing many of them, and forced the rest to flee back to the vacated Masada fortress.

News of this Jerusalem anti-Roman revolt reached the chief deputy of Syria at the time, Gaius Cestius Gallus. He departed

Antioch with an army, determined to put down the rebellion. Marching toward Jerusalem, they plundered villages along the way, burning homes, and killing many Jews and their families. Upon his arrival in Jerusalem, Gallus realized he lacked enough force to overtake it. So he retreated. Roman supremacy over Judea and Galilee was thus temporarily suspended. Meanwhile, patriot rebels prepared to defend against an expected long and bloody retaliatory onslaught from the Roman military.

Galilee had long been a hotbed of rebel patriot resistance. The Zealots there were led by the firebrand warrior, John of Gischala. Key Galilean cities were fortified with trenches, ramparts, and bulwarks. Half the male population of each city was sent to be trained in Roman military tradition. A one-hundred-thousand-man army was assembled.

Upon learning of the Jerusalem revolt, Emperor Nero assigned his top general, Vespasian, to the task of crushing it. Assembling sixty thousand horsemen and infantrymen, he moved first with an attack on Galilee. Although the Galilean rebel forces fought valiantly to defend themselves, it was only a matter of time before their vastly overpowered and poorly trained forces were defeated. By the end of the year 67, all of Galilee had been conquered, with one hundred thousand Galilean Jewish men, women, and children having been killed or sold into slavery. John of Gischala and his military unit managed to escape to Jerusalem under the cover of night. Before laying siege to Jerusalem, Vespasian subdued parts of Judea and then encamped his tired troops for a winter rest in the region of Caesarea.

Meanwhile, Jerusalem had become overcrowded with refugees from all over Judea. Various Jewish factions were battling each other for control ahead of an anticipated siege by the Romans. One faction was led by the extremist Galilean zealot John of Gischala. Another was led by the more moderate

Jerusalem-based zealot Eleazar. A third element was the Judean provisional government and its aristocratic anti-rebel supporters. There were also bands of Sicarii and assassins roaming the streets. John of Gischala, assuming the role of dictator, invited a contingent of twenty thousand Idumean warriors into the city to join in the fray as well.

In AD 69, following a series of assassinations in Rome, the Roman Senate offered the imperial throne to Vespasian. He handed over leadership of the Jewish war effort to his son Titus. Titus amassed what was an unprecedentedly large contingent of soldiers in the history of war in the ancient world. Alexander had established his empire using thirty-two thousand troops. Julius Caesar had conquered Gaul and invaded Britain with fewer than twenty-five thousand legionnaires. Hannibal had later crossed the Alps attempting to defeat the Romans using fewer than fifty thousand soldiers. By contrast, Titus's assault on Jerusalem involved the use of eighty thousand Roman soldiers. The Jewish defense was mounted using fewer than twenty-five thousand fighters.

By the spring of 70, a certain Simon bar Giora and his band of outlaws showed up in arms outside the walls of Jerusalem, having retreated from approaching Roman troops. A council of priests invited him and his contingent into the city to join their fight against the zealot factions. The two competing zealot factions occupied the temple, with John's faction encamped in the outer court and Eleazar's in the inner court. Simon's band of outlaws, meanwhile, positioned themselves outside the temple. These three Jewish factions battled each other continuously. Hoping to starve their opponents, John and Simon both resorted to burning some of the large quantities of stored food supplies. Thousands of Jews lost their lives at the hands of fellow Jews.

Jerusalem Under Siege

On Passover Eve, Roman troops positioned themselves around the walls of Jerusalem to set up their siege. They began building embankments, constructing their battering rams and siege engines. Every tree in every orchard and forest within ten miles was eventually cut down to provide the necessary lumber.

Inside the walls were well over a half million Jews, as the city was crowded with Jewish Passover pilgrims—some from great distances: Egypt, Antioch, the Far East, Cyprus, Asia Minor. Tens of thousands of fearless patriots eagerly awaited the chance to take on their despised oppressors. The competing Jewish factions dropped their internecine strife and united to defend their city.

The Romans' attack was met with a furious resistance unlike anything previously ecnountered. The Jewish freedom fighters not only defended themselves but made fierce counterattacks of their own. Two times they succeeded in burning the Romans' siege engines. Because the city was so strongly fortified and the Jewish fighters so tenacious, the siege turned into a long-drawn-out standoff.

When Rome's initial military maneuvers against the city walls failed, they changed tactics. They resorted to psychological warfare. Multiple times, they used their prominent fellow Jew, Josephus (who had already surrendered), to appeal for their surrender. Titus amassed all his troops in an encircling arrangement on the plain outside the city to give its residents an impressive view of their superior might. He conducted a three-day parade around the walls of Jerusalem. Seventy thousand foot soldiers. Ten thousand mounted cavalry. Thousands of battering rams. Jewish observers on the ramparts responded with a defiant Bronx cheer.

An enraged Titus ordered an attack. For two weeks, Roman siege guns hurled massive boulders at Jerusalem's northern wall. A gaping hole was torn open. Roman soldiers streamed in. Jewish defenders engaged them in two weeks of brutal hand-to-hand combat and eventually drove them out.

Titus now realized he was left with one remaining option: starve the city into surrender with a blockade. He encircled Jerusalem's surrounding stone wall with a new earthen wall, creating a dry moat between the two walls to entrap any Jew attempting to escape. Food supplies began to dwindle. Those Jews caught outside the city wall prowling for food were flogged. Tortured. And taken to the top of the earthen wall to be crucified in full view of the Jews inside Jerusalem. As many as five hundred of their fellow Jews a day could be observed there, writhing on crosses.

The Roman siege of Jerusalem eventually came to its inevitable end. Herod's magnificent temple edifice was reduced to its foundations amid smoldering ruins. The city was a hideous scene of death and devastation. As Josephus, who witnessed the battle, recounted, "The entire Temple Hill seemed to blaze, from the foundation to the top; but the streams of blood were wider than the streams of fire. The ground was hidden by piles of corpses, and the soldiers pursued the living over the heaps of the dead." "It was," he wrote, "hard to believe a human settlement had ever existed on that spot."

The Aftermath

Josephus claimed that more than a million Jewish lives were lost and that tens of thousands who survived the starvation and bloodshed were auctioned off as slaves and sent to die or be mutilated in gladiatorial contests with beasts. As a notorious exaggerator, Josephus's estimates cannot be trusted. But countless Jews no doubt were killed or enslaved or died of starvation or disease during the siege. Some were able to flee to Jewish settlements in Babylon and in the Roman territories of Syria, Asia Minor, North Africa, and Egypt. The overall Palestinian Jewish population was consequently diminished by as much as one-third through this loss of life, enslavement, and migration.

Having been cleared of all Jews, Jerusalem became a military installation, with Roman soldiers now living in barracks on the temple ruins. All conquered territory was proclaimed to be property of the emperor's family. Large tracts of land became royal estates, leased out to Romans, Greeks, and surviving Judeans—who were reduced to impoverished tenant farmers. New, entirely Roman and Greek settlements sprang up. Since the gods of Rome had obviously defeated the God of the Jews, the national Jewish tax that previously supported their temple in Jerusalem was now diverted, repulsively, to supporting the temple of the triumphing god Jupiter in Rome.

Those Jewish communities in Judea and Galilee that had not been attacked or destroyed by the Romans faced a profound existential crisis. The post-war policy of their Roman vanquishers, intent on stamping out their Jewish state, had stripped them of the four foundational elements of their Jewish national identity. Gone was their temple—the very dwelling place of their Most High God. Gone was their high priesthood—the indispensable facilitators of their religious practice. Gone was their beloved ancient Holy City of Jerusalem—the religious and cultural hub of their nation. Gone was the Sanhedrin—their centralizing administrative leadership body. How would they possibly be able to pick up and reassemble the shattered pieces of their economic, social, and religious world?

Rise of Rabbinic Judaism

During the first twenty-five years following the demise of Jerusalem and the temple, foundations were laid for a new centralizing Jewish religious and national authority. Faced with the loss of their physical territory and their ability to protect themselves militarily, they discovered a new way forward. They now focused on defending and protecting their spiritual territory instead. This was the one thing Rome had been unable to take from them.

This new direction revolved around the activity of two influential rabbis: Yohanan ben Zakkai and Gamaliel II. Rabbi Yohanan had been a member of the Jerusalem Sanhedrin and a prominent and influential leader of an academy of scholars in Jerusalem. He had spoken in favor of compromising and accommodating with Rome. Having apparently turned himself in to the Romans during the war, he ended up in the half-Gentile Judean city of Jabneh near the Mediterranean coast. It had served as a place of detention for prominent Jewish groups and individuals who had surrendered.

While there, he was granted permission by the Romans to begin instructing his disciples. Thus, a new academy sprang up in Jabneh. It grew in size and stature, attracting a large gathering of scholars. It began to function as an informal "High Court" that took over some of the religious regulatory functions of the former Jerusalem Sanhedrin. Eventually, this High Court and academy were taken over by Rabbi Gamaliel II, who went on to become officially acknowledged by the Roman government as the first post-Jerusalem head of the Jewish people.

The Jewish religious material that had by this time become accumulated into the Pharisaic "Oral Law" was now too voluminous to be preserved anymore by memory in oral form. For continued preservation, it needed to be written down. These scholars, therefore, organized and systematized it into what would eventually come to be known as the Midrash. This work was eventually completed by a later Sanhedrin in Galilee. This authoritative document, governing many detailed facets of daily Jewish life, became a kind of second Torah. And it functioned as a unifying protective armor for a defenseless people who were desperate to preserve their national and religious identity from destruction.

The old Jewish aristocracy of wealthy landowners and influential priestly families was in this way replaced by a new aristocracy of rabbinical scholarship. The Midrash produced by the rabbis in Galilee became combined with a scholarly work produced by rabbis in Babylon to form the landmark Jewish Talmud—a three-million-word encyclopedic marvel covering Jewish history, prophecy, poetry, medicine, astronomy, astrology, legal code, mythology, folklore, and more. For hundreds of years to come, this work would serve the worldwide Jewish community as a substitute for their lost temple and homeland, providing a core unifying structure for their religious, cultural, and national identity.

What thus resulted was a reconstitution of Judaism centered around the Torah instead of the temple. A religion of temple sacrificial rites was replaced by a religion of Torah compliance. The central ministry function of the priest was replaced by that of the rabbi. The Judaism of temple cultic practices gave way to a Judaism revolving around prayer and good deeds.

The Kokhba Revolt

The Roman emperor Hadrian (reigning 117–138) had a passion for building cities. He decided that the city of Jerusalem, having lain in ruins for forty-seven years, should be rebuilt as a Roman cultural center replete with Roman shrines, idols, theaters, circuses, and a temple devoted to Jupiter. It would serve as a colony for former Roman soldiers. He renamed it Aelia Capitolina in honor of Emperor Aelia Hadrian and Jupiter Capitoline. An altar to Zeus was placed on the site of the former Jewish temple. Jerusalem was now devoted to the worship of the Capitolina gods.

In response to this atrocity, the smoldering fires of Jewish rebellion reignited under the leadership of Simon Bar Kokhba. In 132, he gathered an army of more than one hundred thousand soldiers who operated in small bands dispersed throughout Judea. They conquered hundreds of towns and settlements in Judea, Samaria, and Galilee, decimated two Roman legions, and forced the Romans out of Jerusalem.

Emperor Hadrian answered by sending in half of his worldwide army. And after a three-and-a-half-year battle, five hundred thousand Jews had lost their lives, and vast numbers of captives were sold into slavery and shipped abroad. Archaeological evidence points to total regional destruction following the war. Surviving Jews were expelled from Jerusalem and from Judea in general. Most of them fled to Galilee.

Second-century Roman historian Cassius Dio, using official Roman military records, detailed the devastation: "almost all of Judea was turned into a wilderness." Fifty secret rebel outposts were destroyed. Nine hundred eighty-five towns and villages were razed to the ground. Five hundred eighty-nine thousand fighting men were killed in battle. An incalculable number of inhabitants died, not only as a result of the burning of towns and villages, but also due to disease and starvation. Archaeological evidence has confirmed his report. More than 440 underground hiding settlements in 252 sites have been found in the Judean foothills, the Hebron mountains, and elsewhere.

Rather than forcing the Jews to embrace Roman pagan religion, Hadrian's vengeance took a different tactic. He outlawed the essential Jewish religious practices of circumcision, observing the Sabbath, and studying the Torah in the synagogues. His apparent purpose was to quash their national spirit by attacking its roots—their Jewish religion. These decrees were brutally enforced for the next three years, until rescinded by the next Roman emperor, Antoninus Pius, in 138.

Second-Century Jewish Life in Galilee

Galilee was now the epicenter of what remained of a Jewish population that no longer constituted the majority of Palestine's residents. While comprising just half of the total population of Galilee at the end of the third century, they accounted for less than one-fourth of the population in the rest of Palestine. With the recent influx of Jewish war refugees from Judea, there were now some three hundred thousand Jews inhabiting Galilee—among whom my own Jewish ancestors were likely residing. The majority lived in countryside villages, mostly as peasant farmers and some as craftsmen and merchants. Under Emperor Pius, an extended two-hundred-year-long era of peace began, allowing the Galilean Jews to begin to flourish economically.

They also reconstituted themselves religiously through the emerging framework of Rabbinic Judaism. Recent immigrants from Judea included members of the rabbinical schools. Their insistence on strict adherence to the traditional Jewish purity and tithing laws, however, was not well-accepted by the Galilean farmers. The economic demands associated with these practices were considered too burdensome. In order to gain recognition as the political and religious leaders of the Galilean Jews, the rabbis consequently yielded to the farmers' resistance and discontinued stressing the purity and tithing requirements.

Eventually, a Sanhedrin of sorts—a "Great Court of Law," "The Great Academy"—was constituted in Galilee by the rabbinic scholars. They established the office of patriarch to serve not only as the authoritative head of the Sanhedrin but also as the supreme leader of the entire Jewish community. And in time, the Romans themselves officially recognized his role as the head of all the Jews living under the jurisdiction of Rome. The Jews were thus permitted to form their own administrative structure and exercise self-government regarding their internal affairs.

Fate of "Jewish Christianity" in Palestine

The community of Jesus-followers that had emerged initially in Jerusalem and spread elsewhere within Palestine during its early years faced daunting impediments to its growth and expansion. Having emerged at the margins of Palestinian Jewish society and having been viewed as a radical fringe "anti-religious-establishment" movement, it encountered strong and widespread opposition within the Jewish community from the get-go. The aristocratic temple priesthood authorities responded with violent physical opposition. With mob violence incited against them, early Jesus-followers were hauled before the Sanhedrin and subjected to synagogue floggings and expulsions.

In addition, they soon found themselves occupying a tenuous middle ground between two polarized camps, with one foot in each camp. Imagine two overlapping circles, the one on the left representing an increasingly Gentile Christianity and the one on the right representing Judaism. The Palestinian Jewish Christians are represented by the gradually shrinking area of overlap between these two circles. As Jews, they maintained their identity with historic Judaism. As Jesus-followers, they had joined up with what had initially appeared to them to be a new sect within Judaism. But this new sect had spread beyond Judea and was incorporating Gentiles who were being given a pass on committing to Judaism.

Palestine's Jewish Christians thus found themselves "playing defense" on two fronts. They were caught in a tug of war—feeling pressured to maintain their Judaism while also feeling pressured to refrain from imposing it on new Gentile converts to Jesus. In order to gain additional Palestinian Jewish converts to Messiah Jesus, they needed to avoid being perceived as disloyal to their Jewish heritage with a too-accommodating stance toward the Gentiles. It was a paralyzing catch-22 situation.

As noted earlier, in the aftermath of the Roman defeat of 70, communities of Jewish believers in Jesus had survived in Palestine. But they now suddenly found themselves living in a whole new Jewish reality. The destruction of Jerusalem and the temple, and the demise of the dominating authority of the priesthood, had created a power vacuum within Judaism. A window of opportunity had opened for someone to fill that power vacuum and to assume new leadership for the future direction of Judaism.

The Jewish-Christian community in Palestine, however, was not the only available candidate for filling that leadership vacuum. Simon Bar Kokhba was one such candidate. He took the approach of making messianic claims for himself, mandating that Jesus-followers be tortured and executed if they refused to renounce Jesus as Messiah. They, however, refused to recognize Bar Kokhba's messianic claims and distanced themselves from the goals of his revolutionary movement. We have already noted how his efforts ended in a debacle.

At that point, there was one remaining element within the Judaism of second-century Palestine left to compete with the Jewish-Christian community for the hearts and minds of Palestinian Jews: the rabbinic party. And over time, they were able to seize the upper hand over Jewish Christianity within the existing power vacuum and gain acceptance by the majority of Jews as the leaders of their community. Jewish Christianity was simply unable to convince most of Palestine's Jews of the claims of the Gospel of Jesus.

A major reason was the intense Jewish nationalism present in the first two centuries in Palestine. Jewish Christianity was significantly out of sync with this prevailing spirit of the times. Its emphasis was on the spiritual rather than the physical dimension of the Kingdom of God. Their downplaying of the territorial dimension of Judaism fed the narrative that Jewish Christianity was insufficiently Jewish.

In the end, though, it was the rabbis' ability to marginalize all those who opposed them that led to their success. They essentially set up a closed society of "observant" Jews committed to following their detailed prescriptive oral traditions. And they ostracized everyone else. Categorizing followers of Jesus as "heretics," they sought to exclude them from synagogues and to persuade other Jews to ostracize them from their social and commercial lives. They forbade Rabbinic Jews from eating with Jewish Christians. They issued rulings declaring that Torah scrolls written by Christian scribes were unfit to be used in synagogue worship services. Rabbinic Jews were thus dissuaded from attending synagogues where there was a Christian presence or influence.

Galilean towns such as Sepphoris, Tiberius, Capernaum, and Nazareth—all of which in their time probably contained Jewish Christians—were likely split between rabbinic and non-Rabbinic Jews. As the rabbinic teachings grew in acceptance, the Jewish Christians of such towns likely came under increasing pressure to conform and found themselves becoming more and more "ghettoized." By the latter half of the fourth century, the presence of a Jewish Christianity in Palestine had seemingly disappeared.

Third-Century Roman Empire in Crisis

During the third century and first half of the fourth century, the Palestinian Jews were blindsided by devastating economic developments. A potentially crippling political and economic crisis emerged within the Roman Empire's governmental system. And its aftershocks had a distressing ripple effect on such far-reaching places in the empire as Galilee.

For nearly a half-century (235–284), Rome experienced utter turmoil on the home front—anarchy, civil war, social unrest, assassinations. There were bloody internal power struggles among rivals for the throne, with frequent changes from one ruler to the next. Villages rose up against their ruling cities with support from peasant soldiers.

Away from home, the provinces of Rome's empire were becoming more independent economically. Its central authority became weakened. The old religious system of emperor worship that had helped unite the various parts of the empire was now in decline. The process of economic deterioration would prove to be something from which the Roman Empire would never be able to fully recover.

In response to this crisis, the Roman government debased its coinage. Faced with the need to increase military spending in order to maintain their empire, and lacking the revenues needed to do so, the emperors were forced to continually reduce the silver value of the Roman denarius. The ripple effect was felt by the Palestinian Jewish community: spiraling inflation. Prices and living costs rose astronomically.

Another source of economic devastation for them was the unbearable burden of taxation, confiscation, and forced labor imposed on them by the Roman government. A new Roman policy was initiated whereby local provinces were obligated to furnish provisions for Roman troops in their region. This was particularly onerous for the rural Jewish population of Palestine. It entailed the confiscations of such things as wine, vinegar, olive oil, clothing, and animal fodder. Their domestic animals were appropriated by the army for transporting supplies. Forced labor was imposed for such purposes as road repair projects.

Because of these harsh realities, many Palestinian Jews, even wealthy landowners, were forced to abandon their land and flee the country. A mass migration took place, with a half-deserted Palestine left in its wake. The heyday of Palestinian Judaism was coming to its end.

10

On to Europe

For more than two thousand years—from the time of Abraham to the time of the Roman Empire—the Land of Israel and its surroundings served as the beloved homeland of my Jewish ancestors. And then they were forced to leave, never to return. Arriving at the distant shores of Italy, they found their way northward and crossed the Alps into an underdeveloped Germany. Though the details of this long migratory journey remain obscure, its general contours can be deciphered.

Migration to Italy

Jewish migration from Palestine to Italy occurred in multiple waves over many centuries. Already in the first century BC, a sizable Jewish community had emerged in Rome along the banks of the Tiber River. They resided in the area of an ancient trading center where Greek mariners arrived with their merchandise. This was one of dozens of such Jewish communities scattered throughout the Mediterranean world. They typically were self-contained communities, maintaining their distinctive Jewish ways, while sustaining ties with sister Jewish settlements.

These scattered enclaves were uniquely positioned to participate in the arena of international trade between the Eastern and Western worlds. Two of the dominating trade centers at this time—Babylon in the East and Alexandria, Egypt, in the West—were also prominent and influential Jewish centers. Enterprising Jews consequently became involved in the Mediterranean trade industry. The economic pursuits of such traders likely account for the origination of the Jewish community in Rome.

Many early Jewish settlers, however, came from Palestine to Italy involuntarily. Following Rome's destruction of Jerusalem in AD 70, large numbers were sent over as slaves. Many were settled in Rome, where they were conscripted to construct such public works as the Colosseum. Some were settled in seaport towns in southern Italy. Another wave of Jewish slaves arrived in Italy from Palestine in the second century AD after their capture during the failed Bar Kokhba Jewish revolt.

During the fourth to sixth centuries, the Italian Jewish community developed into what historians have described as the most visible and substantial Jewish community in western antiquity. They were attracted to other cities besides Rome, and also to small, remote villages in the Italian countryside. They were prominently present in southern Italian commercial centers and port cities involved in trade with Greece, North Africa, and the eastern Mediterranean coast. They also settled along the trade routes connecting those Italian port cities with Rome. Although some of this populace were directly involved in the trade industry, most made their living as peddlers of various wares, as tentmakers, tailors, butchers, and other craftsmen. By the beginning of the eighth century, Jewish communities were present in all the important cities of the southern part of the peninsula, while a much sparser representation could be found in northern Italy.

Arab raids on southern Italy during the ninth and tenth centuries and Muslim persecution of the Jewish population there changed all that. Jews in southern Italy fled northward, creating a proliferation of Jewish settlements in growing commercial centers in upper Italy. Most of these inhabitants were traders and merchants, while some were peasant proprietors and craftsmen.

The city of Lucca was among the most important of these centers. A road extending northward from it provided the primary southern approach to a passage across the Alps. This trans-Alps corridor connected Lucca with the western European Rhineland region across the mountains. Lucca thereby became a trading hub between Italy and the regions of Germany and France.

Thanks to Italy's strategic central location in both the Mediterranean basin and on the European continent, it played a leading role in international trade at this time. It became the cornerstone of medieval European commerce. While many Italian Jews were active in the area of trade, they were not, however, an integral part of the international networks that thrust the Italians to the forefront of medieval intercontinental commerce. Their role, rather, both in the southern and northern parts of Italy, was generally limited to engagement in local and regional trade as itinerant merchants.

Italian international trade networks had produced well-used trade routes, both to Italy from the east and within Italy itself. These trade routes appear to have been the path along which Italian Jewish migratory movements were made. New opportunities for trade were about to be opened in the European frontier land across the Alps. A trans-Alps thoroughfare was already in place. Thus, the stage was set for further migration of Jewish merchants northward across the Alps. A vital part of that migratory passageway was a major river flowing out of what is today the Swiss Alps all the way to the North Sea coast of the present-day Netherlands: the Rhine River.

The Rhineland Frontier

Back in the first century BC, the Rhine River region had been of pivotal importance to the Roman Empire. It was the boundary line between two major tribal groups that the Romans sought to add to their burgeoning empire—those in the territory of Gaul to the river's west and those to its east in the territory of Germania. Although Rome was able to conquer Gaul, its efforts to vanquish Germania were eventually abandoned. Consequently, by the beginning of the first century AD, the Rhine River region had become a Roman Empire buffer zone between its conquered and unconquered territories. And Roman legions had established army camps at various places along the Rhine for the protection of their newly acquired territory.

In time, these legions shifted to the non-military task of consolidating their gains. They Romanized their new land, creating the infrastructure necessary for supporting an organized society. Major engineering projects were undertaken. Swamps were drained. Roads, bridges, harbors, canals, fortifications, and aqueducts were built. They founded new settlements, enhanced the cultivation of the land, and fostered the emergence of local industry and commerce.

The Rhineland's geography made it a natural European crossroads. To the north, the Rhine valley provided uninterrupted access to the Scandinavian countries and the British Isles. To the south, it led to access across the Alps into and through Italy to the entire Mediterranean world. To the west, it led into France and beyond to Spain. To the east, a trans-Europe route led to the undeveloped Slavonic lands. This region was ideally suited to become a major center of commerce. Roman soldier settlers and their entourage in this new outpost created an emerging market for merchants who stood ready to supply the wares and commodities they needed.

Rhineland Jewish Settlements

Already in the early fourth century AD, a small well-established Jewish community existed in Cologne, Rome's administrative headquarters along the Rhine. By the fifth century, a handful of additional small Jewish communities and synagogues had sprouted along the waterway. Between the end of the ninth century and the middle of the eleventh they had multiplied into about a dozen settlements. Among them were important Jewish centers in Mainz, Speyer, and Worms, as well as in Cologne. (See map, *Jewish Settlements in the German Rhineland ca. 900-1300,* p. iii). These were literate urban middle-class enclaves, well-organized, synagogue-centered communities, dwelling among the non-Jewish population as ethnically and religiously conspicuous groups. Notably, they enjoyed political freedom and autonomy, and lived in peaceful coexistence with local Roman and Germanic inhabitants.

Jewish merchants apparently initiated these Rhineland communities, paving the way for an influx of additional merchants as well as non-merchant Jewish immigrants to join them. Later non-merchant settlers included wine growers, carpenters, masons, bookbinders, artisans, surgeons, apothecaries, and jeweler-craftsmen in gold, silver, and precious stones. The primary economic pursuits most visible within these communities by the ninth century, though, were the endeavors of landholding and commercial enterprise.

What drew Jewish merchants to settle in this particular place? Economic opportunity. Rivers were the major commercial arteries of the Middle Ages. The Rhine and its tributaries were among the most lucrative of them. Its banks were dotted by the larger towns and cities, political centers where the aristocratic ruling class of nobles and bishops resided. There, a wealthy clientele of counts, barons, village lords, priests, and bishops— the upper tier of ecclesiastical and lay Christian society— provided continual demand for the goods that Jewish merchants had access to. Such staples as salted fish, wine, ready-made clothing, wool, dye-stuffs, copper vessels, horses, and cattle. And luxury items such as furs and animal pelts, gold-threaded garments, medicines and spices, imported gilded vessels, precious metals, and jewelry.

Early Jewish settlers here soon discovered an added bonus. The Rhineland was a vine-growing region. In fact, the area around the Jewish settlements in Mainz, Worms, & Speyer was viewed as the "wine cellar" of the German Empire. Jewish people, of course, had been cultivating vineyards since settling the land of Canaan in 1200 BC. Wine had become for them a staple of everyday life and was required for use in their religious rituals. But it had to be wine untouched by Gentile hands while being produced. Here was a place where they could produce their own kosher wine. And so some in the Jewish community purchased land for planting their own vineyards.

A Burgeoning Wine Trade

The nobility—both secular and ecclesiastical members— had initiated the planting of vineyards along the Rhine in the 700s and 800s. They had a vested interest in maintaining these vineyards so there would be an uninterrupted flow of good wine to their aristocratic meal tables. The consumption of wine in medieval times was a major form of entertainment for those with the means to purchase it. Wine and beer were considered daily necessities, staples of life. Water was considered fitting only for animals and for the poor and destitute. It's been estimated that those able to afford wine likely consumed an average of one to two liters a day per person.

A massive demand for wine existed in the western part of northern Europe, where there were no vineyards. Those regions could only obtain wine through trading with areas able to produce wine, such as the Rhineland. The demand for Rhineland-area wine only grew with the passing of time, making it a very lucrative commodity. There was a major upswing in European trade in the 900s following the end of the Norman invasion. And at the end of the tenth century and during the eleventh century, the Rhineland wine trade mushroomed even further, becoming one of the most important components of international trade in northern Europe.

This rapid and steep growth of wine trade threatened Jewish merchants with economic marginalization. Those Rhineland Jews who owned vineyards in the tenth and eleventh centuries were at a distinct disadvantage. There were not enough Jewish people to provide the necessary labor for expanding their vine-growing operations. Such expansion would have required the hiring of Gentiles to tread their grapes. But this was not an option, as Jewish wine producers refused to derive profit from wine produced through the touch of Gentile hands. Thus, unable to contribute any additional Jewish-produced wine to the growing wine market, Jewish merchants were forced to find another way to tap into its lucrative profits.

Merchants Become Creditors

In the agricultural society of the Middle Ages, Jewish merchants were among the few people who possessed ready cash. They were the ones farmers usually turned to when they were in need of cash. Loans require collateral, and in an agricultural society, that collateral was land. Medieval farmers in need of cash would therefore have to mortgage their fields to their creditors. Creditors were thereby entitled to work their debtor's field and collect a portion of the harvested produce as payment of interest on their loan. These loans were typically long-term (three to twelve years, on average). Jewish merchants, through the extension of credit, thus frequently exercised long-term control over a considerable amount of land and produce.

Rhineland Jewish merchants consequently received many vineyards as collateral with all their produce. And even when they did not receive vineyards as collateral, their loans were generally paid back in wine, which essentially served as legal tender. Even though their religious principles disallowed them from consuming or initiating trade in Gentile wine, they were allowed to receive Gentile wine as payment of debt. They became the middlemen between Gentile vineyards and the wine market, storing the barrels of wine collected in payment on loans, annually bringing it to market as vendors, and accumulating the profits.

Creditors Become Investors

The accumulating capital held by Jewish merchants put them in a very advantageous position. It enabled them to also become investors in the lucrative viticulture industry by financing the maintenance, cultivation, and expansion of the Rhineland's vineyards. Viticulture was not only a labor-intensive enterprise. It was also capital-intensive, having an insatiable need for the infusion of cash.

There was hardly a riskier or more long-term investment to be made in the Middle Ages. Grapevines are a subtropical plant, requiring ample sunshine and stable weather in order to ripen. The Rhineland, by contrast, had a cool climate, cloudy weather, and harsh winters. Such impediments could only be overcome through additional capital outlay. Vineyards in these climates had to be planted on mountain slopes to mitigate the effects of wind chill and frost, and to make use of the required thinner topsoil available there. Vineyard workers labored all year long, sometimes for two to three years, without producing a good crop and no income to defray rapidly mounting expenses.

Expanding vineyards into new vine-growing areas involved even greater financial risk. Hillside terraces had to be built. Once the new vines were planted, it took three to seven years before they produced any fruit. When finally mature, they produced grapes at the same success rate as the old vineyards: one good crop every two or three years. It could thus take as many as seven years after the planting of new vines, seven years of continual cash investment, before any profit was realized. Viticultural expansion thus required even more expertise than the multiple areas of expertise already needed to merely maintain existing vineyards. It called for a combination of viticulture expertise, merchanting know-how, and skillful money management—capabilities more readily present among Jewish merchants than among their Christian counterparts.

While German Jews were known primarily as traders and merchants in the eleventh century, they became known in the thirteenth century primarily as moneylenders and pawnbrokers. This was a natural transition. What began with the extension of credit to vineyard owners by merchant creditors ended up becoming an entrenched Jewish occupation: a predominant involvement of Jewish communities in the general practice of moneylending to the upper levels of non-Jewish society.

Under the Patronage of Charlemagne

The fall of the Western Roman Empire in the fifth century left a power vacuum in its previously held territories. The territory of Gaul to the west of the Rhine was thereafter conquered by the Franks, and in 768, Charlemagne (Charles the Great) succeeded his father as the King of the Franks. By the end of the eighth century, he had conquered the Germanic Saxony territory to the east of the Rhine, forcibly "Christianizing" its pagan inhabitants by forcing them to choose between conversion and death. Much of western, central, and northern Europe was consequently united under this "Father of Europe," the first recognized Western Europe-based emperor since the fall of the Romans three centuries prior.

While securing military power over his subjects, Charlemagne also aligned himself with the spiritual power base of the papacy in Rome. He became the pope's military defender, and the pope, in turn, became his spiritual defender. When Pope Leo III crowned him king in Rome in 800, the Holy Roman Empire (of Italy and Middle Europe) was born. Through this union of spiritual and temporal power, a monolithic Christian state system was created. It would last for centuries and leave the European Jewish communities completely at the mercy of its power, with often tragic consequences.

Although this church-state system early on imposed restrictions on the Jews, their pivotal role in commercial trade continued to provide them a highly valued status. Charlemagne and his successors needed the economic benefits provided by the Jewish communities and therefore took them under their patronage. Emperor Louis the Pious, Charlemagne's successor, issued special documents stipulating that Jews were not to be slandered, nor illegally harassed, nor have special taxes demanded from them, nor have lawfully-acquired property confiscated from them. A "Magistrate of the Jews" was appointed to ensure that the personal rights and communal autonomy of the Jews were not infringed upon. Under Charlemagne and his Carolingian dynasty, the Rhineland experienced rising prosperity, and the Jewish population, its wealth, and its financial influence continued to increase.

By the late ninth century, though, a shift was occurring in the realm of political power. When the Carolingian dynasty was divided among Emperor Louis the Pious' three sons in 843, governmental power in each of their three sections became diminished. Kingly power was decentralized among an assorted feudal system combination of kings and local counts and "herzogs" ("lords" or "princes").

Rise of the Saxon Dynasty

Influential German feudal lords at the beginning of the tenth century proposed one of their own, Heinrich I, Herzog of Saxony, to be their king. Ruling 919–936, he considered his realm of Germany to be more a confederation of several duchies rather than a single nation. He was succeeded as German king by his son Otto I, also known as Otto the Great, who went on to become Holy Roman Emperor in 962 until his death in 973.

Under Saxon rule, the authority and influence of the clergy were increased. City bishops were given expansive administrative and economic power on a par with that of the non-clergy herzogs. Coincidentally, the largest German Jewish communities at this time existed in the bishop cities—those along the Rhine (Metz, Trier, Cologne, Mainz, Worms) and those in the Saxon and Bavarian cities of Magdeburg, Merseburg, and Regensburg.

These Jewish city-dwellers thus now lived under the direct power of the bishops, which played to their advantage. During times when bishops were excluded from the secular power structure, they were often disdainful toward the Jews. Reflecting the contemptuous official mindset of the church, they viewed Jewish people as inferior, recalcitrant rejectors of their superior Christian religion. But when the bishops took on the role of government officials, they sang a different tune. As local governmental authorities, they and their churches were in a position to reap significant financial gain from the Jewish community's sizable contribution to the royal treasury.

Jewish Life in Ninth- to Eleventh-Century Germany

Jewish presence in ninth-century Germany likely consisted of little more than a few dozen families. In the tenth century, they had grown to perhaps as many as a few hundred families, with an estimated total Jewish population of four to five thousand. While a mere five Jewish communities existed between the mid-tenth and mid-eleventh centuries, continued immigration resulted in eight new ones being established during the second half of the eleventh century. Most were in or near the Rhine River valley.

These Jewish inhabitants enjoyed nearly complete autonomy in establishing their communities, with almost no outside interference. They freely structured their communal life as they desired. Highly valuing rabbinic scholarship and Talmudic law, they seized the opportunity to organize all phases of their communal life—social, economic, political, legal—according to their sovereign Jewish principles. Rabbinic law spelled out in elaborate detail a comprehensive system governing all aspects of community organization and administration: enforcement of law and order; security of property and life; regulation of business practices; raising of funds through taxation; provision of charitable, educational, and religious institutions; and political relationships with secular authorities.

The Rhineland Jewish community thereby became an influential center of Talmudic scholarship. The community at Mainz, in particular, became especially notorious. It drew in students from Germany, France, Italy, and Spain, who, after years of study, returned home and became prominent members of their communities. Their studies centered around the text of the Babylonian Talmud and an orally transmitted commentary on every term and phrase of the Talmud. They learned to read its text phrase by phrase, and to insert between each phrase a few exact memorized words of oral interpretation of that phrase. At the end of a section of text, they memorized a sentence or two of explanation of that section. Eventually, they could read through the entire Talmud and recite from memory all the inserted oral interpretations passed on to them by the rabbinic scholars.

The Jewish "Problem"

By the eleventh century, there were probably about twenty to twenty-five thousand Jewish people living in Germany, all residing in urban areas. With a presence of between five hundred and one thousand residents per town, they likely accounted for up to 10 percent or more of the total early urban population in Germany. And as further urbanization generated the formation of more new German towns, there was a corresponding increase in the number of them that housed Jewish communities.

This may have been a relatively small presence, but it was noticeable. These Jewish people were discernibly different from their non-Jewish neighbors—culturally, socially, economically, and religiously. They were dark-skinned people who wore long silk robes. Their men had distinctively cropped beards and mustaches. They spoke a peculiar language. Lived in their own self-contained neighborhoods. Practiced their odd Jewish cultural customs, with what those on the outside looking in might consider an air of pride and aloofness.

By this time, the Western world had decisively fallen under the domination of the monolithic church-state juggernaut of Christendom. It envisioned the ideal of an empire-wide Christian society. Charlemagne had laid the groundwork for this through his "Christianizing" campaigns among Europe's formerly non-Christian populations. He had imposed upon them the choice between baptism and death. The presence of all previous non-Christian European people groups had thereby been erased, most of them having chosen to convert. Except for the Jews. They were now the only remnant of non-Christians left in a sea of Western Christianity.

Why this special exemption for them? Why hadn't they been forced to either convert or be killed as had Europe's non-Christian pagan populations? Why, instead, had the church gone even so far as to protect them? It was because the Jewish people presented a unique dilemma for pre-medieval Western Christendom. Exterminating them was not considered a justifiable option. They needed to be kept alive for the express purpose of allowing them the continued opportunity to convert. Their conversion was considered essential to the integrity of Christianity. Christianity asserted that Jesus was universally divine. If and when the Jewish community were to convert, it would decisively confirm Jesus's universal claim to divinity— for Christians and Jews alike. How would the church ever be able to claim that the Jews, too, had acknowledged Christ to be divine if they were simply killed off and denied the chance to convert? And so the church continued to hold out hope that the Jews would eventually accept Christianity. But Jewish resistance to Christian conversion stubbornly persisted.

With Jewish eradication not a justifiably Christian option to pursue, and with persistent Jewish rejection of Christianity, the church was left with one alternative. Just ignore them. But this, too, was problematic. Wouldn't this be tantamount to admitting that Jesus was, after all, not universally acknowledged as being divine? It's as if the church needed the Jews to convert in order to prove the legitimacy of their Christian faith. Besides, simply closing their eyes to the Jews posed a danger all its own. They sure acted suspiciously. What secret magical rites might they actually be engaging in? Were they perhaps in league with the devil? Might their true intention be to lead Christians astray? They had, after all, murdered their Christian God, Jesus.

To inoculate itself against this threat to the Christian faith, Christendom sought to hold the Jewish community societally at bay. It already had a convenient socio-economic structure in place that could do so. Feudalism—a rigid, highly restrictive, tiered socio-economic system. It boxed all Gentiles inside a fixed, pre-ordained station in society. Either in the nobility class, or in the clergy class, or entrapped as landless serfs with the remaining 95 percent of the population. The Jewish people could not be shoehorned into any of these feudal categories. So they remained on the outside looking in.

They were feudal system misfits, living in a kind of parallel universe. They were literate and highly educated. They owned books which they read and wrote. Their young boys spent hours in school every day. They were knowledgeable about people and cultures in other parts of the world, while their Gentile German neighbors' worldview was limited by the mere distance they could walk in one day. Among them were those who, because they were involved in the world of finance and commerce, were able to live on a par with the nobility in some of the best houses. They constituted a whole different strata of society that the inventors of feudalism had failed to account for: the "merchant class."

Christendom seems to have assumed that by keeping the Jewish people outside this feudal system, it would successfully protect Christians from apostatizing Jewish influences. But in reality, it only further exasperated the "Jewish problem." That's because the creaking machinery of the feudal state was dependent on the lubricating oil that only the Jewish people were able to provide: tradesmen, merchants, artisans, bankers, doctors. There was a good reason why the Jews were granted charters of freedom by popes, emperors, and princes. And, why they were welcomed to settle in Germany's towns and villages. Christendom needed the essential services that only they could provide. It didn't really want to live with the Jews. But neither could it live without them.

While fettered by the straitjacket of feudalism, the Christian peasant world looked upon the Jewish community with envious eyes. How unfair that they were not subject to the same restrictions as everyone else. Judging from their obvious wealth, they appeared to be thriving. Why are they allowed to control so much of the world of finance and commerce while the Gentile masses are enslaved to their feudal lords? Such feelings of jealousy, suspicion, resentment, and a desire to see the Jews "put in their proper place" were inevitable.

Not surprisingly, an undercurrent of social tension and resentment toward Jewish communities began brewing among the general German population during this time. The societal vision promoted by the controlling church-state system was that of a Christendom: an ideal empire-wide, monolithic, homogeneous Christian society. And it became increasingly apparent that the general Christian populace was buying into this vision, sharing an unarticulated yearning for a uniformly Christian society.

Predictably, the Jewish people came to be perceived as an obvious, irksome obstacle to the attainment of an ideal Christian society. They were the one small religious minority group that persistently resisted capitulation to the dominant Christian church-state religion. And their non-conformity to the majority Christian culture was only strengthened and reinforced by their ability to thrive within their independent, self-contained Jewish enclaves. To make matters worse, as a separatist social minority group, they had an outsized economic power and influence among the dominant culture. As they became increasingly perceived as a threat—both economically and ideologically—to the Christian dream of society, there was an increasing potential for a reactionary anti-Jewish outburst.

During the several centuries prior to the eleventh century, relations between Jewish and Christian populations in Germany had been mostly stable and peaceful. This, despite the negative picture of the Jews that was often being promoted by the church. And despite their outsider status among the broader populace. A dramatic shift, however, began near the end of the eleventh century with the launching of the First Crusade in 1096—a watershed event in the history of the German Jewish experience.

11

Surviving Anti-Jewish Terrorism

Assertion of Christian Supremacy

As was noted back in Chapter 8, early Christianity went through a messy divorce with Judaism. The polemical anti-Jewish sermons, diatribes, and dialogues found in second- and third-century Christian literature exhibit an embarrassingly vindictive contempt and ridicule of Jews and Judaism. Unfortunately, subsequent generations of the Roman Church's hierarchical leadership continued spouting a similar vilifying rhetoric.

An undergirding conviction seems to have driven all this anti-Judaism discourse. The fall of Jerusalem, the temple's destruction, the consequent deaths, exile, and enslavement of thousands of Jews were clearly God's punishment for their rejection of Jesus. Unquestionably, God had rejected and abandoned his once-chosen people. Jews had been replaced by Christians as God's new select people. Christianity had superseded Judaism.

But early Christian leaders took this idea a step further. In their opinion, Christianity had not merely superseded Judaism. It had won a decisive victory over it. The heated rivalry between them had produced a clear winner and loser. The winners had secured the position of supremacy. The losers had been consigned to perpetual servitude and subjection under the winner's supremacy. God's design, so they believed, was for Christians to exercise, not just religious, but also socio-economic supremacy over the Jewish people. For the next several centuries, this became the authoritative Roman Church hierarchy's official stance governing Christian-Jewish relationships within Western Christendom. As the medieval Pope Innocent III blatantly declared centuries later in 1205 in his *Esti Judaeos* papal bull: "Jews are consigned to perpetual servitude because they crucified the Lord."

The nonliterate medieval Christian masses, of course, were incapable of reading any such thing handed down from Roman Church officials. Nonetheless, they got the message. It was vividly conveyed to them via the church's widespread visual arts display known as *Ecclesia* and *Synagoga*. These were two female figures appearing side by side, one representing Christianity, and the other Judaism. *Ecclesia* was presented as a crowned, triumphant queen, holding a chalice or scepter, looking confidently forward. *Synagoga*, by contrast, looked disheveled, her head drooping in humiliation and defeat. She was often blindfolded and typically held a broken scepter. They could be seen paired together as large sculpted figures inside churches, at entrances to cathedrals, on church altars, in devotional church paintings, and in public places as well. The message was unmistakable: Christianity has triumphed over Judaism.

A Perception of Jewish Supremacy

But this did not square with the medieval Christian peasantry's real-life experience. To them, the tables appeared to have been turned completely upside down. While they themselves were shackled by an oppressive feudal socio-economic system, their Jewish neighbors had been exempted from it. To make matters worse, the Jewish community had been handed the ability to engage in the profitable economic activity of moneylending that Christians were forbidden from. Because Jews were barred from most other avenues of generating income, moneylending and pawnbroking had become a mainstay of the German Jewish economy. Some within the Jewish communities thereby became rather affluent, and a predominant image of the stereotypical "rich Jew" emerged.

Church leaders, too, were perceiving the same dynamic. Pope Honorius III, writing in 1221, lamented how "Jews were standing in the way of Christians," and that "the slaves" were "having dominion over the masters." A dozen years later, Pope Gregory IX wrote that it was "jarring that blasphemers of Christ should exercise power over Christians." And in a later letter to German church leaders, he asserted that Jews "should not again dare to straighten their neck bent under the yoke of perpetual servitude in insult to the Redeemer." Pope Paul IV, in his 1555 papal bull, stated that it was "improper that Jews . . . attempt to exchange the servitude which they owe to Christians for dominion over them."

As will become evident in this chapter, resentment about this societal upside-downness fed feelings of fear. Fear that Christian society could soon be easily overtaken by this minority immigrant people with all their strange Jesus-denying religious and cultural practices. Wild-eyed, far-fetched conspiratorial replacement theories sprang to life. As we will see, fear of the imagined approaching demise of Christianity propelled medieval Christians into brazen, lethal action on behalf of Jesus. What they deemed to be the noble cause of Jesus, however, turns out to have been nothing more than a thinly-veiled manifestation of tribal impulses.

Christian Tribalism

Charlemagne's "Christianizing" of Europe in the 700s may have quelled a long history of European intertribal conflict, but it failed to purge its inhabitants' tribalist mindset. His top-down imposition of the cultural system of Christendom did little to spiritually transform the hearts of its subjects. Yes, they had renounced their loyalties to their pagan gods and became baptized and confirmed church members. But their knowledge of the teachings of Jesus was woefully limited. They knew the basic contents of the Lord's Prayer and Apostles' Creed, and that was about it. There were no Bibles, and they wouldn't have been able to read them if there had been any. And almost everything they heard spoken at church services was nonsensical Latin.

In a way, their cultural identity and sense of loyalty had shifted to a new "tribe"—one that was now centered around Christendom's mysterious, heroic figure named Jesus. One that still carried the longstanding historical vestiges of "tribal conflict" with its old rival, Judaism. Tribalist-oriented medieval Europeans could easily relate to the Roman Church hierarchy's own "us against the Jews" tribal mindset. They may have had a lamentably deficient understanding of the true person and mission of Jesus, and a largely nominal association with the Church of Rome. But, as we will see, they proudly sported the sign of the cross when going to battle against their newly adopted Jewish tribal rivals.

The Crusade Movement

In 1071, the Sunni Muslim Seljuk Turks expanded their empire eastward, capturing Jerusalem and most of Palestine from the Christian Byzantine Empire. The Byzantine emperor appealed to the West for help. Word was the Muslims had desecrated the Holy Sepulchre of Jesus and other sacred Christian Holy Land sites. Western clergy began stirring up anti-Muslim resentment among European Christians, fueling aspirations to free the holy sites from Muslim control.

In 1095, Pope Urban II, at a gathering of church leaders at the Council of Clermont (France), called for an assembly of princes and knights to go liberate Jerusalem. An especially zealous French priest, later known as Peter the Hermit, responded by amassing an unofficial "Peoples Crusade." A band of thousands of French peasants and low-ranking knights sewed crosses on their garments and prepared to go rescue the Holy Land. In the spring of 1096, before the princes could assemble a regular army, this ragtag band set out on their own pilgrimage to Jerusalem. Ominously, their journey eastward along the great trade routes brought them through the principal Jewish colonies in Germany.

Coming upon the Rhineland Jewish communities, the crusading mob was taken aback by this unexpected encounter. Here were the very people they believed to be responsible for murdering their Jesus. Pent up with anti-Muslim venom and eager to unleash a ravaging rampage, they exploded. Entering one Jewish community after the next, they offered a choice: be baptized or be executed.

Technically wards of the German emperor, these Jewish residents were living under the protection of the local bishops. These bishops were inadequately prepared, however, for what was about to happen. The city of Speyer was struck first. Its bishop successfully prevented the gang from burning the synagogue packed with Jews. But more than a dozen Jews were murdered, two of whom were crucified, for refusing to be baptized.

Having heard of the massacre in Speyer, some Jews in Worms sought refuge in the bishop's castle. Others remained in their homes and entrusted their valuables to Christian neighbors for safekeeping. A rumor arose among the crusading mob that a Jew had murdered a Christian. In response, they murdered those Jews who had stayed in their homes and pillaged their remaining property. Confronted with the option of death or conversion, many opted for death—either by execution or by suicide. After surrounding the castle, the mob entered it only to discover that most of the Jews there had committed suicide. Those who had not were either forced to convert or were murdered. In all, eight hundred Jews were slaughtered in Worms.

When the terrifying reports from Speyer and Worms reached the Jewish community in Mainz, the archbishop offered them refuge in his monastery. But he was ultimately unable to defend them. Hundreds of Jewish men, women, and children were massacred there.

The archbishop of Cologne secretly hid the Jewish residents of his city in seven surrounding villages that he owned. Upon discovering this, the crusaders surrounded each of the villages and murdered four thousand Jews. In the village of Neuss, drunk crusaders tossed more than twenty women and nearly one hundred children into the river, competing to see how far they could hurl a screaming child. At Moers, nearly one thousand Jewish bodies were seen floating in the Rhine. All told, about twelve thousand Rhineland Jews were murdered.

Mounting Fear, Resentment, and Segregation

Political conditions in Germany during the thirteenth century left Jewish communities even more exposed to physical danger. Multiple centers of power were all competing for political control. The papacy in Rome was competing for power with the emperors. The emperors were vying with local authorities—bishops, feudal lords, provincial princes, and autonomous towns. Various factions were competing for the German royal crown, and feudal lords were caught up in power struggles among themselves. Though the emperor's ultimate authority for protecting the Jews had been delegated to local leaders, they were often too preoccupied with their own political survival to provide Jewish communities sufficient protection.

Amid this political turmoil and increased Jewish defenselessness, malicious anti-Jewish rumors were spreading among the general Christian populace. Rumors driven by fear. Fear of an inherent harm posed by the presence of Jewish communities among them. Apprehension penetrated even the highest levels of the church hierarchy. As the Jewish Talmud became better known, Western Christendom's leaders saw menacing red flags in it. They believed it denigrated Jesus and Mary, which was considered blasphemous. Pope Innocent III (1198–1216) became convinced that Judaism was a dangerous threat to Christianity's survival.

Pope Innocent's mindset is revealed in a 1208 letter to the Count of Nevers: "The Jews are condemned just like the fratricidal Cain, to roam the earth like fugitives and wanderers." Rather than protecting them, Christian rulers, he asserted, should "reduce them to slavery." It was wrong for them to admit Jews to their cities and villages, and "utilize their services as usurers to fleece Christians."

In 1215, he convened the Fourth Lateran Council. Of the seventy new church canons it adopted, five dealt with relationships between Christians and Jews. They officially forbade Jews from practicing any Christian occupation, employing any Christians, or even associating with Christians. The implications were unmistakable. Jews must be isolated into the segregated status of social outcasts.

This, of course, would require a way for Christians to tell the difference between themselves and Jews. The council's solution: Jews must distinguish themselves in public by wearing a distinctive attire. While the nature of that attire was not specified, later church legislation called for Jews to wear a yellow circle on their outer garment and caps with horns.

Later provincial church synods underscored this segregationist regulation. The synod of Mainz in 1259, for example, issued a reminder that a special Jewish badge was to be attached to Jewish garments. It further stipulated that Jews, on Good Friday, were not to appear on the street or even at the door or window of their own home.

Such anti-Jewish church canons were assimilated into the thirteenth-century comprehensive German law book known as the *Schwabenspiegel*. It specified that Jews were to differentiate themselves by wearing peaked hats. It banned them from appearing in public during Holy Week, from Thursday through Easter. If a Jew were found cohabitating with a Christian woman, the two of them were to be burned alive. If required to take a vow in court, a Jew was to stand on a pigskin while placing their right hand on a Pentateuch.

These canonical laws, however, were not strictly enforced by the king or by local bishops—much to the chagrin of church authorities in Rome. In a letter to the German clergy in 1233, Pope Gregory IX excoriated them for being too lenient toward the Jews and for failing to abide by the church's canons regarding Christian relationships with Jews.

Fear of Jewish harm to Christianity, though, was not limited to the church hierarchy in Rome. It was palpable among the peasant masses as well and grew more intense during the thirteenth century. Widespread false allegations arose. Jews were suspected of using Christian blood in their Passover rituals. The blood of crucified Christian youngsters. And it was assumed

Jews were consumed by an extreme hatred of Jesus. Their vengeance against Jesus, so it was imagined, was driving them to go so far as to steal church communion wafers—the sacred host, the very body of Jesus himself—so they could mutilate them and thereby re-crucify him.

There was yet an additional source of anti-Jewish angst: the Jewish enterprise of moneylending and pawnbroking. In even the best of circumstances, borrowers tend not to have the most positive feelings toward their moneylenders. In the case of Jewish moneylenders and Christian borrowers, things were even more strained. There was an added ecclesiastical stigma attached to moneylending. The church prohibited Christians from engaging in it. However, if it is wrong for Christians to take interest on loans, how can it also not be wrong for Jews to do so? This Jewish exception to the rules only served to heighten feelings of antipathy toward Jewish moneylenders. And on top of that, a continual cloud of suspicion hung over this enterprise. Might it be that the items these pawnbroking moneylenders supposedly collected as deposits on their loans were obtained instead through theft?

Jewish moneylending created still another point of social tension. Jewish "protectors"—bishops, lords, princes—did not provide their services for free. They charged the Jewish communities a tax for it. And whenever this Jewish tax was increased, the moneylenders had to increase their interest rates on loans. Jewish moneylenders were perceived as an integral part of an oppressive financial system—conduits through which local authorities were indirectly taxing the general population.

All in all, thirteenth-century German Jews experienced increased social and economic marginalization from the Gentile population. They became ghettoized into separate neighborhoods. This only magnified their unwelcome presence, their perceived religious and cultural inferiority, and their imagined danger to the wider Christian populace. Increasingly, they became the objects of the church's intolerance, the greed of local authorities' exploitative taxes, and the permissive lawlessness of angry peasant mobs.

Eruption of Violence

The century ended with a pervasive eruption of anti-Jewish violence. All driven by widespread anti-Jewish conspiracy theories. A false narrative that Jews were desecrating the Christian communion host and murdering Christian children in their Passover rituals. The discovery of the dead body of a Christian child in Mainz in 1283 resulted in the murder of ten Jews. That same year, twenty-six Jews were similarly murdered in Bacharach. In Munich in 1286, a mob set fire to a synagogue and its assembled occupants. In 1298, in the region of Bavaria, a knight named Rindfleisch organized a mob army to carry out his professed assignment from heaven to exterminate the Jews from the earth. This, in righteous revenge for the alleged murder of Gentile children by Jews in their Passover ritual. For more than half a year, this massacring gang murdered every man, woman, and child in up to 140 Jewish communities.

Unfortunately, these slaughtering and pillaging rampages were merely a harbinger of more disastrous things to come. During the fourteenth century, Germany became a place of even more relentless terror for its Jewish residents. The 1330s saw a spate of anti-Jewish outbursts. Gangs of villagers in the Franconia region formed what became known as *Judenschlegers* ("Jew-beaters") and attacked various Jewish communities. In Alsace, an innkeeper named Zimberlin started such a peasant gang, which called themselves the Armleder ("arm leather")—a reference to the leather bands they wore on their sleeves in lieu of the metal armor of knights. Equipping themselves for battle with axes, rakes, and spears, and bearing the sign of the cross, they went on a two-year beating and plundering tear, massacring Jews in almost a hundred communities.

In 1348, the frightening Black Death pandemic swept across Europe. Over the next two to three years, it obliterated nearly half of the entire European population. Thanks to the regimen of their ritual cleansing and dietary laws, loss of life in the Jewish communities was less extensive. This aroused suspicion, however, regarding their possible culpability in the spread of this plague. Many in the Christian populace were inclined to interpret this outbreak as the work of the devil. And no group was seen as being more in league with the devil than the Jews living among them. They were consequently rounded up and tortured into making incriminating "confessions." These fallacious professions of guilt spread widely, feeding vicious rumors that the Jews had poisoned Europe's water supplies in order to kill off the Christians.

A systematic execution of Jews ensued. One after another, entire Jewish communities were rounded up by angry mobs and set on fire. Nearly six hundred such communities in Germany were attacked, pillaged, and inflicted with loss of life. In more than two hundred of them, "Jewish bonfires" utterly annihilated every man, woman, and child. All told, between 1348 and 1351, likely more than half of the German Jewish population was exterminated. Yet, those who survived tenaciously refused to be terrorized into abandoning their Jewish cultural and religious identity.

Continued Jewish Endurance

What was it about these medieval German Jewish communities that enabled them to endure these centuries of deadly terrorism? Their independent self-governing system was key. Representatives assembled in regular gatherings as community councils. They organized, centralized, and regulated the administration of their internal Jewish life. Local rabbis, as revered spiritual leaders, served as the heads of these councils. This internal leadership structure enabled local Jewish communities to remain economically, socially, religiously, and culturally self-sustaining.

The vitality of their religious discipline provided them with the necessary spiritual strength. It integrated all the facets of their personal, family, and social life through a construct of religious ceremonies and cultural customs. And it enabled them to remain fervently devoted to the God of their ancestors, Yahweh, as their refuge and strength. Even providing the necessary fortitude, when threatened by compulsory Christian baptism, to choose martyrdom over abandonment of their Jewish faith.

The synagogue building and the various activities taking place there formed the hub of Jewish everyday life. It served an obvious religious purpose, accommodating Sabbath worship gatherings. At dusk on Fridays, a sexton summoned the people, going door to door banging his wooden hammer three times on the doors or shutters of their homes. The rabbi or a local Talmudist delivered a sermon. Women and men worshipers, separated by a partition, were each led in prayer by their own cantor. The prayers had specific melodies that were passed from one cantor generation to the next.

The synagogue was also where community council meetings were held. Decisions of the council and verdicts of legal cases were announced there. The traditional high value attached to scholarship and the training of their youth persisted. Therefore, a primary synagogue function continued to be—just as it was in ancient times—that of a "house of study" for educating the youth.

The Jewish educational system existed exclusively for boys. Girls received no formal education. The focus for them was learning how to become good housekeepers and pious wives. They learned merely the bare essentials of reading. Enough to enable them to read the Hebrew prayers. But not necessarily enough to comprehend the meaning of the prayers they were reciting. Though not schooled in the Torah as were the boys, it was nevertheless highly prized and revered by them.

The typical Jewish boy in medieval Germany, at the age of four or five, began a seven-year course of formal schooling centered on the teaching of the Talmud. His very first day of school was marked by various ceremonies. He was brought there by his father, wrapped in a prayer shawl. Using a tablet of the Hebrew alphabet, he would point out to the rabbi the spelling of the word "Torah" letter by letter. He was then brought some gingerbread inscribed with these words from Ezekiel 3:3: "'Son of man, eat this scroll I am giving you and fill your stomach with it.' So I ate it, and it tasted as sweet as honey in my mouth." Sometimes a boiled egg inscribed with similar passages was used instead. The passages would be read to and interpreted for the young boy, after which he would eat the gingerbread or egg. It was believed this would invigorate the child's mind and enhance his ability to memorize.

During the first two years of this primary school program, the focus was on learning to read Hebrew and gaining knowledge of the Pentateuch. Once able to read, the student would work his way through the Pentateuch, having the passages orally interpreted for him. He began with the book of Leviticus, which contained the all-important Jewish legal code. During the second two years, he would move on to the other parts of the Hebrew scripture—the Prophets and Writings sections—and would also be taught the Aramaic Targum (interpretive renderings of the Hebrew scripture written in Aramaic). This was to prepare him for studying the part of the Talmud called the Gemara (rabbinical analysis and commentary). During his last three years, he would move on to study selected tractates of the Talmud. Those students having difficulty with this challenging material were encouraged to drop out so as not to hold back the other students.

Upon reaching the age of Bar Mitzvah, this primary school training ended. Those possessing the necessary academic ability continued on to a secondary school program—the yeshiva or Talmudic academy. If none were located in their own Jewish community, they sought out a yeshiva headed by a prominent sage located in another city. Since many of these students were sons of poor people, they were typically supported financially by their local Jewish community or by a wealthy individual townsman.

The academic program in the yeshiva combined lecturing with intellectual exercises. Each day, the rector selected a Talmudic topic to expound on. He read the text of some Gemara selection along with the commentaries, analyzed the topic, offered explanations of it, and proposed questions about it. Then a discussion took place. Students asked their own questions and challenged the teacher's opinion, to which the teacher then responded. Students spent many hours a day outside of the lectures, engaged individually in study. By the age of eighteen, they would complete their study of the Jewish texts and become married.

Marriages typically took place between the ages of fifteen to eighteen. They were prearranged by the parents, using a marriage broker. He considered the lineages and assets of the two families contemplating a union. He helped them decide the dowry to be paid, which of the two families would take on the financial burden of supporting the newlyweds during the early years of their marriage while they were unable to be self-supporting, and which side would provide living quarters for them.

Eastward Migration

Jewish migration to the Rhineland area of Germany from Italy during the early Middle Ages was followed by a one-thousand-year-long pattern of continued migration eastward through German lands. Its initial phases were driven by the economic opportunity afforded them by the emerging eastern frontier. Along this eastward-moving frontier, barbaric German tribes were becoming Christianized and assimilated into the Holy Roman Empire and its economy. The Jewish merchant industry was positioned to play a central role in facilitating this economic development. New Jewish settlements thus continued springing up further and further east along the trade route that extended there from the Rhineland.

This route followed the river valley of a tributary of the Rhine River—the Main River—east to the Saale River. On the Saale River, in the town of Merseburg, a Jewish colony was already present in the tenth century. This route continued along the Saale River to where it then flowed into the Elbe River. Just to the north of this river junction, along the Elbe River, was the town of Magdeburg, where there was also a Jewish community present in the tenth century. The Elbe River continued to the eastern German border region known as the Mark Brandenburg, where there is evidence of a Jewish presence beginning in the twelfth century. The Elbe River remained the eastern border of this frontier for a long time.

Later stages of migration eastward through Germany and on into Slavic lands, however, were prompted by other causes. The horrific suffering unleashed upon Jewish communities through the loss of economic opportunity. The terrifying violence of the twelfth-century crusades. The numerous thirteenth- and fourteenth-century anti-Jewish pogroms and widespread expulsions of Jews from German cities. From the time of the Black Death through the remainder of the fifteenth century, the number of Jewish communities in Germany was significantly reduced as tens of thousands of their residents escaped, seeking hope and refuge in late medieval Poland.

<h1 style="text-align:center">12</h1>

On to Brandenburg and Ostfriesland

Border regions of the medieval German Holy Roman Empire were known as *Markgrafschafts*, or Margraviates. They were ruled by a military commander known as a "Margrave." The Margraviate of Brandenburg (Mark Brandenburg) was one such German principality. It was located in what is today the eastern part of Germany and the western part of Poland. (See map, *Mark Brandenburg circa 1300*, p. iv). It constituted the nucleus of what later emerged as the Prussian monarchy.

Mark Brandenburg Jewish Communities

Jewish merchants likely traversed this area already during the time of its colonization in the twelfth century, while pursuing trading opportunities with the Slavonic-populated borderland to the east across the Elbe River. Early Jewish traders gradually settled in several of the newly formed cities in this German outpost during the thirteenth century, often in apparently small numbers.

There is compelling evidence, as we will soon see, that my own Jewish ancestors were among those who settled in this Mark Brandenburg region. They arrived, perhaps as early as the twelfth century, likely through a gradual migration over time from the Rhineland area. Perhaps they were among the first Jewish settlers there as entrepreneurial, pioneering frontiersmen. Or they may have arrived there later, while escaping persecution further west. One thing is certain. Somehow, they miraculously survived the dreadful widespread slaughtering of tens of thousands of their fellow German Jews during the late Middle Ages.

Mark Brandenburg Jewish residents lived under the authority of the sovereign margraves, who, in exchange for giving them "letters of protection," required from them an annual tax. Because the emerging urban trade and artisan guilds here excluded Jewish participation, Jewish commercial activities became centered primarily around the meat trade and the lending business. Why the meat trade? Since Jewish religious law forbade the eating of certain cattle parts, medieval Jews were customarily allowed to slaughter cattle for their own consumption. They would then typically sell those unused portions to non-Jews. This created an ongoing conflict with non-Jewish butchers in the Mark Brandenburg. They considered this an encroachment on their supposedly exclusive rights to the butchering business.

Over time, the sovereign central authority of the margraves weakened. Local princes and city authorities exerted greater independent control over their local affairs—including Jewish affairs. Occasionally, they imposed an additional tax burden on the Jews so they could capitalize on the profits from their moneylending enterprise as well.

Economic conditions during the fifteenth century led to a calamitous outcome for the entire Mark Brandenburg Jewish population. There was, during this time, among the Mark's Christian population a general increased need for obtaining credit. Knights, lords, and even some municipalities had incurred significant debt. While their financial indebtedness to Jewish moneylenders was increasing, the wealth and economic influence of the Jewish communities were also growing. This triggered a rising widespread anti-Jewish resentment among the Christian community. Their resentful sentiments eventually became vocalized: the Jews should be outright expelled from their territory.

In 1480, landed estate owners openly demanded that their ruling prince, Albrecht Achilles, expel them. Knowing how dependent he was on the tax revenue he received from the Jewish population, and knowing how indispensable they were to the economic life of the Mark, Albrecht refused to accede to this demand. Instead, he tried placating his discontents by placing a limit on Jewish usury. But this failed to stem the mounting indebtedness to Jewish moneylenders. When Prince Joachim I began his reign over the Mark in 1499, he was likewise pressured to expel the Jews from the Mark. He even went so far in 1503 to issue an order of expulsion, describing Judaism as "despised" and a "persecutor of the Christian name." But he never carried it out.

1510 Massacre and Expulsion

When the Roman Catholic sacrament of communion was conducted in medieval Germany, the priest would consecrate the bread (also known as the host). It was believed that through his act of consecration, the bread became literally transformed into the physical body of Jesus himself. The priest then placed this host—considered to be the actual body of Jesus—into a decorative vessel called a monstrance. Upon seeing the host displayed to them in the monstrance, the gathered congregation responded by expressing their adoration and worship of Jesus.

In February of 1510, the church in the village of Knobloch, diocese of Brandenburg, was broken into. A gold-plated monstrance containing two consecrated hosts was stolen. Pieces of the discarded communion bread, along with a knife and metalworking tools, were found in the nearby village of Bernau. The alleged perpetrator, a Christian blacksmith from Bernau named Paul Fromm, fled from his home. In June he returned to Bernau and was arrested. He subsequently confessed—under torture—that he had eaten one of the stolen hosts himself and had sold the other to a Jew named Salomon from the village of Spandau. This "confession" quickly led to further suspicions and accusations which incriminated additional Jewish people.

This theft had also been reported to Prince Joachim I. Likely due to pressure from local estate owners, he had the accused Jew, Salomon, brought from Spandau to Berlin to face his accuser. Under torture, Salomon was forced to confess that he had indeed bought the host from Fromm. And that he had tried to inflict injuries on it, pricking it until it oozed blood, and had spoken curses over it. He had allegedly broken it into three pieces, sent one piece to a Jew, Jacob, in Brandenburg, and a second piece to a Jew, Markus, in Stendal. Purportedly, Markus had baked the third piece in a cake, which he then had hung up in his local synagogue, where it was said to have been found.

Meanwhile, the mayor of Brandenburg, perhaps under the instigation of the clergy, took it upon himself to get the Jew, Jacob of Brandenburg, to incriminate five additional Jews. They were, in turn, forced to incriminate several more Jews. The host allegedly sent to Stendal was said to have been desecrated by six additional Jews there. They, in turn, incriminated thirty-five more Jews.

All told, about a hundred Jewish suspects were rounded up and brought to Berlin to face charges, undergo horrible tortures, and make further forced confessions. A four-week-long "investigation" ensued, as interrogators sought to line up all the individual confessions with each other. Some of the prisoners died under torture. Sixteen of the suspects were accused of participating in child murders related to their Passover celebrations. Thirty-seven were accused of desecrating the host. Among the accused were the wealthiest Jews in the Mark. Surviving local financial records indicate that they had the highest fixed tax rates.

Once in court, Fromm and the Jewish defendants publicly confessed their guilt. A week later, they were back in court again to hear the verdict. The Jewish suspects were all donned with the distinguishing traditional pointed yellow and white "Jewish hats." Fromm and thirty-eight Jews were pronounced guilty of heresy and sorcery. Their sentence: death by fire. Fromm, though, was to be torn apart with glowing pliers prior to his burning. (Their innocence, notably, was later proven in 1539—with the help of Martin Luther's Protestant Reformation cohort, Phillip Melanchthon.)

The thirty-eight Jewish victims were led in fetters through the streets of Berlin to a public square and fastened to a large scaffold. It was underlain with flammable kindling and tar, built just for them. The rabbi recited aloud the Jewish last will and testament. The condemned repeated the prayer and recitation of Psalms to the very end—as they were burned alive.

The die had now been cast. Joachim I's hand had been forced. There was no choice but to expel the Jewish population from his territory. Sometime around the end of 1510 or the beginning of 1511, all four hundred to five hundred Jewish men, women, and children residing in the Mark Brandenburg were escorted to the border and banished from its territory.

Migration to Ostfriesland

Where did they go? The answer is shrouded in mystery. Having resided in the Mark in small enclaves, dispersed among as many as twenty different villages, they most likely scattered in multiple directions. There is evidence, however, that at least a small group of these refugees found their way to the village of Wittmund in the eastern part of the German North Sea coastal region known today as the province of Ostfriesland. (See map, *Ostfriesland Region 1500s*, p. v). There is also evidence that some of these refugees, or their descendants, found their way from Wittmund to the western Ostfriesland town of Emden. A "Memory Book" kept by the Emden Jewish community is reported to have memorialized the 1510 Brandenburg executions in a particularly detailed and heartfelt manner—indicating it was probably an account related by relatives of those who were executed.

This migration of Jewish refugees from the Mark Brandenburg to Wittmund in Ostfriesland was one of two simultaneous Jewish migratory movements that I discovered lying behind the formation of small Jewish enclaves in various parts of Ostfriesland in the sixteenth and seventeenth centuries. The other was a relocation of Jewish moneylenders coming from the German Rhineland area to Emden in western Ostfriesland. My own Ostfriesland Jewish ancestors had thus been among either of these two separate groups of emigrants. But which one? Because my earliest known Jewish ancestor resided in northcentral Ostfriesland, it is not immediately apparent whether it was the western or the eastern migratory path that his family traveled. This was the puzzle I needed to try to solve.

I found further clarity, however, by considering the dynamics of Jewish social status in Ostfriesland at this time. It appears that Jewish migrants who settled in Ostfriesland evidently fell into either of two different categories of official social status. Some were granted "letters of protection," which gave them an official legal status. In return for paying an annual fee to Ostfriesland's Count, they received permission to live in his territory, to trade, to practice their Jewish religion, and to organize their independent communities. In 1645, Count Ulrich II issued an official protection letter specifically naming thirty-two Jewish families who were living at that time in fourteen towns and villages in Ostfriesland. Three of these officially acknowledged Jewish families were living as a synagogue community in Esens. This was just seven miles away from the village of Schweindorf, where my earliest known Jewish ancestor was living at this very same time. No Schweindorf Jewish families, however, were included in Count Ulrich's list.

How could there be a Jewish family residing in Schwiendorf without it being on Ulrich's list? I soon discovered an explanation. There was an additional category of Ostfriesland Jewish residents—so-called undisclosed Jews. They could not afford the required fee for obtaining "letter of protection" privileges. Apparently allowed to remain in Ostfriesland with "unprotected" status, they were left to fend for themselves within their new Gentile cultural surroundings. As people from Jewish backgrounds now living outside their traditional Jewish synagogue communities, they would have to navigate their way into and within a Gentile- Christian-dominated culture. With the burdensome stigma of being seen as "outsiders"—people with a distinctively "foreign" ethnic, religious, and cultural background and identity. Categorized within Ostfriesland society as "unofficially Jewish."

My Family's Earliest Known Jewish Ancestor

An "undisclosed," "unofficial" Jew. This appears to have been the status of the earliest known Einfeld family Jewish ancestor in Ostfriesland: Folkert Jueden. Land transaction documents provide the only extant evidence of his existence. They reveal that he died in 1683 in Schweindorf—a small

Ostfriesland village that had a population of 179 people in 1693. How long had he lived there? When and where was he born? Where did he, his parents, and grandparents come from? Did he have any brothers or sisters? How did he end up in Schweindorf? Who was his wife? Was he still a "practicing Jew?" Or had he been baptized and added to the rolls of the local Lutheran Church? Unfortunately, the historical record leaves all these questions unanswered.

Some inferences can be made, though. His name Jueden tells us that he would have been considered "Jewish" by the people of his small community—if not religiously, for sure ethnically. His residence in Schweindorf indicates he was definitely not among those who enjoyed the status of a "protected Jew," as no Jews from Schweindorf ever appear on any such lists. And even though the overall Ostfriesland-wide Jewish population statistics show a total of fifty-nine families living in its territory in 1671 and seventy-four families in 1690, none of those families are shown as residing in Schweindorf. This is further evidence that whatever Jewish people were living in Schweindorf during the 1600s, they were among the "undisclosed" Jews unable to afford the official "protected Jew" status.

There is evidence, in fact, that others with Jewish backgrounds besides Folkert Jueden were present in Schweindorf during this time as well. A Jewish man named Moses Benjamin is documented as having sold his land in Schweindorf in 1696. And in 1720, this same Moses Benjamin, at that time living in nearby Esens, reported an incident that occurred in Schweindorf at an engagement party for his Jewish nephew Isaac Simon. He related that some other Jews attending that party pressured him to drink wine earlier than what was considered proper. When he refused to do so, four other Jews grabbed him, tore his wig from his head, and beat him before he was able to make a hasty escape.

Although no record of Folkert Jueden's parents has been found, his name "Folkert" provides some clues about his parentage. First, Folkert was a common Ostfriesland name at this time, not the Biblical name that a Jewish mother and father would typically have chosen. Second, if Folkert's parents were following the Ostfriesland culture's system for naming their family members—and it appears that they were—he would have received his second name Jueden from his father's first name. He would thereby have been identified as "Folkert, Jueden's son." His Ostfrieslander first name, Folkert, would likely have come from an Ostfriesland ancestor on his mother's side of the family. This all seems to indicate that his father was Jewish and that his mother was likely a non-Jewish Ostfrieslander.

As to how Folkert Jueden came to reside in the village of Schweindorf, one can only speculate. However, the evidence that there were other Jewish people besides him living there, and that they had a documented connection with Jewish relatives living in the nearby town of Esens, is instructive. A Jewish presence existed in Esens already before 1600. And there is a direct connection between those earliest Jewish settlers in Esens and those who settled in Wittmund in the early 1500s. Esens Jews were reported to have brought their dead to be buried in the Jewish cemetery in Wittmund before they had their own cemetery in Esens.

It seems a migratory process is evident here. Jewish refugees expelled from Brandenburg in 1510 settled in Wittmund, one of the three domains of the central Ostfriesland separatist territory known then as Harlingerland. By the mid-1600s, a small Jewish community—which had a shared history with the Jewish community in Wittmund—had sprung up nine miles to its northwest in Esens, one of the other Harlingerland domains and also its capital. And by the late 1600s, there were Jewish people living seven miles to the southwest of Esens in the village of Schweindorf—also a part of the Esens domain—who had Jewish relatives living back in Esens. It is therefore highly conceivable that Folkert Jueden's Jewish ancestry connects back, by way of this migratory route, to the earlier Wittmund Jewish community.

What is known for sure about him is that he owned land in Schweindorf, had a son named Juede Fokerts (a variant spelling of Folkert), thereby identifying him as "Juede, Fokert's/Folkert's son," and that he died in 1683 in Schweindorf. The source of this information is a handwritten note documenting a financial transaction concerning a parcel of land he owned in Schweindorf. It was the legal practice at that time that when a property was either sold or inherited, the new owner was required to pay a tax in order to complete the transaction. The original handwritten registers of these transactions, dating back to 1554 for the Esens region, of which Schweindorf was a part, have been organized farm by farm and compiled into a 1998 publication of a two-volume work by Heyko Heyken.

There is an entry in Heyken's work listed under "Farm #12" in the village of Schweindorf, dated April 16, 1683, stating that (translating from the German) "Juede Folkers appeared for his father Folkerdt Jueden's land." In other words, he came as the inheritor of his now-deceased father's land to pay the required tax in order to become the new owner of record. But this entry goes on to relate a heartbreaking reality. "Because of his [the son Juede's] poverty he could only finally offer tax payment of 2 Reichstaler [German dollars]. Another person has offered 4 Reichstaler tax payment. Because of poverty he [Juede] is unable to pay the tax. He must now pay 6 Reichstaler." That is to say, he was too poor to inherit his father's land and was instead outbid by another buyer. This was the desperate economic reality for the majority of Jewish people in Germany in the mid-seventeenth century. It has been estimated that 80 percent of them were living at the poorest level of society at this time.

The historical record of this impoverished Juede Fokerts is more extensive than that of his father. The local church parish, of which Schweindorf was a part, was Lutheran. The church was located two-and-a-half miles away from Schweindorf, along the road to Esens, in a village called Ochtersum. The church-state records of the Ochtersum church show that Juede Fokerts was married there in 1681 to a Himke Alberts. The church records the baptisms of the five children they had together from 1682–1690. Then, in 1700, there is another marriage recorded showing that the widower Juede Fokerts married a second wife, Tomke Eimers. The church records indicate that Juede and his second wife, Tomke, had two sons: Jacob Jueden, born and baptized in 1702; and Aymer (a variant spelling of Eimer) Juden, born and baptized in 1706. Notably, it is from Aymer Juden that the Einfeld family has directly descended. (The story of Aymer and his descendants will be told in a forthcoming work.)

From "Jew" to "Christian"

The local Lutheran parish documentation of the marriages of Juede Fokerts and the baptisms of his children indicates he was a member of the church. This raises an intriguing question. Given his Jewish background and ethnic identity in his community, how did that happen? There likely were various contributing factors.

One factor may have been a gradual weakening of his ties with the broader Jewish community. Ostfriesland Jewish residents in the 1600s were typically quite scattered from each other, living in very small, two- to three-family groupings among their Gentile neighbors. Such isolation over time could have resulted in a weakened commitment to maintaining their Jewish religious and cultural traditions. An added factor may have been a growing desire to escape the negative social stigma and discrimination attached to their Jewishness. And finally, it is highly probable that there were very limited options for finding an available Jewish marriage partner, leaving one to choose between either marrying a Gentile or not marrying at all.

Did Juede or his Jewish father or grandparents experience a spiritual conversion to Christianity? There is no way of knowing, and it certainly cannot be ruled out. However, transitioning from Jewish to Christian religious affiliation during this time in Germany was not normally prompted by a spiritual conversion. The typical scenario would have been that Juede's Jewish family had, over time, become nominal non-practicing Jews and had been essentially assimilated into church "membership" by virtue of residing in the local village as "undisclosed" or "unaffiliated" Jews.

There was no distinction or separation between the entities of church and state within the German church-state system of this time. Village residence and church membership were essentially two sides of the same coin. The church also functioned as the local "governmental agency" tasked with keeping all the village's records of births, baptisms, marriages, deaths, and burials—except for those Jews who had letters of protection. The recordings of their vital statistics were instead made by the local synagogue.

This, then, is the culmination of the story of my Jewish ancestors. The outcome of their treacherous thirty-seven-hundred-year-long, three-thousand-mile-long migratory journey. Having arrived in Ostfriesland as displaced refugees fleeing anti-Jewish religious persecution, they became disconnected from any Jewish enclave or local synagogue community. They settled, rather, as an isolated individual Jewish family among a Gentile community. Cultural and religious ties to their Jewish past disappeared. Through intermarriage, they were assimilated into the broader local Ostfriesland Gentile Lutheran community. The only noticeable surviving link to their Jewish past was the family's three-generation-long continued use of the name "Jueden." And an oral tradition kept alive as it passed down from generation to generation, which eventually reached my Aunt Clara, and which she, in turn, seemed compelled to pass along to me.

Enjoyed this book?

Help other readers discover this story by scanning QR code or using link below to leave a review. **Your comment – even just a sentence or two – makes a big difference.**

Amazon Review

Goodreads Review

bit.ly/review-most-high-AMZ   bit.ly/review-most-high-GdRd

For more about Doug and to sign up for his newsletter to receive updates on his forthcoming publications:

http://www.dougeinfeld.com

Afterword

I step back and try to take in a panoramic view of this entire story, the vast span of my Jewish ancestral history. I try to visualize the more than one hundred generations that have come and gone from the time of Abraham to their sixteenth-century arrival in the North Sea coastal region of Germany. I see one unifying overarching theme tying it all together: the constant overshadowing presence of the Most High God, Yahweh.

The words of Psalm 100:5 come to mind: "Yahweh's faithfulness continues through *all* generations." That is more than a mere trite-sounding theological concept. It's an observable reality playing out in human history. Generations have come, and generations have gone. But Yahweh's faithfulness has outlasted them all. It continued unabated during the generations of Old Testament Israel despite all their faithlessness. It persisted during the time of Jesus and the first-century church, even when the Jewish community largely wrote Jesus off as an imposter Messiah. It endured during the first fifteen centuries AD while my own Jewish ancestors continued clinging to their long-held Jewish faith and hope in Yahweh. It was evidenced when, in the seventeenth century, they were enfolded into the German Lutheran church community.

We live in a time when the foundations of Western civilization often seem to be unraveling, a time of great uncertainty about where history is taking us. A time when we especially need reminding that the ever-present Most High God continues to protectively overshadow his people. And that his faithfulness to them will continue, from generation to generation, until the end of time.

Acknowledgements

I am very grateful for the Scriptoria writers workshops, which helped propel me beyond the research and conceptualization phases of this project. A special thanks to its founders, Gary Schmidt and Cynthia Beach, for creating the space where emerging authors like me can be encouraged, equipped, and inspired to pursue their publishing goals. A special thanks to my fellow workshop participants, and particularly to facilitators Michael Stevens, Elizabeth Vanderlei, and Vinita Hampton Wright, who challenged and inspired me to elevate my writing craft to a whole new level.

I want to acknowledge those organizations and institutions which provided access to the wide range of resources upon which my research depended. Thanks to the Ostfriesen Genealogical Society of America – its conferences, publications, and research library were invaluable. Thanks also to my alma mater Calvin University's Heckman Library, a mere half hour's drive from my home, and its substantial, academically respected holdings. I am especially grateful for the services of MeLCat, a statewide resource-sharing service that enabled countless books held in various libraries across the state of Michigan to be sent for me to pick up at my local Coopersville Public Library. Thanks, as well, to the helpful staff there.

I am grateful as well for the publishing guidance I received from consultants Mark Malatesta and Rob Eagar, whose expertise helped bring clarity and direction to the process. My thanks extend to my cover designer, Ares Jun, to Nycole Sinks at Positive Proofing for her editorial work, and to Bree Rose Creative for designing the maps. A special thanks to my sister, Sharon Gould, for her attentive, meticulous perusal of the final proof copy.

I appreciate all the expressions of interest and encouragement I received along the way from family members and friends. Most of all, I thank my wife Nancy, for her unfailing belief, her steady encouragement, and her deep well of patience that made room for this book to be written.

Bibliography

Ackroyd, Peter R. *Israel under Babylon and Persia.* London: Oxford UP, 1970.

Albertz, Rainer. *A History of Israelite Religion in the Old Testament Period (Vol. 1: From the Beginning to the End of the Monarchy).* Louisville, KY: Westminster/John Knox Press, 1994.

Allison, Jr., Dale C. *Constructing Jesus: Memory, Imagination, and History.* Grand Rapids: Baker Academic, 2010.

Alon, Gedaliah. *The Jews in their Land in the Talmudic Age (70–640 ce).* (Vols. 1 & 2). Translated and edited by Gershon Levi. Jerusalem: The Magnes Press, The Hebrew University, 1980 & 1984.

Anglim, Simon. *Fighting Techniques of the Ancient World 3000 bce–500 ce: Equipment, Combat Skills and Tactics.* London: Amber Books, 2013.

Arnold, Bill T. and Richard S. Hess, eds. *Ancient Israel's History: An Introduction to Issues and Sources.* Grand Rapids: Baker Academic, 2014.

Avi-Yonah, Michael. *The Jews under Roman and Byzantine Rule: A Political History of Palestine from the Bar Kokhba War to the Arab Conquest.* Jerusalem: The Magnes Press, The Hebrew University, 1984.

Avi-Yonah, Michael, and Zvi Baras, eds. *Society and Religion in the Second Temple Period.* The World History of the Jewish People, First Series: Ancient Times. Jerusalem: Masada Publishing, 1977.

Barnett, Paul. *The Birth of Christianity: The First Twenty Years.* Grand Rapids: Eerdmans, 2005.

———. *Jesus and the Rise of Early Christianity: A History of New Testament Times.* Downers Grove, IL: Inter-Varsity Press, 1999.

Barstad, Hans M. *The Myth of the Empty Land: A Study in the History and Archaeology of Judah During the 'Exilic' Period.* Stockholm: Scandinavian UP, 1996.

Bauckham, Richard. *Jesus and the Eyewitnesses: The Gospels as Eyewitness Testimony.* Second edition. Grand Rapids: Eerdmans, 2017.

Beard, Mary. *SPQR: A History of Ancient Rome.* New York: Liveright, 2015.

Beasley-Murray, G. R. *Jesus and the Kingdom of God.* Grand Rapids: Eerdmans, 1986.

Bonfil, Robert. "Italy: The North." In *The Middle Ages: The Christian World,* edited by Robert Chazan, 117–28. The Cambridge History of Judaism 6. Cambridge: Cambridge UP, 2018.

Broadhead, Edwin K. *Jewish Ways of Following Jesus: Redrawing the Religious Map of Antiquity.* Tubingen: Mohr Siebeck, 2010.

Buc, Philippe, et al., eds. *Jews and Christians in Medieval Europe: The Historiographic Legacy of Bernhard Blumenkranz.* Turnhout, Belgium: Brepols Publishers, 2016.

Burgess, Tony, ed. *Chronicles of the Jewish People.* New York: Michael Friedman Publishing, 1996.

Byrskog, Samuel. *Story as History—History as Story: The Gospel Tradition in the Context of Ancient Oral History.* Wissenschaftliche Untersuchungen zum Neuen Testament 123. Tubingen: Mohr Siebeck, 2000.

Carlebach, Elisheva. *Divided Souls: Converts from Judaism in Germany, 1500–1750.* New Haven: Yale UP, 2001.

Charlesworth, James H., ed. *The Messiah: Developments in Earliest Judaism and Christianity.* Minneapolis: Fortress Press, 1992.

Chazan, Robert. *The Jews of Medieval Western Christendom, 1000–1500.* New York: Cambridge UP, 2006.

Chilton, Bruce, ed. *The Kingdom of God in the Teaching of Jesus.* Philadelphia: Fortress Press, 1984.

————. *Pure Kingdom: Jesus's Vision of God.* Grand Rapids: Eerdmans, 1996.

Cohen, Shaye J. D. "The Temple and the Synagogue." In *The Early Roman Period,* edited by William Horbury et al., 298–325. The Cambridge History of Judaism 3. Cambridge: Cambridge UP, 1999.

Collins, Adela Yarbor, and John J. Collins. *King and Messiah as Son of God: Divine, Human, and Angelic Messianic Figures in Biblical and Related Literature.* Grand Rapids: Eerdmans, 2008.

Collins, John J., and Daniel C. Harlow, eds. *Early Judaism: A Comprehensive Overview.* Grand Rapids: Eerdmans, 2012.

Davies, W. D. and Louis Finkelstein, eds. *The Hellenistic Age.* The Cambridge History of Judaism 2. Cambridge: Cambridge UP, 1989.

————. *Introduction: The Persian Period.* The Cambridge History of Judaism 1. Cambridge: Cambridge UP, 1984.

Dimont, Max I. *Jews, God and History.* Second Edition. New York: Signet Classics, 2004.

Dubnov, Simon. *History of the Jews (3 Volumes).* Translated by Moshe Spiegel. South Brunswick, NJ: A. S. Barnes, 1967–1969.

Duff, Paul B. *Jesus Followers in the Roman Empire.* Grand Rapids: Eerdmans, 2017.

Dunn, James D. G. *Beginning from Jerusalem.* Christianity in the Making 2. Grand Rapids: Eerdmans, 2009.

————. "From the Crucifixion to the End of the First Century." In *Partings: How Judaism and Christianity Became Two*, edited by Hershel Shanks, 27–53. Washington, DC: Biblical Archaeology Society, 2013.

————. *Jesus, Paul, and the Gospels*. Grand Rapids: Eerdmans, 2011.

————. *Jesus Remembered*. Christianity in the Making 1. Grand Rapids: Eerdmans, 2009.

———— ed. *Jews and Christians: The Parting of the Ways*. Tubingen: J. C. B. Mohr (Paul Siebeck), 1992.

————. *Neither Jew nor Greek: A Contested Identity*. Christianity in the Making 3. Grand Rapids: Eerdmans, 2015.

Edwards, James R. *From Christ to Christianity: How the Jesus Movement Became the Church in Less Than a Century*. Grand Rapids: Baker Academic, 2021.

Elon, Amos. *The Pity of It All: A History of Jews in Germany, 1743–1933*. New York: Metropolitan, 2002.

Eshel, Hanon. "The Bar Kochba Revolt, 132–135." In *The Late Roman-Rabbinic Period*, edited by Steven T. Katz, 105–127. The Cambridge History of Judaism 4. Cambridge: Cambridge UP, 2006.

Evans, Craig A. *From Jesus to the Church: The First Christian Generation*. Louisville: Westminster John Knox Press, 2014.

Fast, Howard. *The Jews: Story of a People*. New York: Dial, 1968. (e-book)

Foster, Raymond S. *The Restoration of Israel*. London: Darton, Longman & Todd, 1970.

Fredriksen, Paula. *Ancient Christianities: The First Five Hundred Years*. Princeton: Princeton UP, 2024.

————. *From Jesus to Christ: The Origins of the New Testament Images of Christ*. Second edition. New Haven: Yale UP, 2000.

————. *Jesus of Nazareth, King of the Jews: A Jewish Life and the Emergence of Christianity.* New York: Knopf, 1999.

————. *Paul: The Pagans' Apostle.* New Haven: Yale UP. 2017.

————. *When Christians Were Jews: The First Generation.* New Haven: Yale UP, 2018.

Freyne, Sean. *Jesus, a Jewish Galilean: A New Reading of the Jesus-Story.* New York: T & T Clark, 2005.

————. *The Jesus Movement and Its Expansion: Meaning and Mission.* Grand Rapids: Eerdmans, 2014.

Fuellenbach, John. *The Kingdom of God: The Message of Jesus Today.* Maryknoll, NY: Orbis, 1997.

Gay, Ruth. *The Jews of Germany: A Historical Portrait.* New Haven: Yale UP, 1992.

Goodblatt, David. "The Political and Social History of the Jewish Community in the Land of Israel, c.235–638." In *The Late Roman-Rabbinic Period,* edited by Steven T. Katz, 404–30. The Cambridge History of Judaism 4. Cambridge: Cambridge UP, 2006.

Goodman, Martin. *State and Society in Roman Galilee, ad 132–212.* Totowa, NJ: Rowman & Allanheld, 1983.

Gottheil, Richard, and A. Freimann. "Brandenburg." *JewishEncyclopedia.com.* https://jewishencyclopedia.com/articles/3632-brandenburg.

Grabbe, Lester L. *The Coming of the Greeks: The Early Hellenistic Period (335–175 bce).* A History of the Jews and Judaism in the Second Temple Period 2. New York: T&T Clark, 2008.

————. *An Introduction to First Century Judaism: Jewish Religion and History in the Second Temple Period.* Edinburgh: T&T Clark, 1996.

————. *Yehud: A History of the Persian Province of Judah*. A History of the Jews and Judaism in the Second Temple Period 1. New York: T&T Clark, 2004.

Grant, Michael. *The Jews in the Roman World*. New York: Scribner's, 1973.

Greer, Jonathan S., et al., eds. *Behind the Scenes of the Old Testament: Cultural, Social, and Historical Contexts*. Grand Rapids: Baker Academic, 2018.

Hanson, K. C., and Douglas E. Oakman. *Palestine in the Time of Jesus: Social Structures and Social Conflicts*. Minneapolis: Fortress Press, 1998.

Harrill, J. Albert. *Paul the Apostle: His Life and Legacy in Their Roman Context*. New York: Cambridge UP, 2012.

Haverkamp, Alfred. "Germany." In *The Middle Ages: The Christian World*, edited by Robert Chazan, 239–81. The Cambridge History of Judaism 6. Cambridge: Cambridge UP, 2018.

Hawkins, Ralph K. *How Israel Became a People*. Nashville: Abingdon, 2013.

Heise, Werner. *Die Juden in der Mark Brandenburg bis zum Jahre 1571*. Berlin: Verlag Dr. Emil Ebering, 1932.

Helbig, Herbert. *Gesellschaft und Wirtschaft der Mark Brandenburg im Mittelalter*. Berlin: Walter de Gruyter, 1973.

Hengel, Martin, and Anna Maria Schwemer. *Jesus and Judaism*. Translated by Wayne Coppins. Waco, TX: Baylor UP, 2019.

Hess, Richard S. *Israelite Religion: An Archaeological and Biblical Survey*. Grand Rapids: Baker Academic, 2007.

Hock, Ronald F. *The Social Context of Paul's Ministry: Tentmaking and Apostleship*. Philadelphia: Fortress, 1980.

Hoffmeier, James K. *Ancient Israel in Sinai: The Evidence for the Authority of the Wilderness Tradition.* New York: Oxford UP, 2005.

———— et al., eds. *"Did I Not Bring Israel Out of Egypt?" Biblical, Archaeological, and Egyptological Perspectives on the Exodus Narratives.* Winona Lake, IN: Eisenbrauns, 2016.

————. *Israel in Egypt: The Evidence for the Authenticity of the Exodus Tradition.* New York: Oxford UP, 1997.

Horbury, William. *Jewish Messianism and the Cult of Christ.* London: SCM, 1998.

———— et al., eds. *The Early Roman Period.* The Cambridge History of Judaism 3. Cambridge: Cambridge UP, 1999.

————. *Messianism Among Jews and Christians: Twelve Biblical and Historical Studies.* New York: T & T Clark, 2003.

Horsley, Richard A. *Jesus and Empire: The Kingdom of God and the New World Disorder.* Minneapolis: Augsburg Fortress, 2003.

Hurtado, Larry W. *Lord Jesus Christ: Devotion to Jesus in Earliest Christianity.* Grand Rapids: Eerdmans, 2003.

Jacobs, Andrew S. *Remains of the Jews: The Holy Land and Christian Empire in Late Antiquity.* Stanford, CA: Stanford UP, 2004.

Kaiser, Walter C., and Paul D. Wegner. *A History of Israel: From the Bronze Age Through the Jewish Wars.* Nashville: B&H Academic, 2016.

Kaplan, Marion A., ed. *Jewish Daily Life in Germany, 1618–1945.* Oxford: Oxford UP, 2005.

Katz, Steven T., ed. *The Late Roman-Rabbinic Period.* The Cambridge History of Judaism 4. Cambridge: Cambridge UP, 2006.

Kaylor, R. David. *Jesus the Prophet: His Vision of the Kingdom on Earth.* Louisville: Westminster/John Knox Press, 1994.

Kim, Seyoon. *Christ and Caesar: The Gospel and the Roman Empire in the Writings of Paul and Luke.* Grand Rapids: Eerdmans, 2008.

Kloppenborg, John S. *Christ's Associations: Connecting and Belonging in the Ancient City.* New Haven: Yale UP, 2019.

Laato, Antti. *A Star is Rising: The Historical Development of the Old Testament Royal Ideology and the Rise of the Jewish Messianic Expectations.* Atlanta: Scholars, 1997.

Latimer, Elizabeth W. *Judea from Cyrus to Titus 573 bc–70 ad.* Chicago: McClurg, 1899.

Leon, Harry J. *The Jews of Ancient Rome.* Philadelphia: The Jewish Publication Society of America, 1960.

Levine, Lee I, ed. *The Galilee in Late Antiquity.* New York: The Jewish Theological Seminary of America, 1992.

Lieu, Judith M. *Image and Reality: The Jews in the World of the Christians in the Second Century.* Edinburgh: T&T Clark, 1996.

Lokers, Jan. *Die Juden in Emden 1530–1806: Ein sozial- und wirtschaftsgeschictliche Studie zur Geschichte der Juden in Norddeutschland vom ausgehenden Mittelalter bis zur Emanzipationsgesetzgebung.* Aurich: Verlag Ostfriesische Landschaft, 1990.

Longenecker, Bruce W., Elizabeth E. Shively, and T. J. Lang, eds. *Behind the Scenes of the New Testament: Cultural, Social, and Historical Contexts.* Grand Rapids: Baker Academic, 2024.

Ludemann, Gerd. *The Acts of the Apostles: What Really Happened in the Earliest Days of the Church.* Amherst, NY: Prometheus, 2005.

Magness, Jodi. *Stone and Dung, Oil and Spit: Jewish Daily Life in the Time of Jesus.* Grand Rapids: Eerdmans, 2011.

Malina, Bruce. *New Testament World Insights from Cultural Anthropology.* Louisville, KY: Westminster/John Knox, 2001.

———. *The Social World of Jesus and the Gospels.* London: Routledge, 1996.

———. *Windows on the World of Jesus: Time Travel to Ancient Judea.* Louisville, KY: Westminster/John Knox, 1993.

Markreich, Max. *Die Juden in Ostfriesland: Zweige sephardischen und askenasischen Judentums.* San Francisco, 1955.

Matthews, Victor H. *A Brief History of Ancient Israel.* Louisville: Westminster John Knox, 2002.

———. *The Cultural World of the Bible: An Illustrated Guide to Manners and Customs.* Grand Rapids: Baker Academic, 2015.

Mears, John. *From Exile to Overthrow: A History of the Jews from the Babylonian Captivity to the Destruction of the Second Temple.* Philadelphia: Presbyterian Board of Publication, 1914.

Meeks, Wayne A. *The First Urban Christians: The Social World of the Apostle Paul.* New Haven: Yale UP, 1983.

Meier, John P. *Companions and Competitors.* A Marginal Jew: Rethinking the Historical Jesus 3. New York: Doubleday, 2001.

———. *Law and Love.* A Marginal Jew: Rethinking the Historical Jesus 4. New Haven: Yale UP, 2009.

———. *Mentor, Message, and Miracles.* A Marginal Jew: Rethinking the Historical Jesus 2. New York: Doubleday, 1994.

————. *Probing the Authenticity of the Parables*. A Marginal Jew: Rethinking the Historical Jesus 5. New Haven: Yale UP, 2016.

————. *The Roots of the Problem and the Person*. A Marginal Jew: Rethinking the Historical Jesus 1. New York: Doubleday, 1991.

Meyer, Michael A., ed. *German Jewish History in Modern Times*. Volumes 1 & 2. New York: Columbia UP, 1996–1997.

Meyers, Eric M. "Living Side by Side in Galilee." In *Partings: How Judaism and Christianity Became Two*, edited by Hershel Shanks, 133–150. Washington, DC: Biblical Archaeology Society, 2013.

Neusner, Jacob. *The Foundations of Judaism*. Philadelphia: Fortress, 1989.

————. *Judaisms and their Messiahs at the Turn of the Christian Era*. New York: Cambridge UP, 1987.

Newmark, Heidi. *Hidden Inheritance: Family Secrets, Memory, and Faith*. Nashville: The United Methodist Publishing House, 2015.

Noy, David. *Foreigners at Rome: Citizens and Strangers*. London: Duckworth, 2000.

Oegema, Gerbern S. *The Anointed and his People: Messianic Expectations from the Maccabees to Bar Kochba*. Sheffield: Sheffield Academic Press, 1998.

Oppenheimer, Aharon. *The 'Am Ha-aretz: A Study in the Social History of the Jewish People in the Hellenistic-Roman Period*. Leiden: E. J. Brill, 1977.

O'Rourke, David K. *The Holy Land as Jesus Knew it: its People, Customs, and Religion*. Liguori, MO: Liguori Publications, 1983.

Page II, Charles R. *Jesus and the Land*. Nashville: Abingdon, 1995.

Paget, J. Carleton. "Jewish Christianity." In *The Early Roman Period*, edited by William Horbury et al., 731–75. The Cambridge History of Judaism 3. Cambridge: Cambridge UP, 1999.

Peppard, Michael. *The Son of God in the Roman World: Divine Sonship in Its Social and Political Context*. New York: Oxford UP, 2011.

Perdue, Leo G., et al. *Families in Ancient Israel*. Louisville: Westminster John Knox Press, 1997.

Porter, Stanley E., ed. *The Messiah in the Old and New Testaments*. Grand Rapids: Eerdmans, 2007.

———. *Paul: Jew, Greek, and Roman*. Pauline Studies 5. Leiden: Brill, 2008.

Pritchard, James B., ed. *Ancient Near Eastern Texts Relating to the Old Testament*. Princeton: Princeton UP, 1969.

Reichwein, Horst. *Die Juden in der ostfrieschichen Herrlichkeiten Dornum (1662–1940)*. Dornum: 1995.

Reuter, Timothy. *Germany in the Early Middle Ages c. 800–1056*. New York: Longman, 1991.

Reyer, Herbert, and Martin Tielke, eds. *Frisia Judaica: Beitrage zur Geschichte der Juden in Ostfriesland*. Aurich: Verlag Ostfriesische Landschaft, 1988.

Rokahr, Gerd. *Die Juden in Esens*. Aurich: Verlag Ostfriesische Landschaft, 1987.

Romer, Thomas. *The Invention of God*. Translated by Raymond Geuss. Cambridge, MA: Harvard UP, 2015.

Rosenfeld, Ben-Zion, and Joseph Menirav. *Markets and Marketing in Roman Palestine*. Translated by Chava Cassel. Leiden: Brill, 2005.

Roth, Cecil, ed. *The Dark Ages: Jews in Christian Europe 711–1096*. The World History of the Jewish People 2. Tel-Aviv: Masada, 1966.

————. *The History of the Jews of Italy.* Philadelphia: The Jewish Publication Society of America, 1946.

Russell, D. S. *The Jews from Alexander to Herod.* London: Oxford UP, 1967.

Rutgers, Leonard Victor. *The Jews in Late Ancient Rome: Evidence of Cultural Interaction in the Roman Diaspora.* Leiden: Brill, 2000.

————. "The Jews of Italy, c.235–638." In *The Late Roman-Rabbinic Period,* edited by Steven T. Katz, 492–508. The Cambridge History of Judaism 4. Cambridge: Cambridge UP, 2006.

Rydelnik, Michael. *The Messianic Hope: Is the Hebrew Bible Really Messianic?* Nashville: B & H Publishing Group, 2010.

Sanders, E. P. *Judaism: Practice and Belief, 63 bce—66 ce.* London: SCM Press, 1992.

Schafer, Peter. *The History of the Jews in Antiquity: The Jews of Palestine from Alexander the Great to the Arab Conquest.* Translated by David Chowcat. Luxembourg: Hardwood Academic Publishers, 1995.

————. *The Jewish Jesus: How Judaism and Christianity Shaped Each Other.* Princeton, NJ: Princeton UP, 2012.

Schaper, Joachim. "The Pharisees." In *The Early Roman Period,* edited by William Horbury et al., 402–27. The Cambridge History of Judaism 3. Cambridge: Cambridge UP, 1999.

Schmidt, T. E. "Mark 15.16–32: The Crucifixion Narrative and the Roman Triumphal Procession." *New Testament Studies.* Vol 41 (1995) 1–18.

Schnelle, Udo. *The First One Hundred Years of Christianity: An Introduction to its History, Literature, and Development.* Translated by James W. Thompson. Grand Rapids: Baker Academic, 2020.

Schubert, Markus. *Juden in Ostfriesland.* Munich: GRIN Verlag, 2003. (ebook)

Schutz, Herbert. *The Romans in Central Europe.* New Haven: Yale UP, 1985.

Schwartz, Seth. *Imperialism and Jewish Society, 200 bce to 64 ce.* Princeton, NJ: Princeton UP, 2001.

Setzer, Claudia J. *Jewish Responses to Early Christians: History and Polemics, 30–150 ce.* Minneapolis: Fortress, 1994.

Shanks, Hershel, ed. *Partings: How Judaism and Christianity Became Two.* Washington, DC: Biblical Archaeology Society, 2013.

Shelton, W. Brian. *Quest for the Historical Apostles: Tracing their Lives and Legacies.* Grand Rapids: Baker Academic, 2018.

Sivan, Hagith. *Palestine in Late Antiquity.* Oxford: Oxford UP, 2008.

Smallwood, E. Mary. *The Jews Under Roman Rule: from Pompey to Diocletian.* Leiden: Brill, 1976.

Soloveitchik, Haym. *Jews and the Wine Trade in Medieval Europe: Principles and Pressures.* Translated by David Louvish. Edited by Leon Wieseltier. London: The Littman Library of Jewish Civilization in association with Liverpool UP, 2024.

Stegemann, Ekkehard, and Wolfgang Stegemann. *The Jesus Movement: A Social History of Its First Century.* Translated by O. C. Dean, Jr. Minneapolis: Fortress, 1999.

Taylor, Joan. *Boy Jesus: Growing Up Judean in Turbulent Times.* Grand Rapids: Zondervan Academic, 2025.

————. "Parting in Palestine." In *Partings: How Judaism and Christianity Became Two,* edited by Hershel Shanks, 87–104. Washington, DC: Biblical Archaeology Society, 2013.

Telushkin, Joseph. *Jewish Literacy.* New York: William Morrow, 1991.

Teter, Magda. *Christian Supremacy: Reckoning with the Roots of Anti-Semitism and Racism.* Princeton, NJ: Princeton UP, 2023.

Toch, Michael. "Demography and Migrations." In *The Middle Ages: The Christian World,* edited by Robert Chazan, 335–56. The Cambridge History of Judaism 6. Cambridge: Cambridge UP, 2018.

———. "Economic Activities." In *The Middle Ages: The Christian World,* edited by Robert Chazan, 357–79. The Cambridge History of Judaism 6. Cambridge: Cambridge UP, 2018.

———. *The Economic History of European Jews: Late Antiquity and Early Middle Ages.* Etudes sur le judaisme medieval. Leiden: Brill, 2013.

Tomson, Peter J., and Joshua Schwartz, eds. *Jews and Christians in the First and Second Centuries: How to Write Their History.* Leiden: Brill, 2014.

Vermes, Geza. *Christian Beginnings: From Nazareth to Nicaea.* New Haven: Yale UP, 2013.

White, L. Michael. *From Jesus to Christianity: How Four Generations of Visionaries and Storytellers Created the New Testament and Christian Faith.* New York: HarperCollins, 2004.

Williams, Margaret H. "Jews and Christians at Rome: An Early Parting of the Ways." In *Partings: How Judaism and Christianity Became Two,* edited by Hershel Shanks, 151–178. Washington, DC: Biblical Archaeology Society, 2013.

Wilson, Marvin R. *Our Father Abraham: Jewish Roots of the Christian Faith,* Second Edition. Grand Rapids: Eerdmans, 2021.

Wright, N. T. *How God Became King: The Forgotten Story of the Gospels.* New York: HarperCollins, 2012.

———. *Paul: A Biography.* New York: HarperCollins, 2018.

———. *Simply Jesus: A New Vision of Who He Was, What He Did, and Why He Matters.* New York: HarperCollins, 2011.

———. *The New Testament in Its World: An Introduction to the History, Literature, and Theology of the First Christians.* Grand Rapids: Zondervan, 2019.

Wylen, Stephen M. *The Jews in the Time of Jesus: An Introduction.* New York: Paulist, 1996.

Zetterholm, Magnus, ed. *The Messiah in Early Judaism and Christianity.* Minneapolis: Fortress, 2007.

www.ingramcontent.com/pod-product-compliance
Lightning Source LLC
Chambersburg PA
CBHW061428150726
47987CB00001B/136